the

BILLY GRAHAM
CHRISTIAN
WORKER'S
HANDBOOK

A TOPICAL GUIDE WITH BIBLICAL ANSWERS TO THE URGENT CONCERNS OF OUR DAY

Original material compiled by the Christian Guidance
department of the Billy Graham Evangelistic Association, in
conjunction with the Counseling and Follow-Up department

Billy Graham
Evangelistic Association

1 Billy Graham Parkway, Charlotte, North Carolina 28201
1-877-2GRAHAM (1-877-247-2426; 24 hours a day)
www.billygraham.org

The Billy Graham Christian Worker's Handbook

Published by the Billy Graham Evangelistic Association
1 Billy Graham Parkway
Charlotte, NC 28201

Scripture quotations, unless otherwise marked, are taken by permission from The Holy Bible, New King James Version, ©1979, 1980, 1982 Thomas Nelson, Inc., Thomas Nelson Publishers, Nashville, Tennessee.

Scripture quotations marked NIV are taken from The Holy Bible, New International Version, ©1973, 1978, 1984 International Bible Society. Used by permission of Zondervan Bible Publishers.

Scripture quotations marked TLB are taken from The Living Bible, ©1971 Tyndale House Publishers, Wheaton, Illinois.

Scripture quotations marked PHILLIPS are taken from The New Testament in Modern English by J.B. Phillips, translator, ©J.B. Phillips, 1958, 1960, 1972 Macmillan Publishing Company, New York, New York, and Collins Publishers, London, England.

Scripture quotations marked KJV are taken from the King James Version of the Bible.

Quotations from Billy Graham are from many sources, including:
Blow, Wind of God, ©1975 Baker Book House
The Challenge, ©1969 Billy Graham
The Holy Spirit, ©1988 Billy Graham
How to Be Born Again, ©1989 Billy Graham
The Jesus Generation, ©1971 Billy Graham
Answers to Life's Problems, ©1988 Doubleday
The Quotable Billy Graham, ©1966 Droke House
Till Armageddon, ©1981 Billy Graham
World Aflame, ©1965 Billy Graham

ISBN 1–59328–036–X

Printed in U.S.A.

05 06 07 08 09 10 11 12 — 12 11 10 9 8

CONTENTS

FOREWORD

You may have received this *Handbook* because you are involved in follow-up work at a telephone ministry center during our Crusade telecasts. Or you may have gotten it simply because you are a concerned Christian who wants to more effectively share the Gospel with your friends and neighbors. In either case, I want to personally commend you for your commitment to the greatest cause of all: proclaiming the Good News of salvation and everlasting life through Jesus Christ.

The *Handbook* was originally designed for our ministry centers. If you have ever been involved at one of these centers, you know something of the long hours our volunteers put in. Men and women from every walk of life willingly give up their evenings to minister in this unheralded way. Without their tireless efforts behind the scenes, our ministry would not be the same.

Each chapter in this *Handbook* is built around what the Bible says about the various topics of concern. I have always been convinced of the power of God's written Word to draw people to Him and to meet their every need from day to day. I trust that your use of this book will deepen your own dependence on and commitment to the Bible.

As you use this book, you will be encountering people at crucial turning points in their lives—people who, through various circumstances and the prompting of the Holy Spirit, are open as perhaps never before to the Gospel. This *Christian Worker's Handbook* comes to you with my heartfelt prayer for God's blessing as you use it for His glory.

—Billy Graham

FOREWORD

INTRODUCTION

The Billy Graham Christian Worker's Handbook was developed for the use of people who volunteer at telephone ministry centers during telecasts of Billy Graham and Franklin Graham Crusades. It has also been used by Christian ministers and laypersons in a wide variety of other witnessing and ministry situations.

Crusade telephone volunteers have found, through the years, that those who call tend to do so for one of three reasons: to respond to the Gospel for the first time, to rededicate themselves to Christ, or to express concern about a special need. This *Handbook* is designed to address those three areas.

- "Steps to Peace with God," page 11, presents the Gospel in a clear and simple way. Your use of "Steps" will, of course, vary according to the personality and special concerns of the person to whom you present it. But you should try to follow the steps given as closely as possible.

- Whenever possible, follow "Steps" with "Confirming the Decision to Receive Christ," page 13. This will help the new believer clarify the decision he or she has made.

- Pages 15–19 contain useful guidelines for talking with the person who has previously made a commitment of faith but has become unsure of his or her salvation or has experienced serious difficulty in following Christ.

- The "Resource Chapters" which comprise the majority of this *Handbook* address the many special concerns people may express during a telephone or personal encounter. *(See below for further details.)*

- "Seven Common Questions" is an in-depth discussion of some commonly raised objections to Christianity.

- "A Comparison of Christianity with Major Religions and Cults" provides a quick reference for talking with people of those faiths.

The "Resource Chapters" form the bulk of this book simply because of the wide variety of problems and concerns expressed by people responding to Christian outreach. These chapters are designed to point such people first and foremost to the Gospel of Jesus Christ. Each "Resource Chapter" includes:

1. A "Background" discussion of the particular problem or concern. These are brief, to facilitate quick review during a phone conversation. Try, however, to familiarize yourself with this material ahead of time. Try also to gather related information from your own research and to be aware of the issues as they are addressed in the popular media. Such knowledge will give you added confidence as you present the Gospel.

2. The "Helping Strategy" section has three main goals:

- *Relating the expressed need to the Gospel.* Each "Strategy" includes suggestions about how to present Christ in that particular situation.
- *Ministering to the person in his or her need.* Whether or not the person responds to the Gospel, we can show Christ's love by listening to the person and then attempting to address the expressed need or concern.
- *Establishing the believer in his or her Christian life.* Whether a first-time decision for Christ, or a renewal of commitment, the person should be encouraged in five basic activities of Christian life: (1) faithful church involvement, (2) daily Bible study, (3) daily prayer, (4) witness for Christ, (5) service in His name. Billy Graham and Franklin Graham have stressed these five commitments to those who respond at Crusades; we encourage you to stress them as well.

Each person you talk with as a Christian witness will, of course, be unique. Use these "Helping Strategies" only to the extent that they truly help. Beyond that, trust God's Word and His indwelling Holy Spirit to guide you.

3. The "Scripture" portion of each chapter lists just a very few of the passages from God's Word that apply to the situation. Mr. Graham has always believed that the inspired words of Scripture have a unique power to speak to all areas of human concern. The passages in this book have been chosen after much thought and prayer, but don't let them be your only Bible resource. As you read your Bible daily, feel free to add your own favorite verses that apply to various topics.

This handbook is designed for the *layperson.* Throughout the book we refer to such people, not as counselors, but as "helpers." We are not professional counselors, but merely Christians desiring to help as best we can. When faced with a situation that is beyond your own experience or knowledge, you are encouraged to refer the person to a pastor or Christian counselor.

Whatever problem or concern you are asked to address, pray for God's guidance as you do so. And focus the discussion on His Word. You will never answer all the needs of anyone you encounter as a Christian helper. But you can at least direct the person to a resource that *can* meet his or her every need.

Thank you for sharing your life in Christ with a needy world.

—Billy Graham Evangelistic Association

STEPS TO PEACE WITH GOD

NOTE: If the individual is immediately ready to receive Christ, skip the four steps and go directly to the section titled, "To receive Christ you need to do four things."

1. God's Plan—Peace and Life

God loves you and wants you to experience His peace and life.

The BIBLE says: *"For God so loved the world that He gave His only begotten Son, that whoever believes in Him should not perish but have everlasting life"* (John 3:16).

2. Our Problem—Separation

Being at peace with God is not automatic, because by nature you are separated from God.

The BIBLE says: *"For all have sinned and fall short of the glory of God"* (Romans 3:23).

3. God's Remedy—The Cross

God's love bridges the gap of separation between God and you. When Jesus Christ died on the cross and rose from the grave, He paid the penalty for your sins.

The BIBLE says: *"He personally carried the load of our sins in his own body when he died on the cross"* (1 Peter 2:24, TLB).

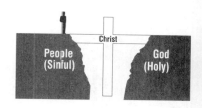

4. Our Response—Receive Christ

You cross the bridge into God's family when you receive Christ by personal invitation.

The BIBLE says: *"But as many as received Him, to them He gave the right to become children of God, even to those who believe in His name"* (John 1:12).

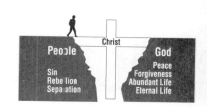

To receive Christ you need to do four things:

1. ADMIT your spiritual need. "I am a sinner."

2. REPENT and be willing to turn from your sin.

3. BELIEVE that Jesus Christ died for you on the cross.

4. RECEIVE, through prayer, Jesus Christ into your heart and life.

11

CHRIST says, *"Behold, I stand at the door and knock. If anyone hears My voice and opens the door, I will come in"* (Revelation 3:20).

The BIBLE says, *"Whoever calls upon the name of the Lord will be saved"* (Romans 10:13).

What to Pray:

Dear Lord Jesus, I know that I am a sinner and need Your forgiveness. I believe that You died for my sins. I want to turn from my sins. I now invite You to come into my heart and life. I want to trust and follow You as Lord and Savior. In Jesus' name, Amen.

* After leading the inquirer in this prayer, discuss with him or her the following pages, "Confirming the Decision to Receive Christ."

CONFIRMING THE DECISION TO RECEIVE CHRIST

You prayed, committing your life to Christ. What does the Bible say happened?

1. You are saved.

JESUS said, *"I am the door. If anyone enters by Me, he will be saved"* (John 10:9).

What did Jesus say about Himself?

I am _____ _____ (to eternal life).

What will happen when a person enters through the door (receives Christ)?

He or she will _____ _____.

The BIBLE says: *"Behold, I stand at the door and knock. If anyone hears My voice and opens the door, I will come in to him and dine with him, and he with Me"* (Revelation 3:20).

The BIBLE says: *"Whoever calls upon the name of the Lord will be saved"* (Romans 10:13).

2. You are a child of God.

The BIBLE says: *"But as many as received Him, to them He gave the right to become children of God, to those who believe in His name"* (John 1:12).

What happened when you received Christ?

I became a _____ _____ _____.

3. You have everlasting life.

The BIBLE says: *"For God so loved the world that He gave His only begotten Son, that whoever believes in Him should not perish but have everlasting life"* (John 3:16).

Now that you believe in Jesus Christ, what can you be certain of?

I have _____ _____.

To summarize, emphasize the following questions and answers:

How do you know . . .   **I know because . . .**

you are saved?   God said it . . . in His Word.

13

you are a child of God?   I believe it . . . in my heart.

you have eternal life?   That settles it . . . in my mind.

Follow-Up Steps

After presenting the Gospel and confirming the decision, suggest these follow-up steps:

1. Take a firm stand for Jesus Christ; make your life count. Tell someone about your decision.

2. Read and study God's Word.

3. Pray every day.

4. Identify with a Bible-teaching church for worship, instruction, fellowship, and service.

5. We would like to send you our Bible study booklet, *Living in Christ*, which will help you in your Christian life and future witness. What is your name and address?

FINDING ASSURANCE OF SALVATION

(For a person who has received Christ, but has doubts.)

CLAIM THESE PROMISES

1. The BIBLE says: *"For God so loved the world that He gave His only begotten Son, that whoever believes in Him should not perish but have everlasting life"* (John 3:16).

What did God give to make everlasting life possible? _____ _____.

What must you do to possess everlasting life? _____ _____ _____.

What does God promise you? _____ _____.

2. The BIBLE says: *"Whoever has God's Son has life. . . . I have written this to you who believe in the Son of God so that you may know that you have eternal life"* (1 John 5:12–13, TLB).

If you believe in Christ, what can you know with certainty?

I have _____ _____.

3. The BIBLE says: *"My sheep hear My voice, and I know them, and they follow Me. And I give them eternal life, and they shall never perish; neither shall anyone snatch them out of My hand. My Father, who gave them to Me, is greater than all; and no one is able to snatch them out of My Father's hand"* (John 10:27–29).

What are you promised?

- "And I give them _____ _____."
- "And they shall _____ _____."
- "Neither shall anyone _____ them out of My _____."
- "No one is able to _____ them out of My Father's _____."

To summarize, emphasize the following questions and answers:

How do you know . . .	I know because . . .
you have eternal life?	God said it . . . in His Word.
you will never perish?	I believe it . . . in my heart.
you are safe in God's hand?	That settles it . . . in my mind.

15

Follow-Up Steps

After discussing assurance of salvation, suggest these follow-up steps:

1. Take a firm stand for Jesus Christ; make your life count. Tell someone about your decision.

2. Read and study God's Word.

3. Pray every day.

4. Identify with a Bible-teaching church for worship, instruction, fellowship, and service.

5. We would like to send you our Bible study booklet, *Living in Christ*, which will help you in your Christian life and future witness. What is your name and address?

SEEKING FORGIVENESS AND RESTORATION

(For a person who has received Christ, but has failed Him and now seeks forgiveness.)

1. Repent and Confess to God

The BIBLE says: *"If we confess our sins, He is faithful and just to forgive us our sins and to cleanse us from all unrighteousness"* (1 John 1:9).

What must we do to be forgiven? _____ _____ _____.

What does God say He will do if we confess? _____ _____ _____.

To confess means to "agree" with God. I agree that I lied or cheated or was unkind or lost my temper. Be specific as you silently confess your sin to God.

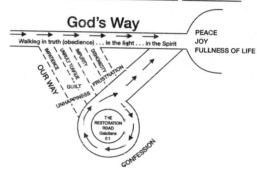

Sin takes us off God's pathway to peace and joy. Confession puts us back on God's pathway.

2. Determine to Forsake Any Known Sin in Your Life

The BIBLE says: *"He who covers his sins will not prosper, but whoever confesses and forsakes them will have mercy"* (Proverbs 28:13).

What happens if we cover our sins?

We _____ _____ _____.

Following confession we must _____ our sins.

3. Make Right Any Known Wrongs

It is important not only to confess and forsake sin, but also to make things right with anyone we may have wronged.

The BIBLE says: *"I strive always to keep my conscience clear before God and man"* (Acts 24:16, NIV).

4. Renewed Fellowship Will Be the Result

The BIBLE says: *"But if we walk in the light, as he is in the light, we have fellowship with one another, and the blood of Jesus, his Son, purifies us from all sin"* (1 John 1:7, NIV).

How do you know . . .	I know because . . .
you are forgiven?	God said it . . . in His Word.
you are cleansed?	I believe it . . . in my heart.
you are restored?	That settles it . . . in my mind.

Follow-Up Steps

After guiding the inquirer to spiritual renewal, share these follow-up steps:

1. Now that you are restored to fellowship with Christ, take a firm stand for Him. Tell someone about your decision.

2. Read and study God's Word faithfully.

3. Pray every day.

4. Identify with a Bible-teaching church for worship, fellowship, and service.

5. We would like to send you our Bible study booklet, *Living in Christ*, which will help you in your Christian life and future witness. What is your name and address?

UNCERTAINTY ABOUT ONE'S RELATIONSHIP WITH CHRIST

Start by asking the basic question: "Has there ever been a time in your life when you trusted Jesus Christ as your personal Lord and Savior?"

1. If the answer is YES, ask him or her to tell you about it in order to determine just where he or she really is.

   A. If you feel that he or she has made a commitment, but is uncertain, go over "Assurance," page 15.

   B. If the person seems firm in the commitment, perhaps he or she needs help with some other spiritual problem. Go over the section called "Seeking Forgiveness and Restoration," page 17.

2. If the answer is NO, then share "Steps to Peace with God," page 11.

3. If the answer is vague—"I have doubts," "I'm not sure"—then ask the question: "If you were to die tonight, would you go to heaven?"

   A. If he or she doesn't know, share "Steps to Peace with God," page 11.

   B. If the person believes that he or she would go to heaven, then share "Assurance," page 15.

   C. If he or she is still vague, using such phrases as "I have always attended church," or "I'm doing the best I can," or "I try to be a moral person," etc., then say:

      (1) "Let me share with you how you can know for sure that if you died tonight you would go to heaven."

      (2) Share "Steps to Peace with God," page 11.

4. Always close your conversation with prayer. Remember to offer the Bible study booklet, *Living in Christ*, which will help in the caller's Christian life and future witness.

ABORTION

Background

Abortion has divided our nation like no other issue in recent times. While people on one side of the issue stress a woman's right to choose whether or not to give birth, people of the other side stress the right of the unborn child to be born. Even sincere Christians may differ on whether or not abortion is ever justified, especially in difficult situations such as rape or incest, or when tests reveal that the unborn child has severe abnormalities.

The Bible places the highest value on human life. It is sacred and of inestimable worth to God, who created it "in His own image" (Genesis 1:26–27); who sustains it (Job 12:10); and who redeemed it (2 Corinthians 5:19). The Bible recognizes the unborn as being fully human: "You saw me before I was born and scheduled each day of my life before I began to breathe. Every day was recorded in your Book!" (Psalm 139:16, TLB).

Helping Strategy

As a Christian helper, there are several aspects of the abortion issue that you may be called upon to deal with: the woman who is considering having an abortion; the guilt of one who has already gone through that experience; parents of a pregnant girl; the unmarried father; medical personnel who have helped with or performed abortions.

The Woman Considering an Abortion:

1. Commend her for calling concerning her anxiety. You are happy to talk with her, and hope you can share some insights which will help her make a final decision.

2. Tactfully remind her that she quite possibly has strong feelings about the moral implications of abortion or she wouldn't have called. Avoid being judgmental about her situation. For example, if she is young and unmarried, her pregnancy could be the result of having sought love, attention, and affection which she never received at home. At the same time, avoid minimizing the wrongness of her sexual conduct, because it is sin.

3. Question her about her feelings on abortion:

   • What prompted you to call about your problem?

   • What are your real feelings about abortion?

- What have you heard from others, Christian or not, regarding abortion?

4. Whether or not she believes abortion is wrong, present the Scriptures discussed above in "Background," along with any others that you think would apply.

5. Ask her to consider the alternatives. If she is considering having an abortion because of the stigma of an illegitimate child, she may only complicate her situation and compound the guilt. Suggest that she consider having the child, asking God to bring good from the experience. He can do this as she commits herself and her problem completely to Him: "And we know that in all things God works for the good of those who love him" (Romans 8:28, NIV).

If she is concerned about not being able to care for or support the child, ask her to consider adoption. There are many couples looking for a child to adopt who are able to provide love and a good home. There are many organizations to which she may turn for help. Suggest that she seek the counsel and advice of a local pastor, who should be able to initiate the process of arranging an adoption.

6. Ask her if she has ever received Jesus Christ as her Lord and Savior. If appropriate, present "Steps to Peace with God," page 11.

7. Suggest that she start reading the Bible. In order to restructure her life according to biblical principles, she needs to read and study God's Word. Offer to send *Living in Christ* to help her get started.

8. Ask if she has a church home. She should try to identify with a Bible-teaching church where she can find fellowship and encouragement, and can grow in her faith.

The Woman Who Has Had an Abortion and Suffers from Guilt:

1. Encourage her by saying that she has made the right choice in seeking help. We care and want to help in any way we can. God has an answer to every human situation, and she can trust Him to work for her good.

2. Don't make a moral issue of her situation; at the same time, don't minimize the seriousness of such a choice. The fact that she is willing to share her feelings of guilt is an indication that God is speaking to her.

3. Dwell on God's forgiveness for those who are willing to repent and confess their sins to the Lord. To the woman taken in the act of adultery, Jesus said, "Neither do I condemn you; go and sin no more" (John 8:11).

4. Should confession result, do not dwell on the past (Philippians 3:13–14).

5. Ask if she has ever received Jesus Christ as her personal Savior. If appropriate, present "Steps to Peace with God," page 11.

6. Suggest that she seek fellowship with God through Bible reading and prayer. Forgiveness is immediate, but a sense of restoration and acceptance will come in due time. Through commitment to this important discipline of prayer and Bible study, she will grow in her relationship with God.

7. Suggest that she seek, or restore, fellowship with a Bible-teaching church. There she can counsel with a pastor, hear God's Word taught, and find strength through Christian relationships.

8. Pray with her. Ask God for forgiveness, commitment, and strength for the future.

Scripture
The Wonder of Life:

"Children are a heritage from the Lord, the fruit of the womb is His reward" (Psalm 127:3).

"You made all the delicate, inner parts of my body, and knit them together in my mother's womb. Thank you for making me so wonderfully complex! It is amazing to think about. Your workmanship is marvelous—and how well I know it. You were there while I was being formed in utter seclusion! You saw me before I was born and scheduled each day of my life before I began to breathe. Every day was recorded in your Book!" (Psalm 139:13–16, TLB).

Forgiveness:

Psalm 32:1–5 (Look up these verses, which were written by one guilty of adultery and murder.)

"Who forgives all your sins and heals all your diseases, who redeems your life from the pit and crowns you with love and compassion" (Psalm 103:3–4, NIV).

"If we confess our sins, He is faithful and just to forgive us our sins and to cleanse us from all unrighteousness" (1 John 1:9).

Courage and Strength to Carry On:

"Why are you downcast, O my soul? Why so disturbed within me? Put your hope in God, for I will yet praise him, my Savior and my God" (Psalm 42:11, NIV).

"But those who wait on the Lord shall renew their strength; they shall mount up with wings like eagles, they shall run and not be weary, they shall walk and not faint" (Isaiah 40:31).

ABUSE, VICTIMS OF

Background

Abused wives, husbands, girlfriends, and boyfriends represent one of the uglier aspects of our society. Only a small percentage of such cases is ever brought to light. The abuse—physical and sexual as well as verbal and emotional—may continue for years. The abused spouse or friend can be found at all socioeconomic levels, and in all educational, racial, and age groups. Not even Christians are immune.

The abuser often masters the "art" of the put-down, foul and abusive language, and threats. At times this abuse is so destructive of personality that the victim feels deserving of any physical battering which follows.

The victim of abuse is characterized by low self-esteem, depression, and a variety of stress-related disorders and psychosomatic illnesses. He or she feels trapped and vulnerable, confused and uncertain. It is impossible to objectively assess one's position or to make decisions. There is a martyr-like endurance and frustration: The victim will often assume responsibility for the abuser's behavior. The vague hope exists that change is "just around the corner," and that "someone will soon come and get me out of all this." At the same time, there is emotional isolation and no real contact with the family.

In the case of a wife, it may take from three to four months of counseling before she can begin to heal emotionally, even after she has been separated from her tormentor. Once she and the children are in a safe place (where the husband cannot reach them) and she has had time to reflect and sort out her feelings, she may be very angry.

The abuser of spouse and family seldom changes unless exposed and subjected to legal action.

Helping Strategy

1. Reassure and encourage. He or she is doing the right thing in talking about the problem. We want to be of help and are happy to listen. He or she is not alone: Many others are experiencing the same bad treatment.

2. Ask questions. It is quite common for abused people to have difficulty in expressing their feelings. Ask:

   • How do you feel about the way you are treated?

   • How long has this been going on?

- Tell me about your spouse. What is he or she like?

- How do you feel about yourself at this point?

- What do you think you can do about all this?

Based on the background of the abused, and the emotional damage suffered, you may have to formulate other questions. The goal is to lead the victim to healthy self-expression and to a realization of his or her God-given rights as a person and as a spouse.

3. Urge the victim not to feel deserving of such treatment. He or she *does not have to be a victim any longer*. Even though the spouse blames the victim and tries to justify the abuse, it is *not* his or her fault.

4. Stress that he or she doesn't have to take the abuse anymore. It must stop! He or she must be decisive and firm. The spouse's conduct is illegal and could even lead to a jail sentence.

5. In order to break the cycle of abuse, the victim must contact a local pastor or family services office and tell the truth about the abuse. They will be able to help the victim sort things out, suggesting legal action if necessary. Separation from the tormentor may be in order.

6. Further counseling and emotional support is a must. Arrangements must be made with a qualified pastor, a Christian professional, or a counseling service. Impress upon the victim that decisions must be made urgently and decisive action must be taken. You may make suggestions, but concrete steps will have to be taken by the victim.

7. Focus on God's love for the abuse victim. Better than anyone else, God understands what the abused person has been going through. Jesus was abused both verbally and physically! Has the inquirer ever received Jesus Christ as Savior and Lord? If not, share "Steps to Peace with God," page 11. If the response is affirmative, share "Assurance," page 15.

8. Encourage the person to start Bible reading and study for solace and spiritual strength. Offer to send *Living in Christ* to get him or her started.

9. Explain the benefits of a good church relationship for the victim and the family. Emotional and spiritual support will be forthcoming as a result of corporate worship, Bible teaching, fellowship, and witness. Counseling might also be available.

10. Pray for strength and understanding, committing the abused person to God's special love and care.

Scripture

"I sought the Lord, and he answered me; he delivered me from all my fears. Those who look to him are radiant; their faces are never covered with shame" (Psalm 34:4–5, NIV).

"Trust in the Lord with all your heart, and lean not on your own understanding; in all your ways acknowledge Him, and He shall direct your paths" (Proverbs 3:5–6).

"You will keep in perfect peace him whose mind is steadfast, because he trusts in you. Trust in the Lord forever, for the Lord, the Lord, is the Rock eternal" (Isaiah 26:3–4, NIV).

"Come to Me, all you who labor and are heavy laden, and I will give you rest" (Matthew 11:28).

"Cast all your anxiety on him because he cares for you" (1 Peter 5:7, NIV).

Other suggested Scriptures:

Psalm 23
Psalm 42:11

THE ABUSIVE PERSON

Background

The abusive person is found in all socioeconomic levels, in all educational, racial, and age groups. There are abusive women as well as abusive men. The following could be applied to either. Though there are similarities in the characteristics of the abuser, we shall briefly list three categories:

The Spouse Abuser

Although case histories vary, there are similar threads running through each. The spouse abuser:

- Has a very "low boiling point" and is able to vent the anger only through the abuse.

- Has little self-esteem, often feeling like a failure.

- Relates poorly to people.

- Is jealous, and accuses the mate of being nonsupportive or unfaithful.

- Tries to control all the spouse's activities and even spies on him or her, believing that such behavior actually promotes the good of the family.

- Often offends without feeling, and admits no guilt on the emotional level even after admitting the problem.

Abusers tend to justify themselves, either feeling that their partners goad them to the point of abuse, or denying that they are abusive. Frustration will trigger abuse: Since the person can't punch his or her boss at work, he or she takes it out on the spouse and children at home. Alcoholism and drug abuse are sometimes causes of the explosive mistreatment.

The Child Abuser

Most of the above symptoms are present in the child abuser. Add to this that the abuser is very demanding, wanting to be obeyed blindly and immediately. He or she is extremely impatient and often vents frustrations—the hurts and pains of his or her own childhood—on the children. Such parents' expectations are far too high for their children, so they berate them or put them down. Often the verbal abuse, accompanied by foul and obscene language, will be so devastating that the children begin to passively accept the physical abuse, feeling that they deserve it.

They become victims. Alcohol and drugs are involved in many cases.

The Sexual Abuser (Incest)

NOTE: Girls are not the only ones suffering sexual abuse; there is much abuse of boys as well.

The characteristics of the spouse abuser are generally true of the sexual abuser. He or she is emotionally isolated, although appearing to be emotionally whole. He or she seems to be passive, but exercises a growing, rigid control over the child's actions. He or she is callous, egocentric, self-indulgent, and sees people only as objects. Alcohol and drug addiction are often related to incest.

Sexual abuse is usually long-term and repetitive, accompanied by intimidation and coercion. When confronted, the abusive adult will deny involvement or responsibility and tends to blame the victim. In all probability, the abuser was also sexually abused as a child.

A spouse who has failed to protect a child from sexual abuse (when actually aware of it) will remain passive and, more often than not, support the spouse's denials or rationalizations. When caught, the offender often promises "not to do it again." Such promises are not to be trusted!

From these three descriptions, you can readily understand that dealing with such an individual is difficult. However, perhaps the following will be helpful.

Helping Strategy

1. Speak in love. Do not be judgmental or accusatory. As you are able to get the conversation around to it, let the Word of God convict the abuser.

2. Assure the abuser that he or she has done the right thing in admitting the problem. You are happy to talk with him or her because the Bible has answers to all human problems, especially those regarding family relationships.

3. Stress that he or she must be willing to face the reality of what he or she has done or of what is happening. Spouses and children have the God-given right to be treated decently and with love and concern for their highest welfare. The abuser must realize that he or she is destroying them. Such actions are punishable by law. But God can help bring control over this behavior.

4. Ask the person if he or she has ever received Jesus Christ as Lord and Savior. Share "Steps to Peace with God," page 11.

NOTE: The abuser must be willing to confess the abusive behavior as sin and look to God for correction and deliverance. God will forgive sin; this is why He sent His Son to the cross. If appropriate, present page 15 on "Assurance."

5. Suggest Bible reading and study. The Bible has answers to all problems of human behavior. Offer to send *Living in Christ,* which will provide a good starting point for serious study.

6. Encourage prayer. If there is any rapport left in the family, prayer will help restore the broken cords of relationship.

7. Recommend finding a good, Bible-teaching church. There, the teaching of the Bible and fellowship with God's people can be healing and corrective factors.

8. Suggest maintaining a close contact with the pastor of the church. The pastor can continue to counsel and monitor behavior in the family.

9. Recommend serious commitment to professional counseling for both the offender and the family. The abusive person has a serious, often deep-rooted problem which can be helped only through prolonged counseling. The effects on the family should also be treated professionally.

Scripture

"Do not be deceived: Neither the sexually immoral nor idolaters nor adulterers nor male prostitutes nor homosexual offenders nor thieves nor the greedy nor drunkards nor slanderers nor swindlers will inherit the kingdom of God. And that is what some of you were. But you were washed, you were sanctified, you were justified in the name of the Lord Jesus Christ and by the Spirit of our God" (1 Corinthians 6:9–11, NIV).

"The Spirit, however, produces in human life fruits such as these: love, joy, peace, patience, kindness, generosity, fidelity, tolerance and self-control—and no law exists against any of them" (Galatians 5:22, PHILLIPS).

"Husbands, love your wives, just as Christ also loved the church and gave Himself for it. . . . So men ought to love their own wives as their own bodies; he who loves his wife loves himself. For no one ever hated his own flesh, but nourishes and cherishes it, just as the Lord does the church" (Ephesians 5:25, 28–29).

"Fathers, do not exasperate your children; instead, bring them up in the training and instruction of the Lord" (Ephesians 6:4, NIV).

Other suggested Scriptures:
1 Peter 3:7

ADULTERY

Background

God's Word makes it clear that marriage is a commitment for life to the one individual chosen as a mate. This commitment means "forsaking all others." "For this reason a man shall leave his father and mother and be joined to his wife, and the two shall become one flesh." (Matthew 19:5).

Sexual unfaithfulness on the part of both husbands and wives has become epidemic, according to polls and reports on sexual practices. Adultery is both forbidden and condemned by God in His Word:

> "Marriage should be honored by all, and the marriage bed kept pure, for God will judge the adulterer and all the sexually immoral" (Hebrews 13:4, NIV).

> "Do you not know that the wicked will not inherit the kingdom of God? Do not be deceived: Neither the sexually immoral nor idolaters nor adulterers . . . will inherit the kingdom of God" (1 Corinthians 6:9–10, NIV).

> "Flee from sexual immorality. All other sins a man [or woman] commits are outside his body, but he who sins sexually sins against his own body" (1 Corinthians 6:18, NIV).

Consider some of the consequences of adultery:

- Emotional: guilt, fear, anxiety, loss of self-esteem, shattered personalities, depression

- Physical: illegitimate births, venereal disease, abortions

- Spiritual: loss in this life and in that which is to come

Billy Graham writes: "How many homes are broken because of men and women who are unfaithful! What sin is committed every day at this point. God will not hold you guiltless! There is a day of reckoning. 'Be sure your sin will find you out' (Numbers 32:23). They will find you out in your own family life here in your relationship with your mate; they will find you out in the life to come."

Adultery is sin, but it is also a symptom that all is not well in a marriage. There are many reasons for adultery:

- Our own sinful, selfish desires: "Each one is tempted when he is

drawn away by his own desires and enticed" (James 1:14).

- Lack of maturity: Fifty percent of teenage marriages come apart in the first five years; however, age is not the only criterion. Immature selfishness at any age can lead to unfaithfulness. Another sign of immaturity is a lack of willingness to accept the responsibility of a family.

- Demanding, critical, scolding, nagging husbands or wives.

- Lack of sexual satisfaction on the part of either mate.

- Transferring to one's mate hostility felt toward a mother or father.

- Meddlesome in-laws who smother a husband and wife with criticism or well-intended advice.

- Lack of adequate sex education.

You should expect no easy solutions in dealing with the problem of adultery. However, God can work the miracle of the new birth for the non-Christian, and spiritual renewal for His own who have fallen away. If you are successful in securing a commitment to Christ, you can be confident that this will bring a new perspective, making it easier to mend lives and to reach permanent solutions.

Helping Strategy
For the Person Involved in Adultery:

1. Try to project yourself as a caring, concerned person, without being patronizing. You are glad to share, and hope that some solution can be reached.

2. Don't be judgmental or assume a "holier than thou" attitude. Don't start out with Scriptures that condemn; these emerge normally as you share Christ at the appropriate time.

3. Encourage the inquirer to talk about the situation so that you can get a complete picture of the circumstances. At the same time, don't press for too much detail.

4. When you feel that enough information has been given, say that you want to work on solutions, but that first you would like to ask if he or she has ever received Jesus Christ as Lord and Savior.

    - If not, share "Steps to Peace with God," page 11.

    - If the person is a fallen Christian, share "Restoration," page 17. Pray for renewed commitment, and then proceed.

5. Ask what solution the person might suggest for the adultery.

6. Make a transition to Scripture. Point out that God not only demands that we confess adultery as sin, but that we put it out of our lives. "He who covers his sins will not prosper, but whoever confesses and forsakes them will have mercy" (Proverbs 28:13).

7. Suggest that the inquirer think about possible reasons for the infidelity and share those reasons with you. You might mention some of the reasons for adultery from the "Background" to stimulate thinking.

8. Recommend that he or she confess the adultery to his or her spouse, demonstrating true remorse and asking forgiveness. Suggest that he or she try to discuss the reasons for the adultery. An honest effort to communicate is the only way that things can be brought to light and the climate provided which will lead to solutions.

9. Suggest initiating regular reading and study of God's Word with the spouse. This will illuminate them both as to their responsibilities, and fortify them against temptation and sin. Also, encourage them to pray together.

10. Encourage them to seek out and identify with a Bible-teaching church. This will provide strength as they fellowship, worship, and study the Bible. Becoming committed Christians should be their goal. The absence of a vital relationship with Christ is the chief factor in this problem.

11. Advise the person guilty of adultery to seek out the pastor for encouragement and counseling. If he or she doesn't find the needed help through the pastor, such help should be sought from a Christian professional counselor or psychiatrist.

For the Partner of the Adulterer:

The adulterer's spouse often feels betrayed, rejected, and hurt. Although only one partner may be guilty of unfaithfulness, often both of them *contributed* to it.

1. Encourage the person to ask:

A. How may I have contributed to my mate's infidelity? Am I supportive, or critical?

B. What circumstances in our marriage might have contributed to the problem?

• Conflict with in-laws?

• Work schedules or absences from home?

- Lack of communication?

- A need for better understanding of each other or of what makes for a good marriage?

C. How may I help to provide a solution to save our relationship?

2. Help determine the best course of action:

A. *Forgiveness.* Things can never be worked out unless there is forgiveness. This may be difficult, but a way can be found. Those involved must ask for God's grace and wisdom to face the reality of the situation. The true extent of their mutual love and concern will be most evident at this point. The guilty spouse must also seek God's forgiveness and the spouse's forgiveness.

B. *Communication.* The couple must make a determined effort to communicate with each other in order to discuss freely all facets of the issue. Lack of communication may have been a contributing factor to the problem. Now is the time to correct this.

C. *Prayer.* The couple should pray together, trusting God to work things out so that the marriage may be saved and grow stronger.

D. *Counseling.* They should be willing to consider professional counseling with a qualified pastor or Christian counselor or psychiatrist. It may take time to work things out.

Scripture

"Take your evil deeds out of my sight! Stop doing wrong, learn to do right! Seek justice, encourage the oppressed. Defend the cause of the fatherless, plead the case of the widow. 'Come now, let us reason together,' says the Lord. 'Though your sins are like scarlet, they shall be as white as snow; though they are red as crimson, they shall be like wool'" (Isaiah 1:16–18, NIV).

Jesus said to the woman accused of adultery, "Neither do I condemn you; go and sin no more" (John 8:11).

"The husband should fulfill his marital duty to his wife, and likewise the wife to her husband. The wife's body does not belong to her alone but also to her husband. In the same way, the husband's body does not belong to him alone but also to his wife" (1 Corinthians 7:3–4, NIV).

"Marriage should be honored by all, and the marriage bed kept pure, for God will judge the adulterer and all the sexually immoral" (Hebrews 13:4, NIV).

"If we confess our sins, He is faithful and just to forgive us our sins and to cleanse us from all unrighteousness" (1 John 1:9).

Other suggested Scriptures:

1 Corinthians 6:15–20

AIDS/HIV

Background

Acquired Immune Deficiency Syndrome (AIDS) is a condition caused by the human immunodeficiency virus (HIV) in which the body's immune system breaks down, rendering it unable to fight disease. The person with AIDS is in perpetual danger from any number of ordinarily curable diseases. Barring the unexpected discovery of a cure, virtually everyone currently diagnosed with the HIV virus will eventually die from an AIDS-related illness.

Approximately a million people in the United States and Canada are currently infected with the HIV virus. Approximately 75 percent of these contracted the virus from homosexual activity. Another 15 percent are intravenous drug users infected by contaminated needles. Others sufferers include hemophiliacs and others infected by blood transfusions, men and women infected through heterosexual contact, and children born to infected parents.

Because of its prevalence in North America among homosexual men, AIDS has come to have stigma attached to it comparable to that associated with leprosy in Bible times.

The caller who is suffering from AIDS or who knows that he or she carries the HIV virus will probably be going through various stages of the grieving process, which for the AIDS victim might look something like this:

1. *Denial.* "I can't believe this is happening to me. Let's run those tests again!" This would be the first reaction of any rational person who discovers that he or she is terminally ill.

2. *Anger turned outward.* This anger may be directed at the person from whom the AIDS was contracted, at doctors or the government for not having found a cure, or at God for allowing such suffering.

3. *Anger turned inward.* The person begins to feel guilty and blame himself or herself for the infection. Even people who contracted the virus through an "innocent" means such as blood transfusion may feel that they are being punished for some unrelated sin.

4. *Genuine grief.* The person begins to realize that he or she has a limited time to live. There's a sense of genuine loss. There's a dread of already worsening problems: physical suffering, social prejudice and isolation, loss of employment, overwhelming medical bills, and the effect of the illness on friends and family.

5. *Resolution.* The final stage of grief comes when the person accepts the fact that he or she is terminally ill and begins making the necessary preparations and emotional adjustments.

Friends or relatives of the AIDS victim may go through a similar grieving process:

- Denial that it could be happening to someone so close.

- Anger directed either toward the victim for his or her lifestyle choices, or towards other parties, whether guilty or innocent.

- Anger turned inward: "It's my fault that he or she got into the situation where AIDS was contracted."

- Genuine grief over a life cut short.

- And finally, accepting the illness and the victim, taking steps to make his or her remaining time as pleasant as possible.

Helping Strategy
For the AIDS/HIV Sufferer:

The AIDS victim who seeks help should be treated with special compassion. He or she may have had to overcome great fear of public exposure just to seek help. He or she may also have a keen awareness of spiritual need, due to the illness and the prospect of death.

If you become aware that the caller contracted AIDS through homosexual conduct, and you question your ability to discuss this area objectively, you should refer the inquirer to another Christian helper.

The following guidelines apply to dealing with any inquirer reporting AIDS or HIV infection:

1. Thank the person for calling, and give assurance of your desire to help in any way you can. Try to empathize with him or her, while realizing—and honestly admitting to the caller—that you will probably not fully understand the anguish he or she must be feeling.

2. At some convenient point in the conversation, ask the inquirer if he or she has ever received Jesus Christ as Lord and Savior. Share "Steps to Peace with God," page 11.

3. If he or she responds affirmatively, pray for a new outlook on life as he or she faces the difficult days ahead. Pray that the blessed hope of everlasting life will become a reality in his or her life, and that God will use this new believer mightily as a witness of His saving grace.

4. Stress the importance of reading and studying God's Word daily to gain a new understanding of life and eternity from God's perspective.

5. Encourage the inquirer to become part of a Bible-teaching church. Recommend that he or she make the pastor aware of his or her situation, so that the pastor can help ensure that the person finds within the church the support and acceptance to grow as a Christian to face the future challenges.

6. Whether or not the person responds to the Gospel, recommend calling a local pastor for referral to a Christian professional counselor and to a Christian agency addressing the needs of AIDS patients. Stress that such an agency would be glad to help the person without regard to his or her religious affiliation.

Questions a Homosexual AIDS Victim Might Ask

1. "Don't Christians believe that all homosexuals are hopeless sinners?" Or, "Don't Christians believe that AIDS is God's judgment on homosexuals?"

Answer: In addressing this question, remember that Christ was always very forthright in confronting people about sin, but He did so lovingly, always with the goal of leading them to repentance and salvation. Don't be afraid to let the caller know that, based on the Bible, you believe that homosexual conduct is sin. Refer to the verses listed under "Scripture" in the chapter on "Homosexuality."

Point out, however, that the Bible also teaches that *all* humans are sinners, no matter what their sexual orientation (Romans 3:23). Emphasize to the caller that you, the same as he or she, are a sinner in God's sight.

Then proceed directly to the great promise of Romans 6:23: "The wages of sin is death, but the gift of God is eternal life in Christ Jesus our Lord." Then read Ephesians 2:8–9: "For by grace you have been saved through faith, and that not of yourselves; it is the gift of God, not of works, lest anyone should boast."

Salvation is based on God's grace, not on a person's moral goodness. Invite the caller to receive the gift of eternal life.

2. "How can I trust a God who would let me suffer this way?"

Answer: Admit that you can't explain all the reasons why God allows us to suffer in this life. But you do know He allowed His only Son, Jesus, to suffer. Read Isaiah 53:1–9 and John 3:16. Even though He was God, Christ suffered more than any human will ever suffer, so He understands how we feel when we suffer. God never promised freedom from suffering during this short time that we call life here on earth. He does, however, promise freedom from suffering for eternity if we trust Christ as Savior. It's very normal to feel bitter when any of us gets a terrible disease, but we should not let such bitterness stand in the way of receiving eternal life through salvation in Christ.

3. "If I trust Christ as Savior, will He cure my AIDS?"

Answer: God can always choose to cure any person of any illness, but history indicates that He usually chooses to let the human suffering do its greater work of making us long for the greater "cure" of eternal life. This assurance of eternal life also helps us endure whatever suffering we must endure in this present life.

4. "Can God forgive a homosexual like me who has AIDS?"

Answer: Say something like, "If God can forgive me of all my selfishness and pride and all the other sins I've committed, He can surely forgive you!" Refer to Proverbs 6:16–19, where homosexuality is not even included in the seven worst sins. Say, "I've committed six of the seven worst sins, and yet God forgave me and saved me, so surely He can forgive you of homosexuality or any other sin." First John 1:9 promises forgiveness for any sin, as long as we are humble enough to confess it. First Corinthians 6:9–11 lists homosexuality as one of the sins the Corinthian Christians had formerly practiced. But the homosexuals at Corinth were forgiven just like the others, when they renounced their sin.

5. "How can I overcome my homosexuality?"

Answer: Encourage the inquirer to seek professional counseling with a Christian psychologist or qualified pastor.

For Family and Friends of the AIDS/HIV Sufferer:

If the caller is seeking comfort or advice concerning a friend or family member who has AIDS, proceed as follows:

1. As early as possible, determine whether or not the inquirer has accepted Christ as Savior and Lord. Share "Steps to Peace with God," page 11. Faith in Christ will give the person a totally new perspective on the person with AIDS.

2. If the friend or family member contracted AIDS through homosexual activity, share insights from points 1 and 4 under "Questions a Homosexual AIDS Victim Might Ask." Make sure the person understands that, in God's sight, homosexual sin is no worse than any other sin.

3. Advise approaching the situation as an opportunity to share the Gospel and to show Christ's love and acceptance.

4. Stress the need to keep the lines of communication open with the AIDS victim, to avoid condemnation, to show acceptance through things like inviting the person with AIDS into your home and including him or her in social activities.

5. Advise encouraging the AIDS sufferer to seek counseling and other available support networks; especially encourage his or her involvement in a Bible-teaching church.

6. Seek counseling for other family members, especially younger children, who may have questions about the illness or may themselves be experiencing prejudice because of their relationship to the AIDS victim.

Scripture
A Christian Perspective on Suffering:

"I am the resurrection and the life. He who believes in Me, though he may die, he shall live" (John 11:25).

"Let not your heart be troubled; you believe in God, believe also in Me. In My Father's house are many mansions; if it were not so, I would have told you. I go to prepare a place for you. And if I go and prepare a place for you, I will come again and receive you to Myself; that where I am, there you may be also" (John 14:1–3).

"For I consider that the sufferings of this present time are not worthy to be compared with the glory which shall be revealed in us. For the earnest expectation of the creation eagerly waits for the revealing of the sons of God. For the creation was subjected to futility, not willingly, but because of Him who subjected it in hope; because the creation itself also will be delivered from the bondage of corruption into the glorious liberty of the children of God. For we know that the whole creation groans and labors with birth pangs together until now. And not only they, but we also who have the firstfruits of the Spirit, even we ourselves groan within ourselves, eagerly awaiting for the adoption, the redemption of our body. . . . And we know that all things work together for good to those who love God, to those who are the called according to His purpose. For whom He foreknew, He also predestined to be conformed to the image of His Son, that He might be the firstborn among many brethren. Moreover whom He predestined, these He also called; whom He called, these He also justified; and whom He justified, these He also glorified. What then shall we say to these things? If God is for us, who can be against us? . . . Who shall separate us from the love of Christ? Shall tribulation, or distress, or persecution, or famine, or nakedness, or peril, or sword? . . . Yet in all these things we are more than conquerors through Him who loved us" (Romans 8:18–23, 28–31, 35, 37).

"For our light affliction, which is but for a moment, is working for us a far more exceeding and eternal weight of glory" (2 Corinthians 4:17).

"To me, to live is Christ, and to die is gain" (Philippians 1:21).

Homosexuality Is Sin, but Is Forgivable as Any Other Sin:

"Do not be deceived: Neither the sexually immoral nor idolaters nor adulterers nor male prostitutes nor homosexual offenders nor thieves nor the greedy nor drunkards nor slanderers nor swindlers will inherit the kingdom of God. And that is what some of you were. But you were washed, you were sanctified, you were justified in the name of the Lord Jesus Christ and by the Spirit of our God" (1 Corinthians 6:9–11, NIV).

"When someone becomes a Christian he becomes a brand new person inside. He is not the same any more. A new life has begun!" (2 Corinthians 5:17, TLB).

See also Homosexuality, Suffering and Adversity, Terminal Illness

ALCOHOLISM

Background

Habitual use of alcohol often results in addiction. The drinker's inadequacies, faults, and problems become intensified, and often personality changes result. Though feeling confident when under the influence of alcohol, he or she is often immature, insecure, and afflicted by guilt and depression. The alcoholic does not feel good about himself or herself and cannot face the addiction and the problems it creates; so he or she denies the problem and is dishonest in covering it up and in blaming it on family members, parents, work supervisors, or the "bad breaks" of life. This deviousness and denial leads to a masquerade in life that at times assumes almost comic, though actually tragic, overtones.

Alcoholics desperately need help. Alcoholics Anonymous maintains that until alcoholics hit rock bottom, admitting their life is out of control, there is little hope of any change. Admitting that there is a problem is the first step on the road to recovery.

There *is* hope for the alcoholic: God is able to deliver from this as well as any other addiction.

Billy Graham writes: "The Bible teaches that there is deliverance from the things that come upon the world . . . not by chemicals, but by Christ, bringing the mind and heart into harmony with God through submission to His will and accepting His forgiveness. . . . In Christ alone there is deliverance from man's tortured thoughts and freedom from the sordid habits which are destroying so many people. Why does the Bible so clearly denounce drunkenness? Because it is an enemy of human life. Anything that is against a person's welfare, God is against."

Helping Strategy

1. If the inquirer is drunk or "high," any help you try to offer will be futile, a conversation with the alcohol and not with the person; it could even be counterproductive for the alcoholic. Arrange a meeting or have him or her telephone the following day when he or she is sober. If the person appears to be out of control, get him or her to a detox center. In some cases, you might ask if there is someone else available to take the person to a center.

2. Because alcoholics are often dishonest and deceivers—con artists—you must evidence a "tough love" in dealing with them. Ask if he or she really wants help. Or did he or she just get in touch with you in order to make excuses or blame the problem on other things and people, while hiding his or her real self and the real problem?

In taking a tough stance, avoid being judgmental and do not use the Bible as a club. Helpful Scripture texts will come out naturally as you present the Gospel. Assure the inquirer that he or she is in touch with the right person because you care and are glad to speak with him or her (unless he or she is drunk).

3. Emphasize that the alcoholic must admit having a problem he or she can't cope with alone, and must be willing to make a commitment to quit drinking for good. Nothing short of this will do! The masquerade must stop, once and for all. He or she must admit being personally responsible for the condition and the problems.

4. This might be the time to ask the person if he or she has ever received Jesus Christ as Lord and Savior. Christ went to the cross specifically for him or her; Christ offers both salvation and reformation. Share "Steps to Peace with God," page 11.

5. Return to the things you were discussing on point number 3; the alcoholic must:

   A. Never again use alcohol. Living one day at a time, he or she must learn to trust God's promise in regard to temptation (1 Corinthians 10:13; see "Scripture").

   B. Sever all relationships that cause enslavement to this pattern of behavior: "Do not be misled: 'Bad company corrupts good character'" (1 Corinthians 15:33, NIV).

   C. Establish new relationships:

      • Seek out a local chapter of Alcoholics Anonymous or other support groups. They are listed in the telephone book.

      • Identify with a Bible-teaching church for the spiritual support of worship, Bible study, and fellowship.

6. Be honest with the alcoholic in warning about possible relapses, but also encourage him or her that a relapse doesn't mean that all is lost. Renewal may be sought on the basis of 1 John 1:9, and the steps of point 5 must be practiced a day at a time.

7. Pray for deliverance from the compulsion and bondage he or she is under, and for a transformation of mind and life by the power of God

(see Romans 12:1–2). Explain the value of a life of prayer.

8. If your inquirer is a Christian who has become a victim of alcohol, use the above steps, then share "Restoration," page 17, emphasizing 1 John 1:9 and 2:1.

9. Whatever the situation, urge the alcoholic to seek further counseling from a pastor or psychologist who understands alcoholism or chemical dependence. Many times it is necessary to deal with the underlying causes of the addiction, such as insecurity, guilt, failure, stress, or deviant sexual behavior.

Scripture

"He who covers his sins will not prosper, but whoever confesses and forsakes them will have mercy" (Proverbs 28:13).

"You will keep him in perfect peace, whose mind is stayed on You, because he trusts in You" (Isaiah 26:3).

"Therefore if the Son makes you free, you shall be free indeed" (John 8:36).

"No temptation has seized you except what is common to man. And God is faithful; he will not let you be tempted beyond what you can bear. But when you are tempted, he will also provide a way out so that you can stand up under it" (1 Corinthians 10:13, NIV).

"Therefore, if anyone is in Christ, he is a new creation; the old has gone, the new has come!" (2 Corinthians 5:17, NIV).

"If we say that we have no sin, we deceive ourselves, and the truth is not in us. If we confess our sins, He is faithful and just to forgive us our sins and to cleanse us from all unrighteousness" (1 John 1:8–9).

Other suggested Scriptures:

Matthew 11:28
John 3:16
Romans 12:1–2
Romans 14:11–12
2 Corinthians 2:14
Galatians 5:22–23

ANGER

Background

Anger is an involuntary reaction to a displeasing situation or event. As long as anger is limited to this involuntary, initial emotion, it may be considered a normal reaction. It is when we respond improperly to anger—when we either lose our temper or store the anger so that it makes us resentful or hostile—that it becomes dangerous. It is here that the Bible calls us to account.

In discussing anger, we must realize that not all anger is wrong. When the Bible mentions anger, it may be focusing on several different emotions. For example:

- Moses was angry when he saw the unfaithfulness and idolatry of his people (Exodus 32:19).

- When He healed the man with the withered hand, Jesus "looked around at them with anger" (Mark 3:5) because He was disturbed by the Pharisees' stubborn hearts.

- Though not explicitly stated, anger is implied in the attitude and actions of our Lord as He drove the profiteers from the temple (Mark 11:15, 17).

- Anger can sometimes be called for in our response to sin: "Be angry, and do not sin" (Ephesians 4:26).

It Is Scriptural to Control Anger

"A fool gives full vent to his anger, but a wise man keeps himself under control" (Proverbs 29:11, NIV). Each person has the right to express his own opinions and to be treated with dignity and respect. At the same time, we should not forget that if Jesus had demanded His "rights," He wouldn't have gone to the cross! The Christian must be careful of his responses, remembering that one's position may be right while the accompanying attitudes may be wrong.

Billy Graham writes: "The Bible does not forbid displeasure, but it sets up two controls. The first is to keep anger clear of bitterness, spite, or hatred. The second is to check daily on how we have handled malevolent feelings. There's an old Latin proverb, 'He who goes angry to bed has the devil for a bedfellow.' Of course, there are many irritations in life. They become prime opportunities for Satan to lead us into evil passion."

Anger Is Excessive or Uncontrolled If It Leads To:

- Outbursts of temper or bad language.

- Bitterness, resentment, and hostility (the urge to "get even").

- Inner turmoil—the loss of one's sense of tranquillity and well-being. Do I have the nagging feeling that my attitude is displeasing to God, or that I "give place to the devil" (Ephesians 4:27)?

- Harm to other people. Does the anger negatively affect my testimony as others observe my bad responses? Are they victims of those responses, physically or emotionally?

How Can We Learn to Control Anger?

1. Don't interpret everything as a personal offense, oversight, or hurt. At the same time, try to pinpoint the things that cause you to become excessively angry.

2. Make your attitudes and responses a matter for serious prayer. Pray also about the irritating behavior of others that has caused your anger. Remember that God uses people and circumstances to refine our character. We may have many rough edges that need to be filed down!

3. Regularly confess excessive anger as sin: "Do not let the sun go down while you are still angry" (Ephesians 4:26, NIV). Learn to balance the books at least by the end of each day.

4. Realize that the Christian must learn to cope with two natures, each striving for supremacy. We must learn to practice the "put off—put on" principle of Ephesians 4:22–24 (NIV):

   A. **"Put off** your old self, which is being corrupted by its deceitful desires" (verse 22, emphasis added).

   B. **"Put on** the new self, created to be like God in true righteousness and holiness" (verse 24, emphasis added).

   C. The effect of practicing the "put off—put on" principle is to "be made new in the attitude of your minds" (verse 23; see 2 Corinthians 5:17).

5. Strive to focus your anger away from yourself, to the problems that are causing it.

6. Surrender each day to the Holy Spirit: "Live by the Spirit, and you will not gratify the desires of the sinful nature" (Galatians 5:16, NIV).

7. Let the Word of God permeate your life as you read, study, and

memorize it: "Let the word of Christ dwell in you richly as you teach and admonish one another with all wisdom" (Colossians 3:16, NIV).

Helping Strategy

1. A personal relationship with Jesus Christ is basic to solving any spiritual problem. Ask the inquirer if he or she has entered into this relationship. Share "Steps to Peace with God," page 11.

2. Ask questions of your Christian inquirer to determine the extent of his or her problem with unresolved or excessive anger. Share from the "Background," emphasizing proper Christian attitudes, daily confession, and the "put off—put on" principle. Suggest writing down the points and Scripture references in order to better remember them.

3. Pray with the inquirer, that he or she may have a "conscience void of offense before God and man"(Acts 24:16), and the faith to trust God for continued victory.

Scripture

"A gentle answer turns away wrath, but a harsh word stirs up anger" (Proverbs 15:1, NIV).

"A fool gives full vent to his anger, but a wise man keeps himself under control" (Proverbs 29:11, NIV).

"You were taught, with regard to your former way of life, to put off your old self, which is being corrupted by its deceitful desires; to be made new in the attitude of your minds; and to put on the new self, created to be like God in true righteousness and holiness" (Ephesians 4:22–24, NIV).

"Put off all these: anger, wrath, malice, blasphemy, filthy language" (Colossians 3:8).

"My dear brothers, take note of this: Everyone should be quick to listen, slow to speak and slow to become angry, for man's anger does not bring about the righteous life that God desires" (James 1:19–20, NIV).

See also Bitterness and Resentment

ANXIETY, WORRY, AND TENSION

Background

The term *anxiety* covers a wide range of problems resulting from unfounded fears. Someone has said that the anxious person and the worrier are so preoccupied about what *may* happen in the future that they forget to cope with the present. It is characteristic of such a person to worry about anything. They build "mountains out of mole hills," as insignificant matters assume great importance in their lives. They are anxious about imagined shortcomings, the future, their health, their families, and their work. They are often unable to pinpoint the reasons for their anxieties and fears.

Many anxious people suffer physical difficulties such as nervousness, sleeplessness, headaches, difficulty in breathing, or excessive sweating. Inability to find relief from the anxiety can lead to more serious consequences, such as a "nervous breakdown." Obviously, such people need our sympathy, our prayers, and whatever help we can offer.

Billy Graham comments: "Mankind has always been beset by worry, and the pressures of modern life have aggravated the problem. . . . Many of you are filled with a thousand anxieties. Bring them to Jesus Christ by faith. . . . I am learning in my own life, day by day, to keep my mind centered on Christ; the worries and anxieties and concerns of the world pass, and nothing but 'perfect peace' is left in the human heart."

Helping Strategy

1. Offer encouragement. The Lord can help! "Why are you cast down, O my soul? And why are you disquieted within me? Hope in God, for I shall yet praise Him for the help of His countenance" (Psalm 42:5). A genuine, healthy fear of God conquers all other fears!

2. Help the inquirer discover the reason for his or her anxiety. Try to offer more than just a temporary relief. As much as possible, seek to get at "root causes." Avoid probing too deeply, however. Limited time for discussion, and the possibility that the person's anxieties are based on traumatic experiences of the past, should limit your questions only to those which will help open the door for presenting Christ as Savior and sustainer. Your questions might include:

- Why are you fearful (about your job, your future, your family, etc.)?

- Why are you nervous? Why do you have headaches? Why can't you sleep?

- Describe the way you feel. Do you feel guilty? What might have caused such feelings?

- Do you think you may be running from something?

Again, these questions should be asked in a friendly, conversational manner. You are discussing these matters as an equal, not as one in the superior position of counselor or spiritual leader.

If the anxiety seems to have been brought on by true feelings of guilt, this could indicate wrong behavior that needs correction. Experiencing God's forgiveness in Christ can remove guilt and guilt feelings, which will contribute to healing. Share "Steps to Peace with God," page 11.

Avoid telling people that if they *think* right they are bound to feel right. To the contrary, some people need to learn that right *living* produces right *feelings*. God alone is the source of positive thoughts. Facing the basic problem—sin—will eventually produce the kind of conduct which pleases God, and will result in better emotional health.

Anxiety about the future may reveal concern about death and future judgment. Again, this opens the door to present Christ.

3. Discuss the necessity of daily Bible study and prayer. We must not only read the Bible, but must assimilate its teachings in such a way that they begin to mold our life and character. Memorizing the Bible is most important. "Thinking God's thoughts" will take the place of worried, anxious concerns.

   Prayer is the companion of Bible study. According to the Bible, we should "be anxious for nothing, but in everything by prayer and supplication, with thanksgiving, let your requests be made known to God" (Philippians 4:6).

4. Share some of the promises of God's Word. God can be trusted to keep His promises. See "Scripture."

5. Advise the inquirer to get involved with a Bible-teaching church. Thinking of and serving with others can be an antidote to negative and unhealthy introspection.

6. Pray with the inquirer for genuine solutions (see Psalm 34:4, next page).

   If you detect deeper problems than you can deal with, suggest that the person consider counseling with a Christian psychologist.

Scripture

"I sought the Lord, and He heard me, and delivered me from all my fears" (Psalm 34:4).

"Why are you downcast, O my soul? Why so disturbed within me? Put your hope in God, for I will yet praise him, my Savior and my God" (Psalm 42:5, NIV).

"But seek first his kingdom and his righteousness, and all these things will be given to you as well. Therefore do not worry about tomorrow, for tomorrow will worry about itself" (Matthew 6:33–34, NIV).

"Do not be anxious about anything, but in everything, by prayer and petition, with thanksgiving, present your requests to God. And the peace of God, which transcends all understanding, will guard your hearts and your minds in Christ Jesus" (Philippians 4:6–7, NIV).

"Casting all your care upon Him, for He cares for you" (1 Peter 5:7).

Other suggested Scriptures:

Psalm 55:22, NIV
Proverbs 3:5–6
Romans 8:28
Philippians 4:13
Philippians 4:19, NIV

ASSURANCE OF SALVATION

Background

Assurance of salvation is the awareness of belonging to Christ and having complete confidence that He has given us everlasting life. Many Christians lack this kind of assurance. Because of ambivalence about their relationship with Christ, they don't really experience the joy of the Lord. The only thing they are entirely sure of is that they have doubts. Uncertainty can stem from any of the following:

- *Not being truly converted.* A Christian is a person who has trusted in Jesus Christ as Lord and Savior:

  "If you confess with your mouth the Lord Jesus and believe in your heart that God has raised Him from the dead, you will be saved. For with the heart one believes to righteousness, and with the mouth confession is made to salvation" (Romans 10:9–10).

  A person who lacks this experience cannot possibly be certain about having eternal life. Salvation is not based on a person's performance, but on his or her relationship with Jesus Christ. Confident Christians can say, "For I know whom I have believed and am persuaded that He is able to keep what I have committed to Him until that Day" (2 Timothy 1:12).

- *Trusting feelings rather than God's Word.* Some people, especially new Christians, expect a sustained, emotional elation; and when this is missing or lags, doubts come. Our eternal relationship with God cannot be based only on emotion. We must rest on facts based on His written Word. We are to commit ourselves to the finished work of Christ on the cross. Having trusted Him, we continue in this relationship, confident that "He who has begun a good work in you will complete it until the day of Jesus Christ" (Philippians 1:6).

- *Sin and disobedience in the life of the Christian.* These will result in ambivalence and uncertainty: "A double-minded man is unstable in all his ways" (James 1:8, KJV). Sin must be acknowledged and confessed in order to maintain unbroken fellowship with God.

The Christian who does not nurture his or her life in the Word of God, prayer, fellowship, and witness will dry up, opening the way to uncertainty and doubts. The biblical admonition to "grow in the grace and knowledge of our Lord and Savior Jesus Christ" (2 Peter 3:18) is not just an idle phrase. We grow or we die.

Helping Strategy

1. *The inquirer who is unsure of salvation:* If the inquirer does not know whether or not he or she has trusted Jesus as Savior and Lord, due to misunderstanding the true nature of Christian conversion or due to dependence on his or her own performance, share "Steps to Peace with God," page 11. Emphasize that salvation means a relationship with Christ through the new birth (John 1:12; 3:3), not through our own efforts (Ephesians 2:9).

2. *The inquirer who has been depending on feelings:* Our experience must rest on the biblical facts of the Gospel, not on emotion. Share "Assurance," page 15.

3. *The Christian who is disobedient, harboring sin in his or her life:* Share "Restoration," page 17. Emphasize 1 John 1:9 and 2:1, and Romans 12:1.

4. *The immature Christian:* If the uncertainty and doubt is the result of arrested spiritual development, stress that either we grow or we die. Share "Restoration," page 17.

5. With all the above, emphasize the need to pursue a vital spiritual relationship with Christ:

   A. Read and study the Bible. Offer to send *Living in Christ* to help the inquirer get started.

   B. Pray. Through prayer, we:

      • worship God

      • confess our sins to Him

      • express our gratitude and thanksgiving

      • remember the needs of others

   C. Seek to develop relationships with other Christians through a Bible-teaching church. This will provide fellowship, Bible study, and opportunities for service to Christ—all necessary to develop the Christian life.

   D. Pray with the inquirer that he or she may begin to know a life of joy and assurance in Christ.

Scripture

Salvation:

"But as many as received Him, to them He gave the right to become children of God, even to those who believe in His name" (John 1:12).

"I tell you the truth, whoever hears my word and believes him who sent me has eternal life and will not be condemned; he has crossed over from death to life" (John 5:24, NIV).

"When someone becomes a Christian he becomes a brand new person inside. He is not the same any more. A new life has begun!" (2 Corinthians 5:17, TLB).

"For by grace you have been saved through faith, and that not of yourselves; it is the gift of God, not of works, lest anyone should boast" (Ephesians 2:8–9).

Salvation Is a Fact, Not Just a Feeling:

"For I am convinced that neither death nor life, neither angels nor demons, neither the present nor the future, nor any powers, neither height nor depth, nor anything else in all creation, will be able to separate us from the love of God that is in Christ Jesus our Lord" (Romans 8 38–39, NIV).

"For God took the sinless Christ and poured into him our sins. Then, in exchange, he poured God's goodness into us!" (2 Corinthians 5:21, TLB).

"And I am sure that God who began the good work within you will keep right on helping you grow in his grace until his task within you is finally finished on that day when Jesus Christ returns" (Philippians 1:6, TLB).

"Yet I am not ashamed, because I know whom I have believed, and am convinced that he is able to guard what I have entrusted to him for that day" (2 Timothy 1:12, NIV).

"And God, in his mighty power, will make sure that you get there safely to receive [eternal life], because you are trusting him. It will be yours in that coming last day for all to see" (1 Peter 1:5, TLB).

"I write these things to you who believe in the name of the Son of God so that you may know that you have eternal life" (1 John 5:13, NIV).

Confession of Sin for Restoration:

"I waited patiently for the Lord; and He inclined to me, and heard my cry. He also brought me up out of a horrible pit, out of the miry clay, and set my feet upon a rock, and established my steps. He has put a new song in my mouth—praise to our God; many will see it and fear, and will trust in the Lord" (Psalm 40:1–3).

"He who covers his sins will not prosper, but whoever confesses and forsakes them will have mercy" (Proverbs 28:13).

"If we confess our sins, He is faithful and just to forgive us our sins and to cleanse us from all unrighteousness" (1 John 1:9).

BACKSLIDING, SPIRITUAL INDIFFERENCE

Background

The dictionary says that to "backslide" means to lapse in morals or religious practice, but backsliding has a deeper spiritual connotation than this would indicate. It means to lose one's fellowship with the Lord, to grow cold and indifferent to spiritual matters, or even to fall away (apostatize) from faith altogether.

There are varying degrees of backsliding:

Apostasy: A falling away because of a conscious rejection of God's truth as revealed in His Word and in His Son.

Sins of the flesh: Habitually giving in to sins such as immorality, drunkenness, or stealing.

Sins of the spirit: Things such as spiritual indifference, lying, cheating, gossip, envy, selfishness, or jealousy (Galatians 5:19–21).

Things That Lead to Backsliding

- Disappointment because of the inconsistencies seen or imagined in other Christians.

- An indifferent relationship with Christ, or ignoring the place of God's Word, prayer, and witnessing in our Christian life.

- Ignorance of the true implications of spiritual responsibility and practice.

- Disobedience to God's revealed will.

- Willful sin which remains unconfessed.

Billy Graham has wisely commented: "If you are a true believer in Christ, you are going to be at war. The lusts of the flesh, the influence of the world, and the devil are going to war against your Christian life. The flesh will fight against the spirit, and the spirit against the flesh, and there will be constant conflict. The only time you will have perfect peace is when you are totally committed and yielded to Christ in every phase of your life. Too many people want to have one foot in the world and one foot in the kingdom of God, and it is like straddling a fence. You are not happy either way. Declare yourself for Christ."

Helping Strategy

You should seek true repentance, confession, and restoration of the inquirer, so that his or her life might be renewed in love for Christ, for the Bible, and for service to others.

In order to accomplish this goal, try to determine how the inquirer has fallen away from fellowship or relationship with the Lord. If he or she seems unsure about his or her original commitment to Christ, review "Steps to Peace with God," page 11. If the person is willing to face certain issues, encourage him or her to:

1. Confess to the Lord all known sin (1 John 1:9).

2. Review with you the "Restoration" section on page 17. By confession he or she can be renewed. There is no sin that God will not forgive in Christ.

3. Start reading and studying the Bible and praying daily. Offer to send *Living in Christ,* which will help launch serious Bible study.

4. Seek a Bible-teaching church for fellowship, instruction, and opportunities for service.

5. Make restitution, if necessary, to make right anything through which others might have been offended or taken advantage of.

Pray with the person for full restoration and blessing. Suggest memorizing Proverbs 3:5–6 and learning to lean on its truth in the days ahead.

Scripture
Repentance and Confession:

"I waited patiently for the Lord; and He inclined to me, and heard my cry. He also brought me up out of a horrible pit, out of the miry clay, and set my feet upon a rock, and established my steps. He has put a new song in my mouth—praise to our God; many will see it and fear, and will trust in the Lord" (Psalm 40:1–3).

"The sacrifices of God are a broken spirit, a broken and a contrite heart— these, O God, You will not despise" (Psalm 51:17).

"He who covers his sins will not prosper, but whoever confesses and forsakes them will have mercy" (Proverbs 28:13).

"If we confess our sins, He is faithful and just to forgive us our sins and to cleanse us from all unrighteousness" (1 John 1:9).

Promise of Forgiveness:

"If My people who are called by My name will humble themselves, and pray and seek My face, and turn from their wicked ways, then I will hear from heaven, and will forgive their sin and heal their land" (2 Chronicles 7:14).

"Let the wicked forsake his way, and the unrighteous man his thoughts; let him return to the Lord, and He will have mercy on him; and to our God, for He will abundantly pardon" (Isaiah 55:7).

Spiritual Growth:

". . . that Christ may dwell in your hearts through faith; that you, being rooted and grounded in love, may be able to comprehend with all the saints what is the width and length and depth and height—to know the love of Christ which passes knowledge; that you may be filled with all the fullness of God" (Ephesians 3:17–19).

"Do not be anxious about anything, but in everything, by prayer and petition, with thanksgiving, present your requests to God. And the peace of God, which transcends all understanding, will guard your hearts and your minds in Christ Jesus" (Philippians 4:6–7, NIV).

"Let the word of Christ dwell in you richly in all wisdom, teaching and admonishing one another in psalms and hymns and spiritual songs, singing with grace in your hearts to the Lord" (Colossians 3:16).

Trust in God for Daily Victory:

"Trust in the Lord with all your heart, and lean not on your own understanding; in all your ways acknowledge Him, and He shall direct your paths" (Proverbs 3:5–6).

"He who did not spare His own Son, but delivered Him up for us all, how shall He not with Him also freely give us all things?" (Romans 8:32).

"Yet in all these things we are more than conquerors through Him who loved us" (Romans 8:37).

BAD HABITS

Background

Human beings are creatures of habit. Many of our practices become automatic; we are sometimes unaware that we do certain things or that we do them in a specific way.

The designation "Bad Habits" covers a wide range of negative behavior and could be defined as anything that inhibits Christian growth or offends others. We may be speaking of the so-called sins of the spirit, such as envy, jealousy, malice, gossip, lying, criticism of others, selfishness, impatience, quarreling, or procrastination. Or, we may be speaking of various compulsive behaviors: overeating, drinking, smoking, overspending, reading and viewing pornography, excessive working, fantasizing and evil thoughts, masturbation, or swearing.

The subject of bad habits assumes special importance in the light of the scriptural demand that Christians "walk in newness of life" (Romans 6:4). As we surrender to the Lord, asking Him to search our hearts and reveal all that is displeasing to Him (Psalm 139:23-24), we will begin to see many ugly things that need to be dealt with. The most important thing to remember with regard to bad habits is that they displease God, but that with His help the bad habits can be broken and replaced with more wholesome alternatives.

None of us is immune to change. The Gospel specializes in change (2 Corinthians 5:17). We know that God can work in our lives in order to bring our conduct into line with what pleases Him: "For we are God's workmanship, created in Christ Jesus to do good works, which God prepared in advance for us to do" (Ephesians 2:10, NIV).

Helping Strategy

1. Commend the inquirer for being sufficiently interested in spiritual values to seek solutions to problems related to bad habits. Change is possible for anyone, regardless of age or other limitations: "I can do all things through Christ who strengthens me" (Philippians 4:13). His help and the prospect of breaking the shackles of the bad habits should provide the motivation for achieving ultimate victory.

2. Ask if the inquirer has ever received Jesus Christ as personal Savior and Lord. One might assume that someone inquiring about conquering bad habits would be a Christian, but don't take it for granted. Is the inquirer confident about having experienced that abiding relationship with Christ

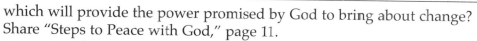

which will provide the power promised by God to bring about change? Share "Steps to Peace with God," page 11.

3. Suggest that the bad habit or habits (sins) be faced in specific terms. It is necessary to identify those areas that need changing. It is a challenge to be faced realistically, because habits are hard to break. They cannot be "wished" away. The use of pious phrases is of little help. We must work at it. The apostle Paul put this in perspective when he said, "O wretched man that I am! Who will deliver me from this body of death?" (Romans 7:24). Cures are neither instantaneous nor easy.

4. Encourage the person to confess his or her bad habits to the Lord as sin, and to seek forgiveness. At the same time, help the person to make a covenant with God to work through to victory. A definite commitment at a given place and time will set the stage for change. Take a stand; be an overcomer. (See Joshua's statement in Joshua 24:15.)

5. Tell the inquirer that bad habits can be broken by practicing the principle of replacement or exchange—what the apostle Paul speaks of as the "put off—put on" principle: "You were taught, with regard to your former way of life, to put off your old self, which is being corrupted by its deceitful desires; to be made new in the attitude of your minds: and to put on the new self, created to be like God in true righteousness and holiness. Therefore each of you must put off falsehood and speak truthfully" (Ephesians 4:22-25, NIV). And, "He who has been stealing must steal no longer, but must work . . ." (Ephesians 4:28, NIV).

Memorized Scripture can be a great help in practicing the "put off—put on" principle of exchange. For the Christian afflicted with the inclination for swearing or bad language, a "replacement Scripture" such as the following would be helpful: "Let no corrupt communication proceed out of your mouth, but what is good for necessary edification, that it may impart grace to the hearers" (Ephesians 4:29). At other times, one might use a word of praise, such as those found in Psalm 34 or 103.

Assure your inquirer that there is a wholesome replacement for each bad habit which is broken!

6. Suggest that daily Bible reading, study, Scripture memorization, and prayer are of great value. As God's thoughts invade our minds, things must begin to change.

7. Suggest that a fellowship link be established with another Christian for mutual sharing of problems, prayers, and victories. This sort of "buddy system" has helped many people.

8. Suggest seeking opportunities to serve Christ. As we begin to share

ourselves, our experiences, and the fruit of our Bible study and personal victories, we are "fortified in the inner man."

9. If the inquirer is not already a member of an active Bible-teaching church, he or she should seek such a relationship. This will give opportunity for fellowship, prayer, Bible study, and opportunities for service.

10. Suggest selecting one bad habit to overcome, and setting some immediate goals.

11. Pray with the inquirer for victory over the bad habit, to the glory of God.

Scripture

"Your word I have hidden in my heart, that I might not sin against You" (Psalm 119:11).

"Then He said to them all, 'If anyone desires to come after Me, let him deny himself, and take up his cross daily, and follow Me'" (Luke 9:23).

"In the same way, count yourselves dead to sin but alive to God in Christ Jesus. Therefore do not let sin reign in your mortal body so that you obey its evil desires. Do not offer the parts of your body to sin, as instruments of wickedness, but rather offer yourselves to God, as those who have been brought from death to life; and offer the parts of your body to him as instruments of righteousness. For sin shall not be your master, because you are not under law, but under grace" (Romans 6:11–14, NIV).

"In all these things we are more than conquerors through Him who loved us" (Romans 8:37).

"For it is God who works in you to will and to act according to his good purpose . . . so that you may become blameless and pure, children of God without fault in a crooked and depraved generation, in which you shine like stars in the universe" (Philippians 2:13, 15, NIV).

"Submit to God. Resist the devil and he will flee from you. Draw near to God and He will draw near to you" (James 4:7–8).

Other suggested Scriptures:

Jeremiah 17:9–10, NIV
Galatians 2:20
2 Timothy 2:15, NIV

THE BIBLE

Background

Some uninformed Christians or sincere doubters question the authority of the Bible, believing that it is just a collection of myths and inaccuracies. Three things characterize almost everyone who has difficulty accepting the authority of the Scripture:

- They seldom, if ever, bother to read the Bible.
- They approach the Bible with prejudiced ideas learned from Bible critics and their writings.
- They are not acquainted with the Bible's "Author."

Can we trust the Bible? Yes!

Billy Graham says: "Long ago I decided to accept the Bible by faith. This should not be difficult for anyone to do. Most of us do not understand nuclear fission, but we accept it. I don't understand television, but I accept it. . . . Why is it so easy to accept all these man-made miracles and so difficult to accept the miracles of the Bible?"

What Is Our Authority for Believing the Bible?

1. The Bible itself claims to be the inspired Word of God:

   "All Scripture is God-breathed and is useful for teaching, rebuking, correcting and training in righteousness, so that the man of God may be thoroughly equipped for every good work" (2 Timothy 3:16–17, NIV).

   "Above all, you must understand that no prophecy of Scripture came about by the prophet's own interpretation. For prophecy never had its origin in the will of man, but men spoke from God as they were carried along by the Holy Spirit" (2 Peter 1:20–21, NIV).

2. Jesus and the apostles confirmed the authenticity of the Old Testament, quoting it scores of times in their writings and ministries. Jesus said, "I tell you the truth, until heaven and earth disappear, not the smallest letter, not the least stroke of a pen, will by any means disappear from the Law until everything is accomplished" (Matthew 5:18, NIV). Peter quoted David's words to substantiate the resurrection of Jesus Christ (Acts 2:29–36).

3. The historical church has recognized and used the Bible as God's

inspired record of Himself and His will. The Bible has always been the ultimate rule of faith and practice for the true church.

4. History and archaeology combine to confirm the accuracy of the Bible. The historical record is obvious and indisputable. Many of the places mentioned in the Bible can easily be identified, even today. Hundreds of archaeological sites have yielded ample evidence to substantiate the Christian's claim that the Bible can be trusted. Many ancient manuscripts of the Bible have been preserved to the present day; among them:

   - *The Dead Sea Scrolls* confirm either fragments of, or the complete text of, all the books of the Old Testament except Esther. Some of these manuscripts go back to the second and third centuries before Christ.

   - The *Septuagint* (Greek Translation of the Old Testament) dates from 250 B.C.

   - *Codex Sinaiticus,* containing the entire New Testament and parts of the Old Testament, dates from about 330 A.D.

   All of these documents, and many more, are available for examination to any interested person.

5. Fulfilled prophecies witness to the Bible's accuracy. For instance, people living hundreds of years before Christ predicted that He would:

   - Be born of a virgin (Isaiah 7:14; see Luke 2:26–35).

   - Be born in Bethlehem (Micah 5:2; see Luke 2:4–7).

   - Live a sinless life (Isaiah 53:9; see 2 Corinthians 5:21).

   - Be put to death (Isaiah 53:5, 7; see Matthew 27:35).

   - Cry from the cross, "My God, My God, why have You forsaken Me?" (Psalm 22:1; see Matthew 27:46).

6. The Bible's remarkable unity and coherence confirm its authenticity. It reveals a single author—the Holy Spirit—behind the diversity of its human writers. The Bible is not just a jumble of characters, places, and dates. It has an amazing continuity, as both the fact and the message of the Bible are closely and amazingly interconnected to reveal God's Son, our Lord and Savior Jesus Christ, and His part in human redemption and restoration. The sixty-six books comprising the Bible fit together as one book with one theme: Jesus Christ.

7. The Bible is confirmed by its power to transform lives. Its message exploded on the human scene in New Testament times to turn the world "upside down" (Acts 17:6). There is power in the Bible's message. From the apostle Paul's time down to the present day, the power of the Gospel

has changed lives. Only those countries affected by the Gospel have seen any real social progress—the guarantee of human rights, fair treatment of children and women, medical advances, and freedom from slavery, among other things.

The Bible is the only book ever written which gives satisfactory answers to life's ultimate questions: Who am I? Where did I come from? Why am I here? Where am I going? What is the purpose of life?

Helping Strategy

Never argue! If the inquirer is open-minded enough to listen, present as much of the "Background" as you can.

1. A person's acceptance of the Bible is directly related to his or her willingness to accept its Author. At some convenient point during the conversation, ask the inquirer if he or she has ever received Jesus Christ as Lord and Savior. Share "Steps to Peace with God," page 11.

2. Suggest that he or she obtain a recent translation of the Bible to read and study. Approaching it with an open mind and asking God to reveal Himself, His will, and His eternal purposes should be a rewarding experience. Offer to send *Living in Christ* to foster the beginning of serious Bible reading and study.

3. Recommend finding a Bible-teaching church for worship, Bible study, and fellowship with others who take the Bible seriously.

4. Pray with the inquirer for spiritual illumination, for faith, and for fulfillment in life through the power of the Word: "And now, brethren, I commend you to God and to the word of His grace, which is able to build you up and give you an inheritance among all those who are sanctified" (Acts 20:32).

Additional Suggestions

1. If the inquirer admits to not having read much of the Bible, challenge him or her to get started at once, following the same method as with any experiment: Approach the Bible impartially and give it a chance in his or her thinking. Suggest starting with the gospel of Luke, then going to Acts, then wherever he or she might choose.

2. Answers to some common objections:

   • "The Bible says that humans have been on the earth for only approximately 6,000 years."

   Answer: Nowhere does the Bible state that people have been here only

6,000 years. This misconception is probably due to Bishop Ussher's chronology, developed in the 1600s. The Bible doesn't say mankind is 6,000 years old, nor 60,000 nor 600,000. It does say, "In the beginning God created the heavens and the earth" (Genesis 1:1).

- "The Bible is filled with inaccuracies."

  Answer: To test the person's knowledge, ask, "What inaccuracies?" Should he or she bring up creation, Noah's ark, Joshua's long day, Jonah's fish, the Virgin Birth, etc., respond that we cannot explain these things, though we believe they are historical. We don't have to defend them. God has spoken. The Bible demands the exercise of faith! Quote Billy Graham from the "Background." Paul the apostle said, in writing of those who have problems with Scripture, "But the natural man does not receive the things of the Spirit of God, for they are foolishness to him; nor can he know them, because they are spiritually discerned [known only through the Holy Spirit]" (1 Corinthians 2:14).

- "I find the Bible hard to believe," or, "I can't understand it."

  Answer: Suggest purchasing a modern translation of the Bible and trying again. Quote Mark Twain: "It's not the things I don't understand about the Bible that bother me; it's the things I do understand that bother me."

If the inquirer seems sincere in his or her doubts, suggest the prayer given by John Stott in his book *Basic Christianity:* "God, if You exist (and I don't know if You do), and if You can hear this prayer (and I don't know if You can), I want to tell You that I am an honest seeker after the truth. Show me if Jesus is Your Son and the Savior of the world. And if You bring conviction to my mind, I will trust Him as my Savior and follow Him as my Lord."

3. You may find it helpful to share with the caller this personal testimony from Dwight L. Moody concerning the power of the Bible's message:

"I prayed for faith, and I thought that some day faith would come down and strike me like lightning. But faith did not come. One day I was reading the tenth chapter of Romans: 'Faith comes by hearing, and hearing by the word of God' (Romans 10:17). I had closed my Bible and prayed for faith. I now opened my Bible, and began to study, and faith has been growing ever since."

Scripture

"For whatever things were written before were written for our learning, that we through the patience and comfort of the Scriptures might have hope" (Romans 15:4).

"For this reason we also thank God without ceasing, because when you received the word of God which you heard from us, you welcomed it not as the word of men, but as it is in truth, the word of God, which also effectively works in you who believe" (1 Thessalonians 2:13).

"The word of God is living and active. Sharper than any double-edged sword, it penetrates even to dividing soul and spirit, joints and marrow; it judges the thoughts and attitudes of the heart" (Hebrews 4:12, NIV).

Other suggested Scriptures:

Acts 20:32
2 Timothy 3:16–17
2 Peter 1:20–21

BITTERNESS AND RESENTMENT

Background

Bitterness is the product of intense animosity, characterized by cynicism and ill will. Resentment is indignant displeasure and ill will which results from a wrong, an insult or injury, either real, imagined, or unintentional. Bitterness and resentment often go together, the dual results of unresolved anger.

Billy Graham says: "The Bible does not forbid displeasure, but it sets up two controls. The first is to keep anger clear of bitterness, spite, and hatred. The second is to check daily to see how we have handled malevolent feelings. There's an old Latin proverb: 'He who goes angry to bed has the devil for a bedfellow.' Of course, there are many irritations in life. They become prime opportunities for Satan to lead us into evil passion."

Professional counselors reveal that a large percentage of those being counseled today are angry, embittered, and resentful. Bottled-up feelings eat away until some become emotional cripples and physically ill. Their ability to function is impaired, diminishing their effectiveness. They often have difficulty sleeping; and their personal relationships, both within and without the family, erode. Some become so obsessed with the urge to "get even" that they may kill someone. The individual who has deep-seated, unresolved anger is not a whole person.

A classic case of the "grudge and get even" syndrome is found in the story of Cain and Abel (Genesis 4:1–16). Cain was angry because his offering was not accepted while his brother's offering was. It really wasn't a matter between Cain and Abel at all, but between Cain and God, for it was God who had rejected Cain's offering. But Cain became resentful and depressed. Instead of repenting and asking forgiveness of the Lord, he turned on his brother.

Many times people will share problems of this nature because they are seeking sympathy or reinforcement. They will tell you how they have been misunderstood, maligned, and mistreated, never realizing the sinful implications behind their own behavior. As the story unfolds and you detect resentment and bitterness, treat it as sin.

God's Word says, "Put off all these: anger, wrath, malice, blasphemy, filthy language" (Colossians 3:8).

Helping Strategy

1. As your inquirer reveals the problem, remain neutral. Assure him or her that God's Word has the solution to any problem.

2. Assure yourself that you are speaking with someone who has truly received Christ. If this is not the case, then share "Steps to Peace with God," page 11.

3. If your inquirer has not yet realized that he or she has a problem with bitterness and resentment, or if he or she is aware of it and sincerely wants to find a solution, make sure he or she understands that bitterness is sin. To ignore this will prevent any real solution.

4. Repentance and confession will result in forgiveness and restoration to fellowship with God. Share "Restoration," page 17, emphasizing 1 John 1:9. Pray together, asking the inquirer to privately confess to God all known bitterness and resentment.

5. If the above is accomplished, then steps toward reconciliation are in order, especially if there has been accusation, recrimination, criticism, and a rupture in a relationship. Victory comes when matters are solved on both the vertical and horizontal planes. The prize is a "conscience without offense toward God and men" (Acts 24:16).

   It is not necessary to make a public issue of it, but Jesus said, "First be reconciled to your brother" (Matthew 5:24).

   The apostle Paul advised, "If it is possible, as far as it depends on you, live at peace with everyone. . . . 'If your enemy is hungry, feed him; if he is thirsty, give him something to drink. In doing this, you will heap burning coals on his head.' Do not be overcome by evil, but overcome evil with good" (Romans 12:18, 20-21, NIV). If there is reconciliation, God will be pleased and both parties will be spiritually healed. If, on the other hand, nothing positive happens, the inquirer will have done all God requires. He or she has been obedient and can live with a clear conscience.

6. Urge your inquirer to pray to be filled with love for the other person, whether or not reconciliation occurs: "Love . . . keeps no record of wrongs. Love does not delight in evil" (1 Corinthians 13:4–6, NIV).

7. If the bitterness and resentment are of long standing, and the inquirer stubbornly maintains the correctness of his or her position, share Paul's admonition: "Get rid of all bitterness, rage and anger, brawling and

slander, along with every form of malice. Be kind and compassionate to one another, forgiving each other, just as in Christ God forgave you" (Ephesians 4:31–32, NIV). Ask him or her to reflect on the passage and to pray for his or her enemies in the light of its truth.

8. Pray with the inquirer.

Scripture

"For if you forgive men when they sin against you, your heavenly Father will also forgive you. But if you do not forgive men their sins, your Father will not forgive your sins" (Matthew 6:14–15, NIV).

"Bless those who persecute you; bless and do not curse. Rejoice with those who rejoice; mourn with those who mourn. Live in harmony with one another. Do not be proud, but be willing to associate with people of low position. Do not be conceited. Do not repay anyone evil for evil. Be careful to do what is right in the eyes of everybody. If it is possible, as far as it depends on you, live at peace with everyone. Do not take revenge, my friends, but leave room for God's wrath, for it is written: 'It is mine to avenge; I will repay,' says the Lord" (Romans 12:14–19, NIV).

"Make every effort to live in peace with all men and to be holy; without holiness no one will see the Lord. See to it that no one misses the grace of God and that no bitter root grows up to cause trouble and defile many" (Hebrews 12:14–15, NIV).

"When they hurled their insults at [Jesus], he did not retaliate; when he suffered, he made no threats. Instead, he entrusted himself to him who judges justly" (1 Peter 2:23, NIV).

See also Anger

CHILD ABUSE

Background

Child abuse is a great American tragedy. Children of domestic violence are found in all socioeconomic, educational, racial, and age groups. Patterns of violence often run in families; the battered becomes the batterer. Abuse falls into several categories: verbal, emotional, physical, and sexual. Any one of these can be so devastating in the life of a child that he or she may never recover from the damage.

Verbal abuse can be degrading, debasing the child. He or she may feel that any physical abuse that follows is deserved. The screaming parent often accompanies these tirades with swearing, foul language, and constant put-downs: "You can't do anything right"; "Stop acting like a child"; "You should be more like so-and-so." This can rob a child of all self-esteem, cause problems with identity, and depress the child to the point of becoming an emotional cripple.

Add physical punishment to this, and the child will be further denied that proper emotional development which produces a normal, responsible adult. It is easy for the abused child to slip into drugs, alcohol, or deviant sexual behavior.

Such children often are depressed, do poorly in school, misbehave, and are delinquent. They are frequently deceptive and lie, steal, cheat, and violate the rights of others. Assuming violence to be a normal behavioral response, the child reverts to it in order to solve problems in school, with peers, and with family. He or she will often be suicidal and may entertain thoughts of murdering his or her parents. A great percentage of our prison population is the product of family violence.

Proper emotional responses in such children are almost impossible; but a tender, loving attitude may at least begin to open a door to solutions.

Helping Strategy

1. Be sensitive, patient, and caring in your approach. You may be speaking to a child who is incapable of comprehension on the emotional level.

2. Reinforce the child's motive in calling:

   - We are glad you called.

   - We are here to help you.

   - God loves you and we love you.

- You are special to Him and to us.
- God knows what you are going through and will help.

3. Ask the child how he or she feels about himself or herself. As he or she reports abuse which may have come from a father, mother, or elder sibling, find out how he or she feels about the constant punishment. Such people may feel that they deserve the physical punishment they have been receiving.

4. Reassure the child that he or she is not necessarily bad. Sometimes parents do not realize that they are being abusive. They do not necessarily need a motive for hurting a child. Seventy percent of abusers were themselves abused as children.

5. Tell the child about the love of Jesus and how He showed it: Jesus died on the cross for him or her. Jesus is preparing a special kingdom for children ("For of such is the kingdom of heaven," Matthew 19:14).

6. Ask if he or she has ever received Jesus as Savior. If not, share "Steps to Peace with God," page 11.

7. Ask if he or she has a Bible. Encourage reading it. If needed, offer to provide a copy of the Bible in a modern translation. Offer to send either *Living in Christ* (12 years and above) or *Jesus Loves Me* (under 12). This will help the child get started in daily Bible study.

8. Does the person go to church? If he or she knows the pastor, suggest telling the pastor about all that he or she is going through, even though it may be very embarrassing to do so. The pastor needs to know about the abuse in order to help. The abusing parent is not likely to change unless faced with the legal implications of his or her behavior. The pastor can confront the parents, arrange for counseling, and contact the necessary authorities if necessary.

9. Pray with the child for further encouragement.

Scripture

"Come to me, all you who are weary and burdened, and I will give you rest" (Matthew 11:28, NIV).

"Jesus said, 'Let the little children come to me, and do not hinder them'" (Matthew 19:14, NIV).

"Let him have all your worries and cares, for he is always thinking about you and watching everything that concerns you" (1 Peter 5:7, TLB).

THE CHURCH

Background

By definition, the church is the "body of Christ," that community of the redeemed of which He is the head: "And He is the head of the body, the church, who is the beginning, the firstborn from the dead, that in all things He may have the preeminence" (Colossians 1:18).

The church is nurtured by Christ's own dynamic life:

"Husbands, love your wives, just as Christ also loved the church and gave Himself for it, that He might sanctify and cleanse it with the washing of water by the word" (Ephesians 5:25–26).

"Christ will come to claim the church as His bride adorned for her husband" (Revelation 21:2), ". . . that He might present it to Himself a glorious church, not having spot or wrinkle or any such thing, but that it should be holy and without blemish" (Ephesians 5:27).

The church's birth was confirmed by the coming of the Holy Spirit (Acts 2:1–11), who also provides the power for its self-perpetuation through witness to the world (Acts 1:8).

The Church Is Both Visible and Invisible

- The *invisible* church is that larger body of believers who, down through the ages, have sincerely trusted Jesus Christ as Lord and Savior: "The Lord knows those who are His" (2 Timothy 2:19). One becomes a member of the invisible church when he or she receives Jesus Christ as Lord and Savior (John 1:12).

- The *visible* church is the present-day universal church, composed of local groups of Christians. In it are both the "wheat and tares" (Matthew 13:25–30)—the truly redeemed, and many who are not.

When a person experiences the new birth, he or she becomes a member of the invisible church. He or she should seek to identify immediately with a local church which honors the Lord and His Word, in order to take an active part in worship, fellowship, evangelism, Bible study, and prayer. This is a responsibility which the Bible teaches: "Let us not give up meeting together, as some are in the habit of doing, but let us encourage one another—and all the more as you see the Day approaching" (Hebrews 10:25, NIV).

(Sadly, there have been many churches down through the centuries that have denied "the faith which was once for all delivered" [Jude 3], and which therefore do very little to nurture the believers committed to their care.)

Billy Graham writes: *"The church is primarily the body of Christ. . . . The Bible says . . . that it was Christ's love for the church that caused Him to go to the cross. If Christ loved the church that much . . . I must love it too. I must pray for it, defend it, work in it, pay my tithes and offerings to it, help to advance it, promote holiness in it, and make it the functional, witnessing body our Lord meant it to be. You go to church with that attitude this Sunday, and nobody will keep you away the next. . . . The family of God contains people of various ethnological, cultural, class, and denominational differences. I have learned that there can be minor disagreements of theology, methods and motives, but that within the true church there is a mysterious unity that overrides all divisive factors."*

Helping Strategy

1. Commend the inquirer for his or her interest in the church. We are being obedient to God when we identify with the local church. In church we are seeking the opportunity to worship, fellowship, evangelize, study the Bible, pray, and participate in the Lord's Supper.

2. Becoming a member of a local church does not save us. We identify with a church *because* we are saved and desire to be obedient. Jesus said, "I am the door. If anyone enters by Me, he will be saved" (John 10:9). Ask the inquirer if he or she has received Jesus Christ as Lord and Savior. Share "Steps to Peace with God," page 11.

3. After trusting Christ, the inquirer should seek to identify immediately with a local church. Suggest that he or she pray for God's guidance in finding the right church, one which exalts Christ, preaches and teaches the Bible, and evangelizes the lost.

4. Once the person becomes a member of a church, faithful attendance is very important.

5. He or she should seek a place of service in the church. Opportunities are always available if we offer ourselves in service to God.

6. Encourage financial support of the church. Other Christian causes and ministries are worthy of our giving but in order to function and grow, the local church should receive a substantial part of its members' tithes and offerings.

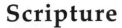

Scripture

The book of Acts presents the birth of the church, its early growth, and the people involved.

The Epistles were directed to the church and provide guidelines for faith and practice.

CULTS

Background

A cult can be defined as a religious group which teaches doctrines or beliefs which deviate from the broad consensus of orthodox Christian doctrine down through the ages. Cults either distort truth or focus on half-truths. The small amount of truth which they do proclaim is often mixed with doctrinal error and is therefore dangerous. Cults succeed in deceiving many. As Paul warned, "The time will come when men will not put up with sound doctrine. . . . They will turn their ears away from the truth and turn aside to myths" (2 Timothy 4:3–4, NIV). Jesus said, "For many will come in My name, saying, 'I am He,' and will deceive many" (Mark 13:6).

What Has Caused the Proliferation of Cults?

Cults thrive on ignorance and uncertainty. Christians who do not know what they believe or why they believe it are especially vulnerable. Churches are lax in their responsibility to teach God's Word and disciple Christians. Paul admonished Timothy to, "Preach the Word; be prepared in season and out of season; correct, rebuke and encourage—with great patience and careful instruction" (2 Timothy 4:2, NIV).

Features Common to All Cults

- *Extra-biblical or special revelation.* To the sixty-six books of the Old and New Testaments, cults typically add their own revelations, which take precedence over the Bible. Or, a limited number of Scripture passages are used completely out of context, resulting in erroneous interpretations. The Bible is explicit in defending its own integrity: "If anybody is preaching to you a gospel other than what you accepted, let him be eternally condemned!" (Galatians 1:9, NIV; see also Revelation 22:18–19).

- *Salvation by works.* Any teaching that encourages people to seek a right relationship with God apart from the person and work of Jesus Christ is in error. This can take the form of a complete rejection of Christ and His work, or a partial rejection that tries to *add to* His work. The Gospel consists of grace—plus nothing and minus nothing (Ephesians 2:8–9).

- *A denial of or lack of full recognition of Jesus Christ as God's Son.* Cults either totally deny Christ or relegate Him to a place that is less than He merits.

"Who is a liar but he who denies that Jesus is the Christ? He is antichrist who denies the Father and the Son" (1 John 2:22).

"For no other foundation can anyone lay than that which is laid, which is Jesus Christ" (1 Corinthians 3:11).

"Christ is the exact likeness of the unseen God. He existed before God made anything at all, and, in fact, Christ himself is the Creator who made everything in heaven and earth" (Colossians 1:15–16, TLB).

"He is before all things, and in him all things hold together" (Colossians 1:17, NIV).

"The Word [Jesus] became flesh and dwelt among us, and we beheld His glory, the glory as of the only begotten of the Father, full of grace and truth" (John 1:14).

"Nor is there salvation in any other, for there is no other name under heaven given among men by which we must be saved" (Acts 4:12).

Helping Strategy

1. The Christian who has been deceived into joining a cult should be encouraged to:

   A. Reassure himself or herself about his or her personal relationship with Jesus Christ. Happy indeed is that believer who can say with the apostle Paul, "For I know whom I have believed and am persuaded that He is able to keep what I have committed to Him until that Day" (2 Timothy 1:12).

   B. Constantly reaffirm his or her faith and commitment by adhering to the teachings of the Bible: "So then, just as you received Christ Jesus as Lord, continue to live in him, rooted and built up in him, strengthened in the faith as you were taught, and overflowing with thankfulness. See to it that no one takes you captive through hollow and deceptive philosophy, which depends on human tradition and the basic principles of this world rather than on Christ" (Colossians 2:6–8, NIV).

   C. Be sure he or she is identified with an evangelical church and takes an active part in the ministry of that church.

   D. Pray with the person for definite deliverance from the cult and commitment to the Lord Jesus Christ and His Word.

2. If you are talking with an aggressive cult member, you will find it necessary to assume command of the conversation; otherwise, you may

be overwhelmed with an endless defense of the cult's false doctrines and organization. If this happens, you might try interrupting with a statement such as, "Yes, I understand that this is very meaningful to you, but let me ask you a few important questions."

Here are some questions you should ask the cultist:

A. What do you think of Jesus? Is He God's Son? Is He the only Savior? (Recite John 3:16 and Acts 4:12.)

B. What do you believe about sin? Are you a sinner? If you don't trust Jesus Christ for forgiveness, how will you find it?

C. Whether you receive positive or negative answers to the above, ask the most important question of all: Have you ever received Jesus Christ as your personal Savior? Or: Do you know God's plan for peace and life? (See page 11.)

D. Encourage the person to take a definite stand for Christ by leaving the cult and former associations. There must be a complete break with the past.

E. Encourage him or her to get into a church that holds to the historical evangelical Christian position, where he or she can begin to study the Bible for what it actually says.

F. Pray with him or her for complete deliverance and for complete commitment to Christ and to the Word of God.

Scripture

False Teachers, False Doctrines Prophesied:

"For such men are false apostles, deceitful workmen, masquerading as apostles of Christ. And no wonder, for Satan himself masquerades as an angel of light. It is not surprising, then, if his servants masquerade as servants of righteousness. Their end will be what their actions deserve" (2 Corinthians 11:13–15, NIV).

"But, dear friends, remember what the apostles of our Lord Jesus Christ foretold. They said to you, 'In the last times there will be scoffers who will follow their own ungodly desires.' These are the men who divide you, who follow mere natural instincts and do not have the Spirit" (Jude 17–19, NIV).

How to Discern Error:

"At that time if anyone says to you, 'Look, here is the Christ!' or, 'Look, there he is!' do not believe it. For false Christs and false prophets will appear and perform signs and miracles to deceive the elect—if that were possible. So be on your guard; I have told you everything ahead of time" (Mark 13:21–23, NIV).

"Evil men and impostors will go from bad to worse, deceiving and being deceived. But as for you, continue in what you have learned and have become convinced of, because you know those from whom you learned it, and how from infancy you have known the holy Scriptures, which are able to make you wise for salvation through faith in Christ Jesus" (2 Timothy 3:13–15, NIV).

"Dear friends, do not believe every spirit, but test the spirits to see whether they are from God, because many false prophets have gone out into the world. This is how you can recognize the Spirit of God: Every spirit that acknowledges that Jesus Christ has come in the flesh is from God, but every spirit that does not acknowledge Jesus is not from God. This is the spirit of the antichrist, which you have heard is coming and even now is already in the world" (1 John 4:1–3, NIV).

How to Resist Error:

"Watch and pray, lest you enter into temptation. The spirit truly is ready, but the flesh is weak" (Mark 14:38).

". . . that you may approve the things that are excellent, that you may be sincere and without offense till the day of Christ, being filled with the fruits of righteousness which are by Jesus Christ, to the glory and praise of God" (Philippians 1:10–11).

"Be diligent to present yourself approved to God, a worker who does not need to be ashamed, rightly dividing the word of truth" (2 Timothy 2:15).

"But you, dear friends, build yourselves up in your most holy faith and pray in the Holy Spirit. Keep yourselves in God's love as you wait for the mercy of our Lord Jesus Christ to bring you to eternal life. Be merciful to those who doubt; snatch others from the fire and save them; to others show mercy, mixed with fear—hating even the clothing stained by corrupted flesh" (Jude 20–23, NIV).

Other suggested Scriptures:
2 Timothy 4:3–5, NIV

See also False Teaching

DEATH

Background

The Bible contains hundreds of references to death. It is a formidable foe: "The last enemy that will be destroyed is death" (1 Corinthians 15:26); but also a conquered foe: "Death is swallowed up in victory" (1 Corinthians 15:54).

Jesus Christ has changed the meaning of death, as Scripture amply shows. At death, the spirit of the believing Christian enters immediately into the presence of the Lord. Physical death is but a transition from life on earth with Christ to life in heaven with Christ. Death does not alter the continuity of relationship; it only enriches it.

"To be with Christ is far better," says Paul (see Philippians 1:23); and he confirms that the transition to that new state is immediate: "We are confident, yes, well pleased rather to be absent from the body and to be present with the Lord" (2 Corinthians 5:8).

The Bible teaches that someday the "dead in Christ" are going to be resurrected, at which time we shall be given new bodies. We don't know exactly what these new bodies will be, except that they will be spiritual, permanent, and glorious: "And just as we have borne the likeness of the earthly man, so shall we bear the likeness of the man from heaven" (1 Corinthians 15:49, NIV). "But we know that when [Christ] is revealed, we shall be like Him, for we shall see Him as He is" (1 John 3:2; see also 1 Corinthians 15:51–58).

Billy Graham writes of the "resurrection that blasts apart the finality of death, providing an alternative to the stifling, settling dust of death and opens the way to new life."

At the second coming of the Lord Jesus, the believing dead will be resurrected and joined immediately to Him: "The dead in Christ will rise first. Then we who are alive and remain shall be caught up together with them in the clouds to meet the Lord in the air. And thus we shall always be with the Lord" (1 Thessalonians 4:16–17).

We have hope beyond the grave! "If only for this life we have hope in Christ, we are to be pitied more than all men" (1 Corinthians 15:19, NIV).

The reuniting of living believers with those who have died before the coming of our Lord is part of the "blessed hope" Christians look forward to (Titus 2:13).

The Christian should be able to confront death realistically yet victoriously. Though inevitable and often unexpected, death should never catch us completely off guard. Death should never be a "great unknown" that produces fear and terror; it should be, rather, the moment when we no longer see "in a mirror, dimly" but "face to face" (1 Corinthians 13:12).

Helping Strategy

1. If the inquirer is a Christian, bear in mind that preparing for death, or enduring bereavement, brings changes and adjustments. Try to be considerate and understanding: "Therefore comfort one another with these words" (1 Thessalonians 4:18). As you share Scriptures from the "Background," suggest that they be noted and later reviewed and possibly memorized for added strength and encouragement. Seek to guide the person to a new commitment and devotion to Christ. If there is any uncertainty about his or her relationship with Christ, share "Steps to Peace with God," page 11.

2. If the inquirer is not a Christian, emphasize that to be properly prepared for death a person must make the all-important decision about his or her eternal relationship during this lifetime. Invite him or her to receive Jesus Christ as Lord and Savior. Share "Steps to Peace with God," page 11.

3. Encourage reading and studying the Bible and cultivating habits of prayer.

4. Recommend becoming involved in a Bible-teaching church for fellowship, worship, and Bible study. This will also help the person to be constantly reassured as to the eternal hope that is ours as Christians.

Scripture

"Yea, though I walk through the valley of the shadow of death, I will fear no evil; for You are with me; Your rod and Your staff, they comfort me" (Psalm 23:4).

"I am the resurrection and the life. He who believes in Me, though he may die, he shall live" (John 11:25).

"Let not your heart be troubled; you believe in God, believe also in Me. In

My Father's house are many mansions; if it were not so, I would have told you. I go to prepare a place for you. And if I go and prepare a place for you, I will come again and receive you to Myself; that where I am, there you may be also" (John 14:1–3).

"But as it is written: 'Eye has not seen, nor ear heard, nor have entered into the heart of man the things which God has prepared for those who love Him.' But God has revealed them to us through His Spirit. For the Spirit searches all things, yes, the deep things of God" (1 Corinthians 2:9–10).

"For to me, to live is Christ, and to die is gain" (Philippians 1:21).

"But our citizenship is in heaven. And we eagerly await a Savior from there, the Lord Jesus Christ, who, by the power that enables him to bring everything under his control, will transform our lowly bodies so that they will be like his glorious body" (Philippians 3:20–21, NIV).

See also **Grief and Bereavement**

DEMONS

Background

In both the religious and secular worlds there is a growing recognition of, and interest in, demonic activity. The Bible recognizes the reality of this activity:

"For our struggle is not against flesh and blood [human beings], but against the rulers, against the authorities, against the powers of this dark world and against the spiritual forces of evil in the heavenly realms" (Ephesians 6:12, NIV).

Demons, also called in Scripture "unclean spirits" (Luke 4:36) and "deceiving spirits" (1 Timothy 4:1), are totally evil, invisible, intelligent spirits.

Like Satan, demons fell into condemnation through pride, and are the adversaries of both God and humankind. Though real and active, the devil and his messengers (demons) are often blamed for many things for which they are not guilty. Some Christians tend to blame all erratic behavior on "demon possession" when, actually, most of it is the result of humankind's sinful, selfish nature. Also, sometimes individuals who are on drugs or who are mentally ill will appear to be afflicted by demons.

The Christian who desires to be used by God to help people with spiritual problems might do well to heed the admonition of the apostle John: "Beloved, do not believe every spirit, but test the spirits, whether they are of God" or "the spirit of the Antichrist" (1 John 4:1, 3). Thus, demons must be discerned, tested, resisted, and rejected by believers. (1 Corinthians 12:10; Ephesians 4:27; 6:10–18; James 4:7; 1 Peter 5:8–9; 1 John 4:1–6.)

Through the victory of Jesus Christ over Satan and his demonic assistants, and in the mighty name of Jesus Christ and in the power of the Holy Spirit, the child of God can overcome Satan and his demons. (Matthew 8:16–17; 12:28; Mark 16:17; Acts 19:15.)

Our resources against the hosts of wickedness are:

- Alertness (1 Peter 5:8).

- Prayer (Matthew 26:41).

- The use of the "full armor of God" (Ephesians 6:10–18).

Helping Strategy
For the Non-Christian:

If the inquirer speaks of spiritual bondage, demonic activity or behavior, or has been involved in the occult or eastern religions, ask questions. Try to discern if the situation is truly as he or she describes it. "Tell me about it," is a phrase to be used and repeated until the actual problem emerges. Do not hesitate to press for answers.

1. Emphasize the sufficiency of the sacrifice of Christ on the cross to solve sinful problems: "The blood of Jesus Christ His Son cleanses us from all sin" (1 John 1:7). Share "Steps to Peace with God," page 11.

2. If he or she receives Christ, encourage reading and studying the Bible every day. Offer to send *Living in Christ* for help in getting started. He or she should also pray daily. These two disciplines usually become established for the inquirer who gets into a local Bible-teaching church where he or she can fellowship, worship the Lord, study the Bible, and learn the joys of a consecrated life.

3. If you find that you are dealing with a person who is truly demonized, follow the steps outlined below in regard to "Dealing with demonization."

For the Christian:

If a true believer in Christ fears demonic activity, proceed as follows:

1. Ask about the circumstances. Why does he or she think demons are involved? Sometimes fears are induced by other well-meaning but mistaken Christians.

2. Remind the person that all God's resources are at our disposal:
   - Satan is a defeated foe (1 John 3:8).
   - Christ lives in the believer (Colossians 1:27).
   - The Holy Spirit empowers (Acts 1:8; 2 Timothy 1:7).
   - The Word of God guides (2 Timothy 3:16–17).

3. See the last two paragraphs of the "Background" for further guidance. The Christian is assured of victory as he or she submits constantly to the lordship of Christ, to the authority and the illumination of the Bible, to the discipline of overcoming prayer, and to involvement with a dynamic group of believers in a Bible-teaching church.

4. It may be that the inquirer is suffering severe guilt from actual unconfessed sin, and is raising the issue of demonic influence in an attempt to transfer the blame instead of facing personal responsibility. True repentance and confession of sin would remove the guilt and also the root causes of the "oppression." Share "Restoration," page 17, emphasizing 1 John 1:9.

5. It may be that you are dealing with a legitimate case of one who is demonized. If so, follow the steps outlined below.

Dealing with Demonization:

Be careful! Seek the help of a professional or pastor. You must be sure that you are dealing with a bona fide case of demonization and not a condition resulting from some physical, psychological, or spiritual disorder. The inquirer could be greatly harmed if told that he or she is demonized when that is actually not the case.

1. Note carefully the symptoms of the disturbed person, depending on the Lord for wisdom and discernment. A demonized person is just that. He or she is either being deeply influenced by or has been invaded by an evil spirit. Extremely bizarre behavior may be present. Sometimes blasphemous or foul and immoral language is used.

2. Dealing with such a person is not to be taken lightly. Resistance is often tenacious and much time may be required to properly deal with the difficulties. Obviously the telephone helper can't spend this amount of time. Suggest that the person seek the help of a qualified pastor or professional Christian counselor.

NOTE: (a) In cases where demonized people have been set free, those involved have been unanimous in stating that much prayer, usually involving a group of Christians called together for the purpose, is a great necessity. (b) One person should assume a leadership role as the spokesperson. (c) As the Spirit of God leads, and at moments that He would indicate, a command should be given in the name of the Lord Jesus Christ and with His authority (Matthew 28:18) in order to expel the evil spirit. (d) On deliverance, victory should immediately be claimed in the name of the Lord Jesus Christ and God be praised for it.

The delivered person should be urged to seek strong friendships in the family of God. He or she can greatly fortify God's work in his or her life by reading and studying God's Word, praying, and beginning to witness to God's marvelous work.

Scripture

"Then Jesus came and spoke to them, saying, 'All authority has been given to Me in heaven and on earth'" (Matthew 28:18).

"Submit to God. Resist the devil and he will flee from you" (James 4:7).

"Be self-controlled and alert. Your enemy the devil prowls around like a roaring lion looking for someone to devour. Resist him, standing firm in the faith, because you know that your brothers throughout the world are undergoing the same kind of sufferings" (1 Peter 5:8–9, NIV).

"Dear friends, do not believe every spirit, but test the spirits to see whether they are from God, because many false prophets have gone out into the world. This is how you can recognize the Spirit of God: Every spirit that acknowledges that Jesus Christ has come in the flesh is from God, but every spirit that does not acknowledge Jesus is not from God. This is the spirit of antichrist, which you have heard is coming and even now is already in the world" (1 John 4:1–6, NIV).

Other suggested Scriptures:

1 John 3:8
Revelation 12:11

DEPRESSION

Background

Depression is possibly responsible for more pain and distress than any other affliction of mankind. It is difficult to define depression, describe its symptoms, or treat it. The dictionary defines depression as an emotional condition, either neurotic or psychotic, characterized by feelings of hopelessness, inadequacy, gloominess, dejection, sadness, difficulty in thinking and concentration, and inactivity. Both Christians and non-Christians can suffer depression.

Depressed people have a negative self-image, often accompanied by feelings of guilt, shame, and self-criticism. Neurotic depression can be linked to wrong conduct or behavior and wrong reactions to such conduct. After a series of improper acts and subsequent faulty reactions, guilt and depression set in. If sin is at the heart of the problem, it should never be minimized. Neither should support be given to the idea that other things and other people are responsible for behavioral problems. Either agreeing with the depressed person in this, or not taking seriously his or her expression of sin and guilt, could prevent any real and lasting solutions.

The depressed person will often be concerned only with feeling better. But this is not the first priority. Rather, he or she must seek the causes which may have contributed to the depression. Putting his or her life in order spiritually will eventually eradicate the depression.

This is the point at which the Bible can be used very effectively. The release of the Holy Spirit's power will inevitably result in positive steps on a road to recovery and wholeness. The Christian witness must seek to be an encourager. Even if no spiritual decision is reached, try to leave your inquirer with a sense of hope and well-being. Be patient. Complex problems for which there are no quick and easy solutions are often involved in depression. The depressed person will not "snap out of it" on command. Often months of professional help are needed.

Be a good listener. Don't probe too deeply, but do ask questions and then wait for something to emerge in the conversation which will provide the "handle" for offering spiritual solutions. Do not try to offer solutions before you are well informed of the problem.

Helping Strategy

For the Non-Christian:

1. Your inquirer may reveal symptoms of depression as a result of such

things as unresolved anger, resentment, real or imagined wrongs, self-pity, guilt, or immorality. Give assurance of your interest and your desire to help find solutions.

2. Ask if he or she has ever trusted in Jesus Christ as Lord and Savior. If appropriate, present "Steps to Peace with God," page 11. Remember that it would be a disservice to the inquirer to minimize in any way the seriousness of sin. In order for him or her to experience forgiveness, there must be recognition and confession of sin.

3. Share the section on "Assurance," page 15. Emphasize that this experience with Christ offers real hope. It should bring new awareness and understanding to the battle against depression.

4. Encourage reading and studying the Bible. This will teach the will and ways of God. It will bring the person's thinking in line with God and will result in inner peace (Isaiah 26:3).

5. Recommend that the depressed person learn to pray and to do so daily. Through prayer we confess our sins and are renewed. We learn to experience God's constant presence and approval. We worship as we praise and thank Him. And we express our own needs and those of others.

6. Suggest that he or she cultivate friendships with people who will provide support and encouragement. Such friends may be found in a Bible-teaching church, a Bible class, or a Christian singles' group. This fellowship may also provide opportunities for Christian service, in which concerns are focused on the needs of others.

7. Encourage seeking out a qualified pastor or Christian psychologist for continued counseling in order that all the facets of the depression may be dealt with in the light of Scripture.

For the Christian:

1. A Christian may suffer from depression in reaction to adverse situations, defeats, and setbacks such as a death in the family, a rebellious son or daughter, or loss of employment:

   A. In such cases you should always offer a loving word of encouragement, such as: "You are not alone in your suffering." "God cares and will not leave you alone." "The Lord Jesus not only bore our sins but also our sorrows and heartaches."

   B. Suggest that the present depression might be due to an inability to trust God fully in all circumstances of life. Rededication to Christ

may be needed, along with a commitment to be responsive and obedient to God's will (Romans 12:1–2).

C. Suggest a recommitment to the disciplines of Bible study and prayer (Proverbs 3:5–6; Isaiah 26:3).

D. Encourage faithfulness in worship and service through the church.

Billy Graham has written: "Discouragement is the very opposite of faith. It is Satan's device to thwart the work of God in our lives. Discouragement blinds our eyes to the mercy of God and makes us perceive only the unfavorable circumstances. I have never met a person who spent time in daily prayer, in the study of the Word of God, and who was strong in faith who was ever discouraged for very long."

---

2. A Christian may also be depressed because of spiritual disobedience and unresolved sin in such areas as anger and bitterness, jealousy, grudges, a divorce, or immorality:

A. As the problem is revealed, assure the inquirer that he or she is right to seek a solution—that the first step back to wholeness is spiritual renewal.

B. Share "Restoration," page 17, emphasizing Proverbs 28:13 and 1 John 1:9.

C. As the person responds to the Scriptures in "Restoration," point out that other steps may be necessary beyond recommitment. For example, he or she may need to mend fences broken down as a result of such things as gossip, criticism, envy, or immorality. In cases where things such as theft or fraud were involved, restitution should be considered.

D. Encourage a serious commitment to Bible study. Learning to think God's thoughts is a valuable aid to spiritual recovery (Romans 12:2; Philippians 4:8).

E. Suggest becoming involved in a Bible-teaching church where worship, fellowship, and opportunities for service are available.

F. Suggest a serious commitment to professional counseling with a qualified pastor or Christian psychologist until all issues involved in the depression are resolved in the light of Scripture.

3. A Christian may also be depressed because of setting standards and goals

beyond his or her ability to attain. This may be true both for economic or spiritual goals; failure brings on depression:

A. Patiently point out that goals which others may set for themselves and seem to attain may not be right for the inquirer. The fact that he or she is depressed may indicate the unattainability of such goals.

B. Point out that success or failure cannot be measured by any human standard. Suggest, instead, the following criteria:

- Does what I desire conform with God's will? Can it be supported by Scripture?

- Is what I desire for the glory of God, or to satisfy some personal whim or selfish ambition?

- Have I been motivated by spiritual pride?

- Is what I desire in line with the guidance given by the apostle Paul:

  * Be what I am—what God has made me: Learn to live with my strengths and limitations: "But by the grace of God I am what I am" (1 Corinthians 15:10).

  * Trying to emulate someone else ("keeping up with the Joneses") is spiritually undesirable and counterproductive (2 Corinthians 10:12, NIV).

4. Suggest that the inquirer renew his or her spiritual commitment: "Seek first the kingdom of God and His righteousness, and all these things shall be added to you" (Matthew 6:33).

5. Encourage learning the disciplines of Bible study and prayer.

6. Suggest rearranging priorities so that they are more in line with his or her abilities.

7. If you sense that follow-up is needed, recommend a serious commitment to professional counseling. A qualified pastor or Christian psychologist should be sought.

Scripture

"Trust in the Lord with all your heart, and lean not on your own understanding; in all your ways acknowledge Him, and He shall direct your paths" (Proverbs 3:5–6).

"A man's spirit sustains him in sickness, but a crushed spirit who can bear?" (Proverbs 18:14, NIV).

"Surely he took up our infirmities and carried our sorrows, yet we considered him stricken by God, smitten by him, and afflicted. But he was pierced for our transgressions, he was crushed for our iniquities; the punishment that brought us peace was upon him, and by his wounds we are healed" (Isaiah 53:4–5, NIV).

"We are hard pressed on every side, yet not crushed; we are perplexed, but not in despair; persecuted, but not forsaken; struck down, but not destroyed" (2 Corinthians 4:8–9).

"I have been crucified with Christ; it is no longer I who live, but Christ lives in me; and the life which I now live in the flesh I live by faith in the Son of God, who loved me and gave Himself for me" (Galatians 2:20).

Other suggested Scriptures:

Psalm 38:1–4, 21–22, NIV

DISCIPLINE FROM GOD

Background

The Bible teaches clearly that the various challenges or hardships Christians face may at times result from God's choosing to discipline us, in order to make us more faithful to Him. From time to time, a conversation will reveal problems and troubles that seem to indicate that God is dealing with the inquirer in this way.

Discipline from the Lord Is a Scriptural Concept

"Blessed is the man you discipline, O Lord; the man you teach from your law; you grant him relief from days of trouble" (Psalm 94:12–13, NIV).

"My son, do not despise the Lord's discipline and do not resent his rebuke, because the Lord disciplines those he loves, as a father the son he delights in" (Proverbs 3:11–12, NIV).

Billy Graham comments: "The Bible says, 'The Lord disciplines those he loves.' If life were all easy, wouldn't we become flabby? When a ship's carpenter needed timber to make a mast for a sailing vessel, he did not cut it in the valley, but upon the mountainside where the trees had been buffeted by the winds. These trees, he knew, were the strongest of all. Hardship is not our choice; but if we face it bravely, it can toughen the fiber of our souls.

"God does not discipline us to subdue us but to condition us for a life of usefulness and blessedness. In His wisdom, He knows that an uncontrolled life is an unhappy life, so He puts reins on our wayward souls that they may be directed into the paths of righteousness."

Discipline Is Desirable, Considering the Alternatives

"So he gave them what they asked for, but sent a wasting disease upon them" (Psalm 106:15, NIV).

"I beat my body and make it my slave so that after I have preached to others, I myself will not be disqualified for the prize" (1 Corinthians 9:27, NIV).

God Has Good Reasons for Disciplining Us

1. He wants to lead us to repentance: "Yet now I am happy, not because

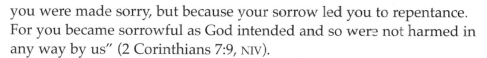

you were made sorry, but because your sorrow led you to repentance. For you became sorrowful as God intended and so were not harmed in any way by us" (2 Corinthians 7:9, NIV).

2. He wants to restore us to fellowship: "That which we have seen and heard we declare to you, that you also may have fellowship with us; and truly our fellowship is with the Father and with His Son Jesus Christ" (1 John 1:3).

3. He wants to make us more faithful: "Now it is required that those who have been given a trust must prove faithful" (1 Corinthians 4:2, NIV).

4. He wants to keep us humble: "To keep me from becoming conceited because of these surpassingly great revelations, there was given me a thorn in my flesh, a messenger of Satan, to torment me. Three times I pleaded with the Lord to take it away from me. But he said to me, 'My grace is sufficient for you, for my power is made perfect in weakness'" (2 Corinthians 12:7–9, NIV).

5. He wants to teach us spiritual discernment: "But if we judged ourselves, we would not come under judgment. When we are judged by the Lord, we are being disciplined so that we will not be condemned with the world" (1 Corinthians 11:31–32, NIV).

6. He wants to prepare us for more effective service: "Therefore, my beloved brethren, be steadfast, immovable, always abounding in the work of the Lord, knowing that your labor is not in vain in the Lord" (1 Corinthians 15:58).

Helping Strategy

1. Encourage the inquirer. He or she can be thankful for the Lord's disciplining. By disciplining, God is not discarding His child or disowning him or her, but rather:

   A. He is confirming His love for you: "For whom the Lord loves He chastens" (Hebrews 12:6).

   B. He is confirming His relationship with you: "If you are not disciplined (and everyone undergoes discipline), then you are illegitimate children and not true sons" (Hebrews 12:8, NIV).

   C. He wants you to respond in obedience and faithfulness to Him: "Before I was afflicted I went astray, but now I keep Your word" (Psalm 119:67).

2. Help the individual to open up to the Lord in the manner of the psalmist:

"Search me, O God, and know my heart; try me, and know my anxieties; and see if there is any wicked way in me, and lead me in the way everlasting" (Psalm 139:23–24).

Some questions might help, for example:

- Why do you feel that God is disciplining you?

- Do you feel that there is some disobedience or sin in your life that God is dealing with?

3. In no way minimize the sin or disobedience the person admits. This is the basis on which you can ask him or her to repent, confess, and be restored to fellowship.

4. Go over the section on "Restoration," page 17, especially emphasizing 1 John 1:9.

5. Encourage the person to start and continue a daily devotional experience with God through reading His Word and praying.

6. Encourage seeking God's direction and discovering His purpose for life. After receiving God's discipline, one can go on to obedience and blessing and opportunities to live for and serve Christ.

7. Recommend finding a good church where there is a biblically oriented fellowship. Christian friends help to make us stronger!

8. Pray for complete restoration and renewal.

Scripture

Psalm 94:12–13
Proverbs 3:11–12
1 Corinthians 9:27

DIVORCE

Background

Divorce could be described as a married couple deciding they no longer want to fulfill their commitment to marriage. Although usually only one of the two partners initiates the action, both may have contributed to the breakup to some degree.

Divorce is a shattering experience, and its wounds heal slowly. It takes time for the parties to get things sorted out so that they are able to deal objectively with themselves and their situation. It may be difficult for them to cut through all the feelings of alienation, rejection, bitterness, and confusion. With a high percentage of our nation's marriages ending in divorce, it is probable that a helper will be challenged with this problem.

Billy Graham comments: "I am opposed to divorce and regard the increase in divorces today as one of the most alarming problems in society. However, I know that the Lord can forgive and heal, even when great sin may have been involved. The church is made up of sinners. When Paul wrote to the Corinthians he gave a long list of evils and then added: 'And such were some of you' (1 Corinthians 6:11). They had been forgiven and had become a part of the church, the body of Christ."

Helping Strategy

1. Encouragement is greatly needed. The inquirer may feel rejected, having lost his or her sense of personal worth. This is common for divorced people. Tell the person that you appreciate the call, that you want to talk with him or her. God loves and accepts us just as we are.

2. Question the inquirer about his or her relationship with Jesus Christ. Has he or she ever received Jesus as Lord and Savior? If indicated, share "Steps to Peace with God," page 11. Although the caller may feel rejected, alienated, and devastated, emphasize that God can make all things new (2 Corinthians 5:17). What has been done—the divorce—perhaps cannot be undone. The inquirer must begin where he or she is to build life on a new foundation. That foundation is Jesus Christ.

3. Talk about the importance of Bible reading and prayer as sources of strength. Does he or she have a Bible? If not, suggest going to a local

Christian bookstore to obtain an easy-to-understand translation of the Bible. Ask if we may send *Living in Christ* to encourage him or her in starting to study the Bible.

4. Suggest that the person seek a Bible-teaching church for fellowship, worship, and opportunities for service. If the church has a singles group, this may provide a setting where he or she can find encouragement and understanding, and build new relationships.

5. Pray for healing of emotions, peace of mind, restored confidence, strength, and spiritual understanding.

6. Suggest special counseling if he or she feels the need for it. A pastor or a Christian psychologist may be helpful.

Points to Remember as You Talk with the Divorced Person

1. What has been done is past. Start where your inquirer is now and go on from there.

2. Try to guide the conversation so that he or she won't feel it necessary to engage in any "postmortems" of the experience. Try rather to direct attention to God, who can help the divorced person reach real solutions.

3. Remain neutral. Do not assume that your inquirer is either guilty or innocent. A judgmental or "holier than thou" attitude will close doors to witnessing.

4. If your inquirer is truly a Christian, encourage him or her to:

   A. Confess any bitterness, anger, or other sin and, if necessary, face realistically any wrong attitudes that contributed to the divorce. Share "Restoration," page 17. Emphasize 1 John 1:9.

   B. Develop a new interest in reading and studying the Bible and in prayer: "Casting all your care upon Him, for He cares for you" (1 Peter 5:7).

   C. Establish or renew a relationship with a church, in spite of feelings of guilt or fear of criticism. He or she needs the church now more than ever. Perhaps the church has a singles group which would be helpful.

   D. Pray with the person for healing, peace of mind, and the ability to make the necessary adjustments to a different lifestyle.

Scripture

Encouragement to Walk with the Lord:

"Trust in the Lord with all your heart, and lean not on your own understanding; in all your ways acknowledge Him, and He shall direct your paths" (Proverbs 3:5–6).

"Do not be anxious about anything, but in everything, by prayer and petition, with thanksgiving, present your requests to God" (Philippians 4:6, NIV).

"Do your best to present yourself to God as one approved, a workman who does not need to be ashamed and who correctly handles the word of truth" (2 Timothy 2:15, NIV).

"Grow in the grace and knowledge of our Lord and Savior Jesus Christ" (2 Peter 3:18).

Healing the Wounds:

"Praise the Lord, O my soul, and forget not all his benefits—who forgives all your sins and heals all your diseases, who redeems your life from the pit and crowns you with love and compassion, who satisfies your desires with good things so that your youth is renewed like the eagle's" (Psalm 103:2–5, NIV).

"Heal me, O Lord, and I will be healed; save me and I will be saved, for you are the one I praise" (Jeremiah 17:14, NIV).

Other suggested Scriptures:

Psalm 23:3
2 Timothy 1:7

DIVORCE, CONTEMPLATING

Background

Divorce, the legal dissolution of marriage, is a departure from what God intended and is not endorsed by Scripture except under limited conditions. Divorce is the result of sin in the lives of one or both of the partners. More often than not, both are to blame to some degree. Pride and selfishness often contribute to the conditions that lead to divorce.

Divorce is often the product of inflexible wills: "Jesus replied, 'Moses permitted you to divorce your wives because your hearts were hard. But it was not this way from the beginning'" (Matthew 19:8, NIV). Divorce was not part of God's original design for marriage.

No manipulation of Scripture or rationalization makes divorce right. Scripture states:

"Therefore a man shall leave his father and mother and be joined to his wife, and they shall become one flesh" (Genesis 2:24).

The apostle Paul wrote: "To the married I give this command (not I, but the Lord): A wife must not separate from her husband. . . . And a husband must not divorce his wife" (1 Corinthians 7:10–11, NIV).

"Has not the Lord made them one? In flesh and spirit they are his. . . . So guard yourself in your spirit, and do not break faith with the wife of your youth. 'I hate divorce,' says the Lord God of Israel" (Malachi 2:15–16, NIV).

Conditions Under Which Divorce May Be Permitted

- When a spouse is guilty of sexual immorality such as adultery or homosexuality and has no intention of repenting or seeking God's forgiveness, and living in faithfulness to his or her spouse (Matthew 19:9).

- When one partner deserts the other, especially when an unbelieving partner deserts a Christian spouse (1 Corinthians 7:15).

Having an unbelieving spouse is not, however, automatic grounds for divorce. To the contrary, the Christian spouse is encouraged to "live in peace" with the unbelieving partner, with the goal of winning him or her to faith in Christ (1 Corinthians 7:12–16).

If the person has divorced and remarried, he or she should try to make a successful second marriage. Leaving the second spouse to return to the first would be wrong. Two wrongs never make a right.

Count the Cost of Divorce

- Is it displeasing to God? (Malachi 2:15–16).

- Will it disrupt the continuity of life and adversely affect other people: children, parents, extended families?

- Will it really solve any problems, or will it rather create many new ones? Divorce is an emotionally traumatic experience.

Exhaust Every Other Option Before Considering Divorce

1. Try to work things out on a personal level, in a spirit of humility and forgiveness (Matthew 18:21–22).

2. Submit to serious counseling with a Christian marriage counselor or a qualified pastor.

3. If necessary, consider a trial separation while searching for a redemptive solution. In a case of physical or psychological abuse, homosexuality, drunkenness, drugs, etc., a separation might be advisable.

Helping Strategy

1. Demonstrate a loving, caring attitude. Reassure the inquirer by saying that you are glad to assist in his or her search for a solution. You want to be a friend and share any insights you can.

2. Listen attentively, letting the caller tell the story and ventilate feelings until you feel you have a grasp of the situation.

3. Avoid playing judge. Don't take sides. Your goal should be to present a scriptural point of view and challenge the inquirer to make the decision, knowing that he or she will have to live with it for life.

   Remember the example of Jesus. He dealt gently with the woman at the well, even though He knew that she had had five husbands and was then living with a man who was not her husband. He revealed Himself as Savior, and offered her "living water" (John 4:9–42).

4. Tell the inquirer that receiving God's help means committing his or her life to Christ, whatever the cost. This commitment must be permanent, regardless of the outcome of the present dilemma. Ask if he or she has

ever received Jesus Christ as Lord and Savior. If indicated, explain "Steps to Peace with God," page 11.

5. After receiving Christ, the inquirer can rightfully expect the Lord's help. He or she will now find a new dimension to life and a new perspective which should be helpful in reaching solutions. For new insights into the divorce situation, he or she should begin to read and study God's Word, and talk with God in prayer. Prayer and Bible study will bring new dimensions to the person's own disposition and personality, and will help bring restoration with the spouse through repentance and confession.

6. Encourage him or her to exhaust all options in the search for a scriptural solution.

7. Pray for God's intervention in putting the marriage back together according to Scripture.

8. If the caller is a Christian, share thoughts from "Restoration," page 17, emphasizing 1 John 1:9 and Romans 12:1–2.

Scripture

"He who finds a wife finds a good thing, and obtains favor from the Lord" (Proverbs 18:22).

"When a woman marries, the law binds her to her husband as long as he is alive. But if he dies, she is no longer bound to him; the laws of marriage no longer apply to her. Then she can marry someone else if she wants to. That would be wrong while he was alive, but it is perfectly all right after he dies" (Romans 7:2, TLB).

"The man should give his wife all that is her right as a married woman, and the wife should do the same for her husband: for a girl who marries no longer has full right to her own body, for her husband then has his rights to it, too; and in the same way the husband no longer has full right to his own body, for it belongs also to his wife" (1 Corinthians 7:3–4, TLB).

"Do nothing out of selfish ambition or vain conceit, but in humility consider others better than yourselves. Each of you should look not only to your own interests, but also to the interests of others. Your attitude should be the same as that of Christ Jesus" (Philippians 2:3–5, NIV).

"Husbands, in the same way be considerate as you live with your wives, and treat them with respect as the weaker partner and as heirs with you of the gracious gift of life, so that nothing will hinder your prayers" (1 Peter 3:7, NIV).

DIVORCE AFTER YEARS OF MARRIAGE

Background

It is difficult to describe the sense of shock, hurt, bewilderment, emptiness, anger, rejection, isolation, and loss of self-worth felt when someone has been deserted or divorced after many years of marriage. The person wonders: Can this really be happening to me? How could he or she do this to me? Where did I fail? What could I have done differently? The most important question is, What do I do now?

In spite of the trauma of the divorce, the person must be helped to realize that life goes on. The fact of the divorce must be accepted; he or she is now single and must face the future as such. It is futile to continually dredge up the past and try to relive it. Facts cannot be changed by self-torturing questions. It is entirely possible that he or she couldn't have done anything differently to save the marriage.

An emotionally healthy person will leave the past behind and go on and grow in the present. The apostle Paul provides the example:

"One thing I do, forgetting those things which are behind and reaching forward to those things which are ahead" (Philippians 3:13).

The divorced person must look at the experience as transitional, as a time to make adjustments, of expanding personality through reading, reflection, and building or rebuilding friendships which will help him or her grow.

If the person needs professional counseling during the transition, he or she should look for a qualified pastor or a Christian psychiatrist or psychologist who can approach the problems in the light of Scripture.

Helping Strategy

1. Encourage the inquirer by projecting love and understanding. The hurts, emptiness, and sense of rejection may be very deep.

2. Be a good listener, trying to get the whole picture before offering any comment. Sometimes we respond too quickly with advice, when a question to stimulate conversation would be more in order.

3. When you feel you have a proper understanding of the situation,

reassure the caller with the verses from "Scripture" at the end of this section. Emphasize that God loves him or her and cares about what is happening. Jesus knows what grief and sorrow are: "He [was] despised and rejected by men" (Isaiah 53:3). Ask the inquirer if he or she has ever received Jesus Christ as Lord and Savior. Explain "Steps to Peace with God," page 11.

4. Explain the value of Bible reading and study. This will give the inquirer perspective and insight as he or she tries to adjust to a new lifestyle and grow in the Lord.

5. Urge the person to pray every day: "Do not be anxious about anything, but in everything, by prayer and petition, with thanksgiving, present your requests to God. And the peace of God, which transcends all understanding, will guard your hearts and your minds in Christ Jesus" (Philippians 4:6–7, NIV).

6. Recommend becoming involved in a Bible-teaching church. Often a Christian singles group can be found which will provide opportunities to share experiences, to grow, and to serve.

7. Pray with the inquirer for the Lord's help in this difficult time of transition as he or she seeks to build a new life.

Scripture

"You have made known to me the path of life; you will fill me with joy in your presence, with eternal pleasures at your right hand" (Psalm 16:11, NIV).

"How precious to me are your thoughts, O God! How vast is the sum of them! Were I to count them, they would outnumber the grains of sand. When I awake, I am still with you" (Psalm 139:17–18, NIV).

"Because the Sovereign Lord helps me, I will not be disgraced. Therefore have I set my face like flint, and I know I will not be put to shame" (Isaiah 50:7, NIV).

"'For I know the plans I have for you,' declares the Lord, 'plans to prosper you and not to harm you, plans to give you hope and a future'" (Jeremiah 29:11, NIV).

Other suggested Scriptures:
Psalm 16:8
Psalm 18:2

DOUBT

Background

Doubts can be debilitating. Hesitation is characteristic of the doubter. Uncertainty throws the doubter off balance and interferes with his or her decision making. James mentions the "double-minded" person as being unstable in all he or she does: "That man should not think he will receive anything from the Lord" (James 1:7–8, NIV).

Yet it is not unusual for even a Christian to experience doubts. When the sincere Christian hears critics attack the Bible, there may be increased temptation to doubt God's Word. In confusion over unanswered prayers, he or she may wonder, "Is God real? Does He really answer prayer?" When confronted with the reality of sinful, selfish desires, he or she may question, "Has God really saved me?"

Billy Graham writes: "Probably everyone has had doubts and uncertainties at times in his or her religious experience. When Moses went up on Mt. Sinai to receive the tablets of the Law from the hand of God, and when he had been a long time out of the sight of the Hebrews who stood anxiously awaiting his return, they finally became doubtful of his return. And they erected a golden calf to worship (Exodus 32:8). Their apostasy was the result of the doubting and uncertainty."

In spite of this tendency to doubt, honest questioning can become the threshold to a more solid faith and a deeper commitment to Christ.

The opposite of doubt, of course, is faith. James encouraged those who were passing through trials to ask of God and to ask in faith (James 1:5–6). We must remember that doubt can be an effective tool for Satan. He brought uncertainty to Eve by asking, "Has God indeed said . . . ?" (Genesis 3:1). He will afflict us with doubts where we are the most vulnerable. Spiritual disobedience, disappointment, depression, illness, and even advancing age can trigger doubts.

Helping Strategy
Those Who May Doubt Their Salvation:

1. Commend the inquirer for being concerned about something so important. God's Word has real encouragement for the doubter.

2. If you discern that he or she has been trusting in things other than a personal relationship with Jesus Christ, share "Steps to Peace with God," page 11.

3. If the inquirer is convinced that he or she has previously made a genuine commitment to Jesus Christ, ask further:

   A. "Are you being deliberately sinful or disobedient?" If this is the case, explain "Restoration," page 17. Emphasize 1 John 1:9.

   B. "Have you been indifferent to spiritual things? Not faithful in attending church? Not reading the Bible? Not praying?" If this is the case, explain "Restoration," page 17. Emphasize 1 John 1:9 and Romans 12:1–2.

   C. Encourage the inquirer to step out anew in faith, to believe God (Acts 27:25), to take a definite stand for Christ, to get into the Word of God, to learn the discipline of prayer, and to get to work for Christ in a local Bible-teaching church. Offer to send *Living in Christ*.

   D. Pray for a stronger relationship with God by faith.

Those Disillusioned by Disappointments:

Disappointment can occur through divorce, a death in the family, a wayward son or daughter, unanswered prayer, or betrayal by another Christian.

1. Offer a word of encouragement. God does love and care for us. He wants the inquirer also to learn to walk with Him by faith.

2. Help identify the source of the doubts, emphasizing that it is not wrong to ask why in life.

3. Remind him or her that God has never promised freedom from adversity in life. It may be that the doubter needs to get the focus off his or her problems and back on God—to see beyond the circumstances of life to what God is trying to teach through those circumstances. God is faithful. The intrusion of doubts doesn't mean that God has ceased to care.

4. The inquirer needs to reflect on God's goodness demonstrated in the past, to remember evidences of God's faithfulness in his or her own life and in the lives of others. This will help to reassure him or her. A renewal of faith is in order. He or she needs to begin to trust God's promises again, to dwell on the Bible, and to believe God. Jesus said, "Blessed are those who have not seen and yet have believed" (John 20:29).

5. Pray for renewal, asking that the caller confess any doubts to God and pray for a dynamic faith.

6. Encourage faithfulness in worshiping with God's people. The cultivation of relationships with other Christians will be helpful. Getting involved in service for Christ through a local Bible-teaching church will strengthen commitment.

Reassurance for Older Christians:

For those who, due to a number of changes that accompany advancing age, need to be reassured as to their salvation and eternal relationship with God, there are three areas to remember:

1. Older people, like anyone else, can continue to trust unquestioningly the Lord Jesus Christ as their Lord and Savior: "For I am convinced that neither death nor life, neither angels nor demons, neither the present nor the future, nor any powers, neither height nor depth, nor anything else in all creation, will be able to separate us from the love of God that is in Christ Jesus our Lord" (Romans 8:38–39, NIV).

2. They can trust unquestioningly their relationship with their heavenly Father: "But as many as received Him, to them He gave the right to become children of God, to those who believe in His name" (John 1:12).

3. They may also trust unquestioningly the Word of God: "Your word, O Lord, is eternal; it stands firm in the heavens. Your faithfulness continues through all generations" (Psalm 119:89–90, NIV).

Scripture

"The fool has said in his heart, 'There is no God'" (Psalm 14:1).

"But without faith it is impossible to please Him, for he who comes to God must believe that He is, and that He is a rewarder of those who diligently seek Him" (Hebrews 11:6).

"Therefore we also, since we are surrounded by so great a cloud of witnesses, let us lay aside every weight, and the sin which so easily ensnares us, and let us run with endurance the race that is set before us, looking unto Jesus, the author and finisher of our faith, who for the joy that was set before Him endured the cross, despising the shame, and has sat down at the right hand of the throne of God" (Hebrews 12:1–2).

"If any of you lacks wisdom, let him ask of God, who gives to all liberally and without reproach, and it will be given to him. But let him ask in faith, with no doubting, for he who doubts is like a wave of the sea driven and tossed by the wind. For let not that man suppose that he will receive anything from the Lord; he is a double-minded man, unstable in all his ways" (James 1:5–8)

DRUG ABUSE

Background

A drug is any substance which produces physical, mental, or psychological changes in the user. Since earliest times, people have experimented with drugs in an effort to escape reality. Today hundreds of millions of people are involved in drugs which range all the way from mildly addictive caffeine to illegal, deeply addictive drugs such as heroin and cocaine.

Anyone can become physically and psychologically addicted to any drug if exposed to high dosages for a sufficient period of time.

Drug users come from all walks of life. Many of the roots of dependency are to be found in insecurity, fear, guilt, disappointments, immorality and deviant sexual behavior, frustration, stress, peer pressures, and intense competition, as exemplified in professional sports. Add to these the great spiritual vacuum which has resulted in a breakdown of moral standards, the disintegration of the home, four major wars in this century, and the staggering availability of drugs of every kind to every age group, including grade school children.

Drug dependency is a problem of the whole person—spiritual, physical, emotional, and social. Once addicted, the dependent lives in an illusory world characterized by paralyzed feelings and emotional responses, mental denials and delusions, social isolation, and spiritual limbo. For many it is a helpless state, a life of no return.

The effort to withdraw from a drug addiction can be very painful, both physically and psychologically. Unmonitored withdrawal can be dangerous. Getting free from dependency, and the subsequent rehabilitation, is usually a long-term process. A strong support system involving the spiritual, emotional, mental, and physical is needed.

In order to be helped spiritually, the drug dependent must desire to be helped and must take some initial step to seek such help. This is where the Christian helper comes in. We should seek his or her commitment to Jesus Christ as Savior and Lord. This initial step of faith should lead to a new perspective and motivation for the drug user, which will lead, hopefully, to rehabilitation and a life of wholeness.

Even after commitment to Christ, however, there is often a need to work on the personal issues that led to the addiction, such as a poor self-image, insecurity, incest, homosexuality, immorality, fear, or guilt.

Helping Strategy

We can contribute in three ways to helping a person become free of a drug dependency:

- Help the individual spiritually, by seeking his or her commitment to Christ.

- Put him or her in touch with a local drug rehabilitation center, where he or she can begin the process of withdrawal and recovery.

- Stay with the person in order to offer support and encouragement until he or she has a deeper understanding of what it means to make a commitment to Christ.

1. Do not moralize about the evils of drugs or the person's addiction. Use the Scriptures on sin only as opportunities to do so occur naturally in your presentation of the Gospel.

2. Be cordial. Be compassionate. Encourage him or her by saying that you are sympathetic and willing to listen and offer help.

3. Hear the person out, giving ample opportunity for the expression of feelings and opinions. Offer reassurance of God's love. God's grace is sufficient to meet any need in his or her life. (A definition of grace: God loves us with no strings attached.)

4. The inquirer will need to be faced with his or her responsibility for the addiction. At some point, he or she made a conscious choice to take drugs. He or she has moral responsibility for the behavior which led to the addiction. If there is an effort to lay the blame for the problem at the feet of circumstances, other people, society, etc., always bring the discussion gently back to the issue of personal and moral responsibility: "But each one is tempted when, by his own evil desire, he is dragged away and enticed" (James 1:14, NIV).

5. At the opportune moment, share "Steps to Peace with God," page 11.

6. Continue to "Follow-Up Steps," if indicated: Start reading and studying God's Word. Learn to pray. Begin to fellowship with a Bible-teaching church.

7. The drug-dependent person must abandon the people and surroundings that have tied him or her to drugs. He or she must stop all use of drugs. This will probably mean treatment at a drug rehab center where withdrawal and early rehabilitation can be properly monitored. Around-the-clock supervision is often needed.

NOTE: You will often need to take the initiative to help the dependent find a center for treatment and check in, or perhaps assist the addict's family in doing this. Indicate that you intend to do this. The addict cannot be trusted to handle this alone. He or she may promise, but never follow through. Both during and following treatment, the helper should be as supportive as possible. Visit frequently. Start the recovering addict in the reading and study of God's Word and prayer. Assist in finding a support group of Christian ex-addicts, if such is available. Get the person involved in the life of a caring, Bible-teaching church. Get him or her in touch with a Christian professional counselor or group experienced in the treatment of addicts. He or she will need ongoing help with those personal problems which led to addiction in the first place.

CAUTION: Do not promise help in finding treatment, only that you will do the best you can.

8. Pray with the drug-dependent person for courage, for commitment, and for the power of the Holy Spirit to be released. All these are necessary in the redemptive process: "For God has not given us a spirit of fear, but of power and of love and of a sound mind" (2 Timothy 1:7).

Scripture

"The Spirit of the Lord is upon Me, because He has anointed Me to preach the gospel to the poor. He has sent Me to heal the brokenhearted, to preach deliverance to the captives. . . . And He began to say to them, 'Today this Scripture is fulfilled in your hearing.' . . . So they were all amazed and spoke among themselves, saying, 'What a word this is! For with authority and power He commands the unclean spirits, and they come out'" (Luke 4:18, 21, 36).

"Therefore if the Son makes you free, you shall be free indeed" (John 8:36).

"In the same way, count yourselves dead to sin but alive to God in Christ Jesus. Therefore do not let sin reign in your mortal body so that you obey its evil desires. Do not offer the parts of your body to sin, as instruments of wickedness, but rather offer yourselves to God, as those who have been brought from death to life; and offer the parts of your body to him as instruments of righteousness" (Romans 6:11–13, NIV).

"But each one is tempted when he is drawn away by his own desires and enticed. Then, when desire has conceived, it gives birth to sin; and sin, when it is full-grown, brings forth death" (James 1:14–15).

"For you have spent enough time in the past doing what pagans choose to do—living in debauchery, lust, drunkenness, orgies, carousing and detestable idolatry" (1 Peter 4:3, NIV).

EMPLOYMENT, LOSS OF

Background

We need to be sensitive to the trauma confronting an individual who has lost a job, who can't find another, whose bills continue to mount, whose mortgage payments may be in default. Such people feel a loss of personal worth, discouragement, frustration, and even depression. Recent statistics show that, with every 1 percent rise in unemployment:

- 4.3 percent more men and 2.3 percent more women are admitted to mental hospitals for the first time.

- 4.1 percent more people commit suicide.

- 4.7 percent more people are murdered.

- 4 percent more people end up in prisons.

- 1.9 percent more people die of heart disease, cirrhosis of the liver, and other stress-related ailments.

- Child abuse increases.

Helping Strategy

1. Offer encouragement by telling the individual you are glad he or she called, that we care, and that you are happy to spend time with him or her to talk about the problem.

2. Remind the person that he or she is not alone, that many others are going through the same difficulty. Employment loss is not unusual. In the light of this, he or she shouldn't feel "singled out" or take the loss of employment personally.

3. Tell the inquirer he or she shouldn't feel any less worthy. There is no reason to lose self-respect or to feel inadequate.

4. Tell him or her to remain confident and not to panic because God knows, loves, and cares. We must learn to trust Him.

5. Encourage praying that God will help him or her to weather the financial strain, provide for family needs, and open a new door of employment.

6. Suggest that he or she share the problem with Christian friends who may also pray, and with a sympathetic pastor who may be able to offer help in seeking employment opportunities.

7. Discourage taking out frustrations on the spouse or children. They will stand by the jobless person in the emergency. All are in it together, and the crisis can actually serve to strengthen family solidarity. They should find it helpful to pray together as a family.

8. Introduce the inquirer to Jesus Christ as Lord and Savior, if the conversation reveals that he or she does not know Him. Share "Steps to Peace with God," page 11.

Scripture

"I was young and now I am old, yet I have never seen the righteous forsaken or their children begging bread" (Psalm 37:25, NIV).

"Do not be anxious about anything, but in everything, by prayer and petition, with thanksgiving, present your requests to God. And the peace of God, which transcends all understanding, will guard your hearts and your minds in Christ Jesus" (Philippians 4:6–7, NIV).

"I can do everything through him who gives me strength. . . . And my God will meet all your needs according to his glorious riches in Christ Jesus" (Philippians 4:13, 19, NIV).

ENEMIES

Background

An enemy is anyone who may show hostility or ill will toward us, or seek to harm us. None of us is entirely free from the unhappiness caused by the wrongs of others. Our inclination may be to retaliate or "get even." But the Word of God always speaks of a different kind of response:

- "Live at peace with everyone" (Romans 12:18, NIV).

- "Repay no one evil for evil" (Romans 12:17).

- "Do not take revenge" (Romans 12:19, NIV).

- "Love your enemies, bless those who curse you, do good to those who hate you, and pray for those who spitefully use you and persecute you" (Matthew 5:44).

Certain attitudes and actions tend to create enemies or widen differences:

- Selfish actions or lack of sensitivity toward others.

- Unwillingness to realize that we may be the "offender" rather than the "offended."

- Talking *about* people rather than to them; "putting them down" or criticizing their attitudes and actions instead of humbly confronting them.

- Deliberately ignoring a tense situation rather than trying to correct it.

- Believing that we are morally superior because we have found something to condemn in someone else.

- Refusing to "go the second mile" or to "turn the other cheek" as taught in Scripture. Forgiveness is the essence of the redeemed life: "Forgive, and you will be forgiven" (Luke 6:37).

- Disobeying God's directive to love our enemies, bless them, do good to them, and pray for them (Matthew 5:44).

Billy Graham writes: "God can and will give you a forgiving spirit when you accept His forgiveness through Jesus Christ. When you do, you will realize that He has forgiven you so much that you will desire to forgive any wrong done to you. In the world, the policy of getting even with the other fellow is generally accepted. Among Christians, it is the policy to endure wrongs for the sake of Christ, forgiving that others might discover through us the grace of God in forgiving the sinner."

Helping Strategy

1. Reassure the inquirer that God is mindful of us in every situation. His Word has something to say about enemies.

2. Ask if he or she has ever received Jesus Christ as Lord and Savior. If not, share "Steps to Peace with God," page 11.

3. If the inquirer is a Christian, encourage a renewal of commitment to Christ. Use "Restoration," page 17, emphasizing 1 John 1:9 and Romans 12:1. A new or renewed relationship with Christ should help to bring a new perspective to feelings about enemies.

4. Ask the following questions, which may open some windows of understanding about reconciliation. Make an effort to understand the situation. Request information about the people and problems involved:

   A. What caused the break in the relationship?

   B. Has the inquirer contributed to the problem?

   C. As far as he or she can determine, what is the attitude of the other person? Is the inquirer being totally honest in trying to evaluate the situation?

   D. Ask how he or she feels about the "enemy": resentful? embittered? harboring ill will?

   E. Emphasize that he or she has the obligation to forgive, with all that this implies. He or she is to take the first step toward reconciliation. The mature Christian will always assume the responsibility for being a peacemaker. Highlight the attitude of Christ, who never demanded His "rights." Though He was reviled and spat upon, He didn't retaliate.

   F. Stress that it is in the inquirer's best interest to clear up the situation as early as possible: "Settle matters quickly with your adversary who is taking you to court . . . or he may hand you over to the judge . . . and you may be thrown into prison. . . . You will not get out until you have paid the last penny" (Matthew 5:25–26, NIV).

   G. Any approach to reconciliation must be made with humility, remembering that none of us is without sin: "A soft answer turns away wrath" (Proverbs 15:1). "Speaking the truth in love" (Ephesians 4:15).

H. Prayer must be sincerely offered for the other person, with one's own heart open to solutions.

I. Pray with the inquirer, asking God to intervene by working with both parties for a successful solution.

J. Ask what he or she intends to do as the first step toward reconciliation; delayed action will hinder reconciliation.

Scripture

"When a man's ways please the Lord, He makes even his enemies to be at peace with him" (Proverbs 16:7).

"But I say to you, love your enemies, bless those who curse you, do good to those who hate you, and pray for those who spitefully use you and persecute you, that you may be sons of your Father in heaven; for He makes His sun rise on the evil and on the good, and sends rain on the just and on the unjust. For if you love those who love you, what reward have you? Do not even the tax collectors do the same?" (Matthew 5:44–46).

"Then Jesus said, 'Father, forgive them, for they do not know what they do'" (Luke 23:34).

"If it is possible, as much as depends on you, live peaceably with all men" (Romans 12:18).

"Let him turn away from evil and do good; let him seek peace and pursue it" (1 Peter 3:11).

Other suggested Scriptures:

Psalm 34:14

Romans 14:17–19

2 Timothy 2:22

See also **Forgiveness**

ENVY, JEALOUSY, AND COVETOUSNESS

Background

Envy, jealousy, and covetousness are interrelated evils. Discontent with our position and possessions often indicates a self-centered attitude which leads to intolerant, resentful, and even malicious feelings toward a real or imagined rival. We may covet the success, personality, material possessions, good looks, or position of another. Then, in order to compensate for a frustrated ego, we make unkind and destructive remarks and submerge ourselves in self-pity, anger, bitterness, and depression.

Cain envied Abel because Abel's offering was accepted by God while Cain's was not. He became jealous, coveting what had been denied him (Genesis 4:3–8). Anger, bitterness, depression, and murder followed: "For where you have envy and selfish ambition, there you find disorder and every evil practice" (James 3:16, NIV).

Envy and jealous ambition motivated Lucifer to rebel against God: "I will ascend to heaven; I will raise my throne above the stars of God. . . . I will make myself like the Most High" (Isaiah 14:13–14, NIV).

Billy Graham writes: "You cannot have a full-orbed personality and harbor envy in your heart. We are told in Proverbs 14:30, 'A sound heart is life to the body, but envy is rottenness to the bones.' Envy is not a defensive weapon; it is an offensive instrument used in spiritual ambush. It wounds for the sake of wounding and hurts for the sake of hurting."

The apostle Paul gives the all-time antidote to the sins of envy, jealousy, and covetousness: "I have learned the secret of being content in any and every situation, whether well fed or hungry, whether living in plenty or in want. I can do everything through him who gives me strength" (Philippians 4:12–13, NIV).

Helping Strategy
For the Non-Christian:

1. If you detect envy, jealousy, or covetousness in the inquirer, carefully but

firmly point out that these attitudes are displeasing to God. Explain "Steps to Peace with God," page 11.

2. Encourage the inquirer to seek deliverance from envy, jealousy, and covetousness. Now that Christ has come into his or her life, the inquirer can begin learning to redirect thoughts and actions in ways that reflect newness of life in Christ. Envy, jealousy, and covetousness should be confessed as sin, and daily forgiveness and cleansing claimed.

3. Envy, jealousy, and covetousness should be converted into "fruits worthy of repentance" (Luke 3:8; see also Philippians 2:3–4):

   • Pray for those once envied.

   • Look for the good in others.

   • Get to know those once envied; learn to appreciate their assets and qualities which formerly produced negative responses and sin in you.

4. Suggest Bible reading, study, and memorization. As the Word of God begins to occupy our thinking, it crowds out the works of the flesh (Galatians 5:17–21).

5. Discuss the value of daily prayer.

6. Recommend becoming involved with a Bible-teaching church for worship, fellowship, and opportunities for service.

7. Pray with the caller for victory over envy, jealousy, and covetousness. Pray also for a transformed life through commitment to Christ.

For the Christian:

1. Encourage breaking his or her vicious line of thinking by openly recognizing the problem. He or she should focus on the real causes for the sin rather than on other people, circumstances, "bad luck," lack of acceptance, or failures to "get ahead." He or she should develop a mind-set which will enable facing issues squarely.

2. Help him or her to repent and confess this sin. Share "Restoration," page 17, emphasizing 1 John 1:9 and 2:1. He or she should be open and specific with God.

3. Encourage getting into the Word of God, reading and studying it. Dwight L. Moody said: "Either sin will keep you from this Book, or this Book will keep you from sin." Suggest searching for texts that speak to the problems, then praying over them, asking God to reinforce their truth. God's Word brings conviction, but also relief, as we learn to obey it.

4. Treat these sins as "bad habits" that need to be broken. Begin to practice the "put off—put on" principle (see the chapter on "Bad Habits"). This will be of great help. He or she should start with one aspect of the problem, focusing on it until it is under control, and then tackle successively other aspects until further progress is noted. It is often helpful to enlist one's spouse or a Christian friend to help monitor progress. Praying with this person on specific issues is also helpful.

5. Recommend getting involved in some form of Christian service through a Bible-teaching church. This could lead to more objective and constructive thinking which will aid in bringing his or her attitudes under control.

6. Encourage developing a thankful attitude toward life and toward the people who cross his or her path. Substituting praise for criticism is a good practice that provides encouraging results.

7. Pray with him or her personally for victory and a newfound joy in the Christian life.

Scripture

"A sound heart is life to the body, but envy is rottenness to the bones" (Proverbs 14:30).

"Since, then, you have been raised with Christ, set your hearts on things above, where Christ is seated at the right hand of God. Set your minds on things above, not on earthly things. For you died, and your life is now hidden with Christ in God. When Christ, who is your life, appears, then you also will appear with him in glory" (Colossians 3:1–4, NIV).

"And let us consider how we may spur one another on toward love and good deeds. Let us not give up meeting together, as some are in the habit of doing, but let us encourage one another—and all the more as you see the Day approaching" (Hebrews 10:24–25, NIV).

"Let your conduct be without covetousness, and be content with such things as you have. For He Himself has said, 'I will never leave you nor forsake you'" (Hebrews 13:5).

Other suggested Scriptures:

Proverbs 27:4
1 Corinthians 3:3

FAITH, LACK OF

Background

Inquirers often express the need for more faith. We could define faith as a total commitment to everything God is, does, and says. It is staking our life on the reality of His trustworthiness. But unless faith becomes operative in our own life, it is only a word. The most well-known definition of faith in Scripture is a functional one; it does not tell us what faith actually is, but what it will do for us:

"Now faith is being sure of what we hope for and certain of what we do not see" (Hebrews 11:1, NIV).

The Gospel is a way of faith. The Christian life is a walk of faith. Faith pleases God and He rewards it: "And without faith it is impossible to please God, because anyone who comes to him must believe that he exists and that he rewards those who earnestly seek him" (Hebrews 11:6, NIV).

Billy Graham has said, "Faith will manifest itself in three ways: in doctrine, worship, and fellowship. It will manifest itself in morality in the way we live and behave. The Bible also teaches that faith does not end with trust in Christ for our salvation. Faith continues! Faith grows! It may be weak at first, but it will become stronger as we begin to read the Bible, pray, go to church, and experience God's faithfulness in our Christian life."

Helping Strategy
For the Non-Christian:

If your inquirer speaks of faith in such a way as to reveal that he or she lacks understanding of saving faith, share "Steps to Peace with God," page 11. Emphasize that only by faith can we know God. Entering into a right relationship with Him through Jesus Christ means a commitment by faith to His person and work as expressed in His death on the cross and His resurrection: "So then faith comes by hearing, and hearing by the word of God" (Romans 10:17). "For by grace you have been saved through faith, and that not of yourselves; it is the gift of God, not of works, lest anyone should boast" (Ephesians 2:8–9). Share "Assurance," page 15, and the chapter on "Assurance of Salvation."

For the Christian:

If your inquirer is a Christian who expresses concern about his or her lack of faith, or who desires to have more faith:

1. Ask:

   • Why do you want more faith?

   • What do you want faith to do for you?

   The problem may be a lack of certainty in his or her relationship with Christ. If this surfaces, share "Assurance," page 15, and read and discuss Ephesians 2:8–9.

2. If he or she seems to have a good understanding of salvation by faith in Christ, then share ideas on increasing faith:

   A. A life of faith doesn't develop instantaneously through some mysterious process. Spiritual discipline leads to deeper faith.

   B. Confess your lack of faith to God as sin: "Whatever is not from faith is sin" (Romans 14:23). "Beware, brethren, lest there be in any of you an evil heart of unbelief in departing from the living God" (Hebrews 3:12).

   C. Highlight the Bible as the source book on faith. There are approximately 500 references to "faith," "belief," etc., in the New Testament alone. Read it and study it! Write down every reference to faith, then study each one in its context to determine what God is saying about faith and how you can apply it to your life.

   D. Explain the need to exercise faith through a life of prayer. There are references relating faith to prayer, for example Matthew 17:20 and James 5:15. Faith will grow as you experience victories in prayer.

   E. Use what you learn about faith, putting it to the test in your life. For example, in Proverbs 3:5–6 God promises His guidance if we meet certain conditions. If you desire the leading of the Lord for some decision you need to make or action you need to take, determine from this passage what God's conditions are, and meet those conditions, in order to experience the promised guidance.

   F. Begin challenging your faith by daring to believe God more and more and by acting on that belief. True faith is dynamic; it results in action! The great heroes of faith (Hebrews 11) were on the move for God! Get involved in Christian service: "Therefore, my beloved brethren, be steadfast, immovable, always abounding in the work of the Lord, knowing that your labor is not in vain in the Lord" (1 Corinthians 15:58).

Scripture

"I say to you, if you have faith as a mustard seed, you will say to this mountain, 'Move from here to there,' and it will move; and nothing will be impossible for you" (Matthew 17:20).

"So Jesus answered and said to them, 'Have faith in God'" (Mark 11:22).

"Therefore, having been justified by faith, we have peace with God through our Lord Jesus Christ" (Romans 5:1).

"In this you greatly rejoice, though now for a little while, if need be, you have been grieved by various trials, that the genuineness of your faith, being much more precious than gold that perishes, though it is tested by fire, may be found to praise, honor, and glory at the revelation of Jesus Christ, whom having not seen you love. Though now you do not see Him, yet believing, you rejoice with joy inexpressible and full of glory, receiving the end of your faith—the salvation of your souls" (1 Peter 1:6–9).

FALSE TEACHING

Background

The apostle John wrote in his second letter, "For if you wander beyond the teaching of Christ, you will leave God behind; while if you are loyal to Christ's teachings, you will have God too" (2 John 9, TLB).

Billy Graham has written, "All the way through the Bible we are warned against false prophets and false teachers 'who come to you in sheep's clothing, but inwardly they are ravenous wolves' (Matthew 7:15). Sometimes it is extremely difficult for Christians to discern a false prophet. . . . Jesus spoke of 'false prophets' . . . who will 'show great signs and wonders . . . to deceive, if possible, even the elect' (Matthew 24:24)."

The underlying principle of all Satan's tactics is deception. He is crafty and has clever disguises. His deception began in the Garden of Eden and continues to this day. He invades the theological seminary and even the pulpit. He invades the church under cover of orthodox vocabulary, emptying sacred terms of their biblical sense.

What is a false teaching? It is any teaching which is contrary to the basic doctrines of God's Word, such as those having to do with the Trinity, the virgin birth of Christ, His atoning death, His bodily resurrection and second coming, salvation by grace through faith, the bodily resurrection of all believers, and the reality of heaven and hell.

Helping Strategy
For the Non-Christian:

1. Commend the inquirer on wanting to share his or her thoughts and discover the truth. Tell him or her that you hope you can be of help as you talk together.

2. If the inquirer seems to have a difficult time accepting the Bible at face value, it may be that he or she has never received Jesus Christ as Lord and Savior. Emphasize that this step is crucial in understanding the Scripture (1 Corinthians 2:14; 2 Corinthians 4:4). Share "Steps to Peace with God," page 11, and invite the inquirer to receive Christ.

3. If the response is positive, share other follow-up steps:

   A. Encourage reading and studying the Bible. Offer to send *Living in*

Christ, which contains the gospel of John along with helpful Bible studies. Stress that he or she should read the Gospel text thoroughly before completing the study portion.

B. If the inquirer is influenced by or connected with a sect or cult, recommend leaving it immediately and severing all ties with the group. In its place, he or she should identify with a Bible-teaching church for worship, prayer, and fellowship with born-again believers and instruction in God's Word.

4. Pray with him or her for a clear understanding of the Bible—for "the mind of Christ" (1 Corinthians 2:16) in all things concerning God's Word.

For the Christian:

It is not uncommon for an apparently knowledgeable Christian to be influenced by false teaching.

1. Take care not to offend the inquirer by suggesting that he or she is in error or has been gullible. Remember that Satan often disguises himself as an "angel of light" (2 Corinthians 11:14). Do not suggest at the outset that he or she leave the cult or sect.

2. Trusting the Holy Spirit to lead you, consult other resources that give information about the doctrinal issues involved. Perhaps something in the chapter on "Cults" in this book, or the section in the back titled "A Comparison of Christianity with Major Religions and Cults," will be of help. Use your own knowledge of the Bible and your experience to help the person.

3. Ask your inquirer to write down the information and accompanying Scriptures you share, for future reflection and study. Offer to send *Living in Christ* for help in Bible study.

4. Finally, pray with him or her for an open mind and for a knowledge of God's will as he or she seeks to know the Bible.

5. If, at this point, your inquirer asks you to recommend a church, simply suggest that he or she seek to identify with a group of believers where God's Word is preached and taught. Then trust the Holy Spirit to guide to the right place. Do not suggest a specific denomination or church unless the inquirer requests this information.

Scripture

"There is a way that seems right to a man, but its end is the way of death" (Proverbs 16:25).

"Beware lest anyone cheat you through philosophy and empty deceit, according to the tradition of men, according to the basic principles of the world, and not according to Christ. For in Him dwells all the fullness of the Godhead bodily" (Colossians 2:8–9).

"Now the Spirit expressly says that in latter times some will depart from the faith, giving heed to deceiving spirits and doctrines of demons, speaking lies in hypocrisy, having their own conscience seared with a hot iron" (1 Timothy 4:1–2).

"Be diligent to present yourself approved to God, a worker who does not need to be ashamed, rightly dividing the word of truth" (2 Timothy 2:15).

"Beloved, do not believe every spirit, but test the spirits, whether they are of God; because many false prophets have gone out into the world. By this you know the Spirit of God: Every spirit that confesses that Jesus Christ has come in the flesh is of God, and every spirit that does not confess that Jesus Christ has come in the flesh is not of God. And this is the spirit of the Antichrist, which you have heard was coming, and is now already in the world" (1 John 4:1–3).

See also **Cults, The Bible, The Trinity**

FEAR

Background

A moderate sense of fear may be considered normal, even healthy. It may be simply an awareness of impending danger—a defense mechanism. It may be just the pounding heart, flushed face, and sweaty palms in anticipation of being called on in class or being asked to make a speech at a meeting. Fears may be in reaction to imagined or real circumstances. They can be acute or chronic. Many fearful people tend to infect others with their anxieties and tensions.

When faced with a fearful person, you must demonstrate love and try to discover the causes for the fears. There may be no easy or instantaneous solutions to the total problem; but you can suggest a proper relationship with Jesus Christ, dependence on the Holy Spirit, and a life focused on the Word of God as necessary steps to freedom from fear.

The expressions "fear of God" or "fear God" in the Bible don't mean that God expects us to cringe in terror before Him in anticipation of punishment, but that we owe Him our reverential respect and trust. Solomon said,

"The fear of the Lord is the beginning of wisdom" (Proverbs 9:10).

The fear of God is the one fear (a trustful, worshipful attitude) which removes all other fears!

"I sought the Lord, and He heard me, and delivered me from all my fears" (Psalm 34:4).

Billy Graham writes, "Jesus said we are not to fear; we are not to be anxious; we are not to fret; we are not to worry. The Bible teaches that this type of fear is sin. 'Peace I leave with you, My peace I give to you. . . . Let not your heart be troubled, neither let it be afraid'" (John 14:27).

Helping Strategy
For the Non-Christian:

If the inquirer is a non-Christian expressing an unhealthy fear of God because of a guilty conscience or fear of punishment (future judgment), you are probably dealing with unresolved sin for which there is a remedy. Share "Steps to Peace with God," page 11. Emphasize that:

1. God can cleanse our conscience: "How much more, then, will the blood of Christ, who through the eternal Spirit offered himself unblemished to God, cleanse our consciences from acts that lead to death, so that we may serve the living God!" (Hebrews 9:14, NIV).

2. God delivers from fears of future punishment: "Therefore, there is now no condemnation for those who are in Christ Jesus, because through Christ Jesus the law of the Spirit of life set me free from the law of sin and death" (Romans 8:1–2, NIV). Share "Assurance," page 15.

For the Christian:

If the inquirer is a Christian whose greatest fear is *personal inadequacy*—failing, or not measuring up—share the following:

1. God doesn't ask you to be successful, only to please Him! "Delight yourself also in the Lord, and He shall give you the desires of your heart" (Psalm 37:4).

2. Learn to accept yourself as you are, not making excessive personal demands. Paul said, "By the grace of God I am what I am" (1 Corinthians 15:10). The Lord told Paul that "My grace is sufficient for you, for My strength is made perfect in weakness" (2 Corinthians 12:9).

3. Don't compare yourself with others. Just be you: "We do not dare to classify or compare ourselves with some who commend themselves. When they measure themselves by themselves and compare themselves with themselves, they are not wise" (2 Corinthians 10:12, NIV).

4. God has given you all you need to be confident: "God has not given us a spirit of fear, but of power [sufficiency] and of love and of a sound mind" (2 Timothy 1:7).

5. Learn to trust God implicitly for what you want to be and do: "Trust in the Lord with all your heart, and lean not on your own understanding; in all your ways acknowledge Him, and He shall direct your paths" (Proverbs 3:5–6).

6. Make your fears a definite matter for prayer: "Do not be anxious about anything, but in everything, by prayer and petition, with thanksgiving, present your requests to God. And the peace of God, which transcends all understanding, will guard your hearts and your minds in Christ Jesus" (Philippians 4:6–7, NIV).

If the inquirer is a Christian with a sense of uneasiness or anxiety about the *uncertainties of life and the future,* offer encouragement w_th the following:

1. The Lord is mindful of us.

   "I am the good shepherd; I know my sheep and my sheep know me" (John 10:14, NIV).

   "'For I know the plans I have for you,' declares the Lord, 'plans to prosper you and not to harm you, plans to give you hope and a future'" (Jeremiah 29:11, NIV).

2. He has promised:

   - *His presence:* "Keep your lives free from the love of money and be content with what you have, because God has said, 'Never will I leave you; never will I forsake you'" (Hebrews 13 5, NIV).

   - *His provision:* "I was young and now I am old, yet I have never seen the righteous forsaken or their children begging bread" (Psalm 37:25, NIV).

   - *His protection:* "The Lord is my light and my salvation; whom shall I fear? The Lord is the strength of my life; of whom shall I be afraid?" (Psalm 27:1).

3. Point out that love is the antithesis of fear: "There is no fear in love. But perfect love drives out fear, because fear has to do with punishment. The one who fears is not made perfect in love" (1 John 4:18, NIV).

If the inquirer is a Christian with a fear of *witnessing* for Christ, encourage him or her to:

1. Be completely sure of his or her own relationship with Christ: "For I know whom I have believed and am persuaded that He is able to keep what I have committed to Him until that Day" (2 Timothy 1:12).

2. Make a conscious moral commitment to God: "Present your bodies a living sacrifice . . . to God, which is your reasonable service" (Romans 12:1).

3. Trust God implicitly both to be with and to work through him or her: "My grace is sufficient for you, for My strength is made perfect in weakness" (2 Corinthians 12:9). "'Do not be afraid of their faces, for I am with you to deliver you,' says the Lord" (Jeremiah 1:3).

4. Be faithful in witnessing in the small things. Demonstrate your Christian faith through such things as acts of kindness, watching one's attitudes, and thanking God for a meal in a public place.

5. Seek the companionship and strength of a stronger Christian so they may witness together. Confidence is gained as one becomes a part of

evangelism: "Make plans by seeking advice; if you wage war, obtain guidance" (Proverbs 20:18, NIV).

6. Take a course in personal evangelism that is available through his or her own or another church.

7. Pray for a consuming compassion for the lost: "Yet when I preach the gospel, I cannot boast, for I am compelled to preach. Woe to me if I do not preach the gospel!" (1 Corinthians 9:16, NIV).

If the inquirer is fearful of *death,* refer to the chapter on "Death."

Scripture

"I sought the Lord, and He heard me, and delivered me from all my fears" (Psalm 34:4).

"Whoever listens to me will dwell safely, and will be secure, without fear of evil" (Proverbs 1:33).

"Fear not, for I am with you; be not dismayed, for I am your God. I will strengthen you, yes, I will help you, I will uphold you with My righteous right hand" (Isaiah 41:10).

"Fear not, for I have redeemed you; I have called you by your name; you are Mine. When you pass through the waters, I will be with you; and through the rivers, they shall not overflow you. When you walk through the fire, you shall not be burned" (Isaiah 43:1–2).

"For you did not receive a spirit that makes you a slave again to fear, but you received the Spirit of sonship. And by him we cry, 'Abba, Father.' The Spirit himself testifies with our spirit that we are God's children" (Romans 8:15–16, NIV).

See also **Anxiety, Worry, and Tension**

FINANCIAL DIFFICULTIES

Background

Understanding and correctly handling finances should be a high priority for all people. Much of our tension, family friction, and frustrations are caused, directly or indirectly, by money. High on the list of causes of divorce is financial disagreement. The Christian family is not immune. If a family cannot or does not pay its bills, or is beset by other problems related to money, it is a poor testimony to nonbelievers. Too few churches offer training for their people in the area of financial accountability.

Chief Causes of Financial Problems

- *Wrong attitudes toward money.* Greed and covetousness quickly lead to all kinds of evil (1 Timothy 6:10). The "get rich quick" syndrome of speculative investment often leads to disaster.

- *Living beyond one's income.* Failure to "count the cost" will result in chronic overspending (Luke 14:28–30). Some people seem to have a great susceptibility to advertising, succumbing to attractive products and seemingly advantageous credit offers.

- *Credit buying.* The best possible advice for those in financial trouble is to stay away from stores and showrooms and to destroy all their credit cards.

- *Self-indulgent living.* Purchase of unnecessary things, consumption of alcoholic beverages, tobacco, and junk or gourmet foods are self-indulgent habits. For example, in a home where both husband and wife smoke heavily, as much as $2,000 yearly can be spent on cigarettes!

- *The misbelief that material things bring happiness.* "Then [Jesus] said to them, 'Watch out! Be on your guard against all kinds of greed; a man's life does not consist in the abundance of his possessions'" (Luke 12:15, NIV).

- *Lack of a budget* for projecting and monitoring expenses. Any given person's income will go just so far. Allowing for some variation in the actual percentages, a typical budget for a small family might include:

Tithe 10%	Housing 30%
Food 14%	Transportation 13%
Insurance 4%	Debts 5%
Recreation and Vacations 5%	Clothing 5%

Medical and Dental 5%   Savings 5%

Miscellaneous 4%

Biblical Principles for Handling Money

- The use of material resources is basically a spiritual matter; therefore, an understanding of the lordship of Jesus Christ is essential. Money brings into perspective the totality of life as it relates to God's will and the issues of eternity:

  "The earth is the Lord's, and everything in it" (1 Corinthians 10:26, NIV).

  "You are not your own. . . . You were bought at a price" (1 Corinthians 6:19–20).

  "Offer your bodies as living sacrifices, holy and pleasing to God. . . . Do not conform any longer to the pattern of this world, but be transformed by the renewing of your mind. Then you will be able to test and approve what God's will is—his good, pleasing and perfect will" (Romans 12:1–2, NIV).

- We must understand that we are stewards (managers) of all that God has put under our care. We are not owners. Our lives, our time, and our assets are gifts from God. We are responsible to God for them, and He will hold us accountable (Matthew 25:14–30).

- God wants us to depend on Him, not on material possessions. "Command those who are rich in this present world not to be arrogant nor to put their hope in wealth, which is so uncertain, but to put their hope in God, who richly provides us with everything for our enjoyment" (1 Timothy 6:17, NIV; see also Psalm 37:25; Proverbs 3:5–6; Philippians 4:19).

- It is God's plan that stewards give a portion of their income to Him and His work: "'Bring all the tithes into the storehouse, that there may be food in My house, and prove Me now in this,' says the Lord of hosts, 'If I will not open for you the windows of heaven and pour out for you such blessing that there will not be room enough to receive it'" (Malachi 3:10; see also Proverbs 3:9; Luke 12:34).

Billy Graham says: "Although all our money actually belongs to God, the Bible suggests the tithe as a minimum response in gratitude to God. . . . You cannot get around it; the Bible promises material and spiritual blessing to the person who gives to God. You cannot outgive God. I challenge you to try it and see."

Helping Strategy

1. If the inquirer admits to financial difficulty, suggest that a person needs the perspective which comes through an eternal relationship with Jesus Christ as Lord and Savior. We must know Him personally before we can expect to have His help. Share "Steps to Peace with God," page 11.

2. After the inquirer has explained the financial problem, suggest looking on it as basically a spiritual problem. Don't look just for a temporary solution, but bring God into the center of life—even into his or her financial dealings. Only this will bring lasting solutions. It wouldn't be in the best interests of the inquirer for you to accept explanations or excuses for the financial problems, such as, for example, the problems of the national economy. Many people are in trouble because they mismanage.

3. How financial problems are dealt with in the future will depend on one's attitude toward the principles of Scripture (see "Background"). Go over these, one by one. Then, question the caller about the cause of the financial problem. Is it:

   - Wrong attitudes about money?
   - Credit purchases?
   - Living beyond his or her means?
   - Self-indulgent living?
   - Lack of a budget or improper planning?

4. Stress the need to bring personal finances and life into line, making whatever adjustments or sacrifices that may be necessary. The person's own future and that of his or her family will depend on such decisive action.

5. If the proposed financial solutions seem beyond the inquirer's ability even after he or she has tried to honor biblical principles, suggest that he or she ask a pastor to recommend a professional counselor or financial planner who can work out steps to recovery; or go directly to a counselor, if he or she knows whom to contact.

   CAUTION: Avoid financial institutions which offer to consolidate debts. Such "consolidation" can actually increase one's indebtedness.

Scripture

"'Will a man rob God? Yet you have robbed Me! But you say, "In what way have we robbed You?" In tithes and offerings. You are cursed with a curse, for you have robbed Me, even this whole nation. Bring all the tithes into the storehouse, that there may be food in My house, and prove Me now in this,' says the Lord of hosts, 'If I will not open for you the windows of

heaven and pour out for you such blessing that there will not be room enough to receive it'" (Malachi 3:8–10).

"Seek first the kingdom of God and His righteousness, and all these things shall be added to you" (Matthew 6:33).

"And my God shall supply all your need according to His riches in glory by Christ Jesus" (Philippians 4:19).

FORGIVENESS

Background

Forgiveness is one of the most beautiful words in the human vocabulary. How much pain and unhappy consequences could be avoided if we all learned the meaning of this word! King David shared some of the emotion he personally experienced after he asked God to "wash me thoroughly from my iniquity, and cleanse me from my sin" (Psalm 51:2).

Elsewhere he says,

> "Blessed is he whose transgressions are forgiven, whose sins are covered. Blessed is the man whose sin the Lord does not count against him and in whose spirit is no deceit" (Psalm 32:1–2, NIV).

In one bold stroke, forgiveness obliterates the past and permits us to enter the land of new beginnings.

Billy Graham says: "God's forgiveness is not just a casual statement; it is the complete blotting out of all the dirt and degradation of our past, present, and future. The only reason our sins can be forgiven is that, on the cross, Jesus Christ paid their full penalty. [But] only as we bow at the foot of the cross, in contrition, confession, and repentance, can we find forgiveness."

The Basis for Forgiveness

1. Own up to what we are and have done (repentance): "For I acknowledge my transgressions, and my sin is ever before me. Against You, You only, have I sinned, and done this evil in Your sight" (Psalm 51:3–4).

2. Ask for forgiveness: "Purge me with hyssop, and I shall be clean; wash me, and I shall be whiter than snow. . . . Hide Your face from my sins, and blot out all my iniquities" (Psalm 51:7, 9).

The Results of Forgiveness:

1. *Reconciliation.* When God forgives, there is an immediate and complete change in relationship. Instead of hostility, there is love and acceptance. Instead of enmity, there is friendship. God is always in the business of "reconciling the world to himself in Christ, not counting men's sins against them" (2 Corinthians 5:19, NIV).

2. *Purification*. The very essence of forgiveness is being restored to our original standing before God: "Purge me . . . and I shall be clean; wash me, and I shall be whiter than snow" (Psalm 51:7; see also Romans 4:7; 1 John 1:9).

When God forgives us and purifies us of our sin, He also forgets it: "For I will forgive their wickedness and will remember their sins no more" (Hebrews 8:12, NIV; see also Psalm 103:12; Isaiah 38:17).

3. *Remission*. Forgiveness results in God's dropping the charges against us. He will not enforce judgment because of our sins. Jesus said to the woman taken in adultery, "Neither do I condemn you; go and sin no more" (John 8:11; see also Romans 8:1).

What a great privilege you have as you share with inquirers the joy of God's forgiveness!

Helping Strategy

We shall consider three areas: forgiveness from God, forgiving those who have wronged us, and forgiving ourselves by putting our past behind us.

For the Non-Christian:

1. Reassure a nonbeliever by saying that God understands sin and knows how to deal with it. He forgives sin. And the inquirer, too, can know the joy of pardon.

2. Explain "Steps to Peace with God," page 11. Emphasize the "Results of Forgiveness" mentioned in the "Background."

3. Share "Assurance," page 15.

   NOTE: If your inquirer insists that he or she can't be forgiven, having committed the "unpardonable sin," turn to the chapter on that subject.

4. Encourage him or her to start reading and studying the Bible. This will bring great reassurance of forgiveness (1 John 3:19). Ask if he or she would like to receive *Living in Christ*, which will provide a good starting place for Bible reading and study.

5. Recommend seeking fellowship with a group of Bible-believing Christians. A good church will provide Bible teaching, worship, and opportunities for service and witnessing as well.

6. Encourage daily prayer and confession (1 John 1:9) as a prerequisite for daily forgiveness and renewal.

7. Pray with him or her for a full understanding of commitment to Christ and its implications in everyday life.

For the Christian Who is Bitter or Resentful:

1. Gently point out the sinfulness of such an attitude. He or she needs first of all to put his or her own house in order, confessing the bitterness and resentment to God as sin.

2. Encourage forgiveness of those who have offended or hurt. This may be difficult, but God commands it! "Bear with each other and forgive whatever grievances you may have against one another. Forgive as the Lord forgave you" (Colossians 3:13, NIV). Sometimes those who deserve forgiveness the least need it the most! Forgiving as the Lord forgave implies forgetting. This may be difficult and may require time, but God can change our attitudes. Jesus' answer of "seventy times seven" to Peter's question, "How often shall my brother sin against me, and I forgive him?" implies that the Christian must be ready, even eager, to forgive (Matthew 18:21–35).

3. Recommend seeking to restore the broken relationship in the spirit of Colossians 3:13. In all probability, this will mean "going the second mile" (Matthew 5:41), but this may be necessary in order to renew the relationship. The Gospel always cuts across the grain of human reactions and conduct. Until one of the parties involved takes the initiative toward forgiveness and restoration, the broken relationship will continue.

For the Christian Who Cannot Forgive Himself or Herself:

1. Ask if he or she is truly repentant and has confessed, frankly and transparently, all sin to God. If so, share "Restoration," page 17, emphasizing 1 John 1:9.

2. If the above step has been taken but the self-punishment continues, point out that he or she is guilty of unbelief: If God has forgiven (1 John 1:9), it is wrong to doubt God. We must take God at His word. Share David's testimony from Psalm 32:1–2: "Blessed is he whose transgression is forgiven, whose sin is covered. Blessed is the man to whom the Lord does not impute iniquity, and in whose spirit there is no guile."

False humility could be involved. Self-flagellation makes some people feel better, while others take pleasure in reviewing the past. This is like the scribes and Pharisees: "Even so you . . . appear righteous to men, but inside you are full of hypocrisy and lawlessness" (Matthew 23:28).

3. If the person is truly repentant, talk about how we need to see ourselves as God sees us—as a new creature in Christ Jesus (2 Corinthians 5:17). God understands sin and knows how to deal with it. He will forgive sin

if we repent and confess. Paul's wisdom needs to be practiced: "Forgetting those things which are behind and reaching forward to those things which are ahead, I press toward the goal for the prize of the upward call of God in Christ Jesus" (Philippians 3:13–14).

Scripture

"I, even I, am He who blots out your transgressions for My own sake; and I will not remember your sins" (Isaiah 43:25).

"For if you forgive men their trespasses, your heavenly Father will also forgive you. But if you do not forgive men their trespasses, neither will your Father forgive your trespasses" (Matthew 6:14–15).

"Father, forgive them, for they do not know what they do" (Luke 23:34).

"Therefore if the Son makes you free, you shall be free indeed" (John 8:36).

Other suggested Scriptures:

Psalm 51

GAMBLING

Background

People gamble in many different ways. Some forms of gambling seem quite innocent, and sometimes a percentage of the profits are used for a good cause. God's Word, however, indicates that gambling in any form is contrary to His will for the Christian:

- First, gambling or betting puts faith in chance or luck rather than in the care and provision of God.

- Second, one who gambles seeks to profit from another's loss. This borders on stealing.

- Third, gambling promotes a greedy spirit. It emphasizes getting rather than giving, selfish interest rather than self-sacrifice. It erodes the moral fiber of society.

The Bible indicates that there are three legitimate ways to accumulate material goods:

- Work: "If anyone will not work, neither shall he eat" (2 Thessalonians 3:10).

- Wise investments (see the parable of the talents, Luke 19:11–27).

- Gifts or inheritance: "Children ought not to lay up for the parents, but the parents for the children" (2 Corinthians 12:14).

Billy Graham writes, "The appeal of gambling is somewhat understandable. There is something alluring about getting something for nothing. . . . And that is where the sin lies. Gambling of any kind amounts to theft by permission. The coin is flipped, the dice are rolled, or the horses run, and somebody rakes in that which belongs to another. The Bible says, 'In the sweat of your face you shall eat bread' (Genesis 3:19). It doesn't say, 'By the flip of a coin you shall eat your bread.' I realize that in most petty gambling no harm is intended, but the principle is the same as in big gambling. The difference is only in the amount of money involved."

The experience of the gambler is similar to that of the alcoholic. He or she experiences the delusion of being master of his or her own life, when in truth, life is out of control. He or she denies having any problem, even while family ties disintegrate. He or she ends up with enormous debts and often steals to cover the gambling losses.

The gambler may promise to quit, but he or she rarely follows through unless disaster strikes, bringing an unavoidable confrontation with reality.

An encounter with Jesus Christ is the only solution for many gamblers; some who are converted experience immediate freedom from their addiction. In other cases, complete victory and healing is a longer process. Many of the emotional problems of the alcoholic are also present in the gambler, and the underlying causes must be dealt with in the light of God's Word.

Gamblers Anonymous, the National Council on Compulsive Gambling, and other recovery groups try to minister to those addicted to gambling. Gamblers Anonymous has chapters in many cities across the nation, and they usually have a listing in the phone book.

Helping Strategy

1. A compassionate but "tough" stance must be assumed by the helper. The gambling addiction is very real. The victim must be confronted with the fact that life is out of control and that he or she must assume personal responsibility for the situation. Does he or she really want help? Then, the gambling must stop. Nothing short of this will solve the problem.

2. Has he or she ever received Christ as Lord and Savior? Share "Steps to Peace with God," page 11. Christ can break the shackles of sin, making all things new (2 Corinthians 5:17).

3. Emphasize that the gambler must make a clean break, resolving never to return to the gambling table, purchase lottery tickets, play slot machines, or engage in other gambling-related activities. Living one day at a time, he or she must learn to trust God in regard to the temptation: "But remember this—the wrong desires that come into your life aren't anything new and different. Many others have faced exactly the same problems before you. And no temptation is irresistible. You can trust God to keep the temptation from becoming so strong that you can't stand up against it, for he has promised this and will do what he says. He will show you how to escape temptation's power so that you can bear up patiently against it" (1 Corinthians 10:13, TLB).

4. The repentant gambler must abandon the old haunts and sever all relationships related to gambling, and establish new relationships. Attendance at a support group for gamblers could bring very positive results. He or she should identify with a local Bible-teaching church for worship, Bible study, prayer, and the building of new friendships that will help rebuild his or her life.

5. Pray with the inquirer for complete deliverance from the bondage to gambling. Stress the importance of going to the Lord in prayer daily. The practice of prayer will encourage increasing dependence on God, rather than on luck!

6. Stress the importance of reading and studying the Bible on a personal basis. As one assimilates God's thoughts, a gradual transformation of the mind and life takes place. You may offer *Living in Christ* at this point.

7. If further help is needed, suggest talking with a qualified pastor or Christian psychologist. Underlying causes that led to the addiction must often be dealt with in depth.

If the inquiry is about bingo, lotteries, or raffles, and the person tries to justify such activities because they are sometimes sponsored by a church or are harmless and serve good causes, refer to the "Background." Then, proceed as follows:

1. Ask if he or she has ever received Jesus Christ as Lord and Savior. Explain "Steps to Peace with God," page 11.

2. Emphasize that God's work is to be supported by the sacrificial giving of God's people, not by such thing as raffles, bingo, or lotteries.

Scripture

"You shall not steal. You shall not covet . . . anything that is your neighbor's" (Exodus 20:15, 17).

"Therefore, I urge you, brothers, in view of God's mercy, to offer your bodies as living sacrifices, holy and pleasing to God—this is your spiritual act of worship" (Romans 12:1, NIV).

"All things are lawful for me, but all things are not helpful. All things are lawful for me, but I will not be brought under the power of any" (1 Corinthians 6:12).

"Therefore, whether you eat or drink, or whatever you do, do all to the glory of God" (1 Corinthians 10:31).

"Set your mind on things above, not on things on the earth. . . . Put to death your members which are on the earth: fornication, uncleanness, passion, evil desire, and covetousness, which is idolatry. Because of these things the wrath of God is coming upon the sons of disobedience" (Colossians 3:2, 5–6).

GRIEF AND BEREAVEMENT

Background

Grief is an intense emotional suffering caused by personal loss. It involves acute sorrow, deep sadness, suffering, pain, and anguish. Bereavement can be defined more specifically as the grief that follows the death of a loved one. This chapter will focus primarily on that aspect of grief.

Bereavement is a difficult time. The bereaved person will often feel that his or her experience is unique, that no one has ever endured such a loss or suffered as he or she is suffering. There are cycles of healing to the pattern of grief, which permit the sorrowing person to recover in due time. For some, however, complete recovery never comes.

The cycle of healing from grief usually proceeds as follows:

1. *The initial shock of death:* that intense emotional impact which sometimes leaves a person with a seeming paralysis.

2. *Emotional release:* a time characterized by weeping.

3. *Loneliness and depression:* a sense of loss, often related to the degree of dependence on the deceased.

4. *Guilt:* a feeling of guilt characterized by second-guessing: "I could have done more," or, "I should have done something differently."

5. *Anger, hostility:* "Why did God do this to me?"

6. *Inertia:* Listlessness: "I can't get on with it," or, "I couldn't care less."

7. *A gradual return to hope:* "Life will go on." "I will be able to cope." "God will help me get over this."

8. *The return to reality and normality:* admitting the loss and adjusting to it.

We must remember, however, that grief is not predictable nor can it be catalogued. Sometimes the stages of grief will seem to merge and overlap. The bereaved may feel release from a certain "phase" of suffering, only to have it return.

Helping grieving people calls for genuineness, special sensitivity and tenderness, sympathy, and empathy. We must depend on the Holy Spirit for guidance. Convenient, glib, or pat answers have the ring of brass. Our words must be sincere and meaningful, "tailor-made for the situation," because real comfort for the bereaving person depends on where he or she actually is in the grieving process.

Don't pretend to have an answer for everything. Admit that you do not understand why or how God does what He does.

Don't be the "cheerleader" type, trying to pump up the bereaved with cheer and good will.

Don't offer cliches or trite phrases about death and suffering.

Don't suggest that if the grieving one were more spiritual or closer to God, the pain might be less.

Remember that one short session will not meet all the needs of the inquirer. Do what you can to share Jesus Christ and the message of Scripture, and trust God to do His work.

Helping Strategy

1. Tell the inquirer you care and want to help. Encourage him or her to tell you about the loss and how he or she feels about it. Be a patient listener. It helps to ventilate feelings when one is grieving.

2. Explain that it is healthy to mourn and grieve. This is a universal human experience through which we all must pass. Someone has said that grief is a "gift from God." It may be His way of helping us react to the tremendous shock of death and its emotional aftermath. Jesus said, "Blessed are those who mourn, for they shall be comforted" (Matthew 5:4). Jesus Himself wept at the grave of Lazarus (John 11:35).

3. Stress that it is good to express feelings of guilt, anger, confusion, or despair. These feelings should not be repressed by the sorrower or rejected by the helper. Encourage honest talk about feelings.

4. Point out that the things he or she is feeling are often normal to the grieving process, and that acceptance and healing will come, though perhaps slowly. God wants to bear our heartaches and losses and give us His comfort, hope, and encouragement. Life may seem valueless at this point, but remember—Christ is permanent, the Solid Rock, the foundation on which to rebuild a life.

5. Ask if he or she has ever received Jesus Christ as Lord and Savior. If indicated, explain "Steps to Peace with God," page 11.

Billy Graham says: "Our confidence in the future is based firmly on the fact of what God has done for us in Christ. Because Christ is alive we need never despair, no matter what our situation may be. 'Now if we died with Christ, we believe that we shall also live with Him. . . . For the wages of sin is death, but the gift of God is eternal life in Christ Jesus our Lord' (Romans 6:8, 23)."

---

6. Remind the bereaved person that, for the Christian, death is not the end of life. Through His death and resurrection, Christ has defeated sin and death, so that to believe in Him now means:

- We "shall never die" (John 11:25–26).

- We have everlasting life (John 3:16).

- We have a place assured in heaven (John 14:1–6).

- We shall take part in the bodily resurrection (1 Corinthians 15:51–52).

And, there will be a glorious reunion some day between us and all those in the Lord whom we hold dear: "If we believe that Jesus died and rose again, even so God will bring with Him those who sleep in Jesus" (1 Thessalonians 4:14).

Encourage the inquirer to read and study the Bible. It is a great source of comfort and strength.

7. Stress that God sees our earthly life as preparation for the greater joys of heaven (Mark 8:36). Thus, He permits trials, sufferings, and the death of loved ones to come into our lives so that we might see our need to trust Him: "Yet we believe now that we had this sense of impending disaster so that we might learn to trust, not in ourselves, but in God who can raise the dead" (2 Corinthians 1:9, PHILLIPS).

8. If the bereaved expresses guilt over some aspect of the death of the loved one (this is common in the case of suicides), advise not to second-guess the situation at this point. He or she should not carry guilt for something that should or should not have been done. The death and all that may have preceded it is past, and the bereaved person needs to leave all regrets with the Lord. If he or she has something to confess to God, do so, but then accept the reality of His forgiveness (1 John 1:9).

9. If the caller seems overwhelmed with a sense of loss, of loneliness, or of uncertainty about the future, suggest confiding in family or friends, trusting them for emotional support and encouragement. Involvement in a church can do a great deal to fill the areas left void. The pastor may be able to offer substantial emotional support.

Learning to accept God's will for what has happened, having a thankful heart for the years of love shared during the life of the loved one and for the promise of the eternal life to come, and reaching out in Christian love to help others who are hurting will all be great therapy and will help the bereaved in learning to live fully again.

10. Pray with the inquirer for understanding, comfort, and blessing in his or her life.

The Death of Children:

The death of a child is especially difficult for surviving parents and families. Death after such a short life span often produces feelings of guilt, melancholy, and a lot of questions. In addition to the foregoing "Helping Strategy," the following may be helpful:

1. Though we cannot know why the child died, we do know that children are especially precious to God. Referring to children, Jesus said, "Of such is the kingdom of heaven" (Matthew 19:14). Interpreted in the light of Scripture as a whole, this passage has led some scholars to believe that children who die are taken immediately into God's presence.

2. If we believe that Jesus died and rose again, and trust in Him as our Lord and Savior, we have the blessed hope of seeing our loved one again. When King David's child was taken from him in death, he said, "Can I bring him back again? I shall go to him, but he shall not return to me" (2 Samuel 12:23).

Scripture

"Jesus said to her, 'I am the resurrection and the life. He who believes in Me, though he may die, he shall live. And whoever lives and believes in Me shall never die. Do you believe this?'" (John 11:25–26).

"Let not your heart be troubled; you believe in God, believe also in Me. In My Father's house are many mansions; if it were not so, I would have told you. I go to prepare a place for you. And if I go and prepare a place for you, I will come again and receive you to Myself; that where I am, there you may be also" (John 14:1–3).

"For we know that if our earthly house, this tent, is destroyed, we have a building from God, a house not made with hands, eternal in the heavens" (2 Corinthians 5:1).

"For to me, to live is Christ, and to die is gain. . . . For I am hard pressed between the two, having a desire to depart and be with Christ, which is far better" (Philippians 1:21, 23).

"Blessed be the God and Father of our Lord Jesus Christ, who according to His abundant mercy has begotten us again to a living hope through the resurrection of Jesus Christ from the dead, to an inheritance incorruptible and undefiled and that does not fade away, reserved in heaven for you, who are kept by the power of God through faith for salvation ready to be revealed in the last time" (1 Peter 1:3–5).

"And God will wipe away every tear from their eyes; there shall be no more death, nor sorrow, nor crying; and there shall be no more pain, for the former things have passed away" (Revelation 21:4).

Other suggested Scriptures:

Psalm 23:4–6

See also Death

GUILT

Background

When using the term *guilt,* people can mean one of two things: true guilt, or the guilty feelings that real or imagined guilt can produce.

True guilt, or sin, comes as a result of breaking God's Law. When the sinner is unwilling to face the issue squarely in God's way—in order to experience forgiveness—he or she suffers the consequences, both in this life and in eternity.

Feelings of guilt arise when our conscience tells us we have violated God's standards, when we wrongly think we have done so, or when we simply fail to measure up to our own expectations or the standards other people set for us.

Adam and Eve in the Garden of Eden provide an example of both real guilt and guilt feelings. Their sin (disobedience) resulted in real guilt. Their relationship with God was broken and they knew it, so guilt *feelings* followed. They ran from God, trying to hide so that they would not have to face the consequences of their behavior. When God found them, they tried to deny their guilt, with Adam blaming Eve and Eve blaming the serpent. They tried to "cover up" their sin by making fig-leaf aprons, but God asked, "Who told you that you were naked?" (Genesis 3:11). By so doing He forced them to deal with their guilt feelings. Then, He dealt with their *real* guilt by killing an animal to make clothes for them, providing a "covering" or atonement for their sin (Genesis 3:21). In so doing He established the principle of sacrifice which would eventually lead to Christ's sacrifice of Himself on the cross.

Another illustration of dealing with real guilt is Nathan's openly confronting David with his sins of adultery and murder, thus opening the way for his repentance and confession (2 Samuel 11:1–12:25; Psalm 51).

Guilt feelings are often associated with emotional illness stemming from negative experiences, many times in childhood. Even Christians who have the assurance that God has forgiven them and that they are His children continue to suffer from "false guilt." Such people usually have a very low self-image, feelings of inadequacy (they can't do anything right or can't measure up), and suffer from depression. They cannot seem to find freedom from guilt even though they seek it, as in the case of Esau who "found no place for repentance, though he sought it diligently with tears" (Hebrews 12:17).

Guilt feelings will manifest themselves in various and complex ways:

- Deep depression from constant self-blame.
- Chronic fatigue and headaches, or other illnesses.
- Extreme self-denial and self-punishment.
- A feeling of being constantly watched and criticized by others.
- Constant criticism of others for their own sins and shortcomings.
- Because of defeatist attitudes, actually sinking deeper into sin in order to feel more guilty.

Billy Graham has said of this complex problem: "The human conscience is often beyond the grasp of a psychiatrist. With all his or her techniques, he or she cannot sound its depravity and depth. Humans are helpless to detach themselves from the gnawing guilt of a heart bowed down with the weight of sin. But where humans have failed, God has succeeded."

Helping Strategy
For the Non-Christian:

1. Offer hope to the inquirer by assuring that God can take care of any problem. God is able not only to forgive, but also to blot out any sin and guilt.

2. Do not excuse or minimize in any way the sins he or she reports. There is disobedience and sinful behavior in every human, which needs to be dealt with in God's way; that is, it needs to be confessed and forgiven. We can never expect to find solutions to guilt if we try to cover up our sin: "He who covers his sins will not prosper, but whoever confesses and forsakes them will have mercy" (Proverbs 28:13).

3. Ask the inquirer if he or she has ever received Jesus Christ as Lord and Savior. Share "Steps to Peace with God," page 11. Emphasize that freedom from guilt is included in Jesus' death on the cross, but we must trust Him to cleanse us.

4. Encourage reading and studying the Bible, beginning with the gospels. Offer to send *Living in Christ*, which will facilitate getting started.

5. Recommend cultivating the habit of daily prayer. While praying, he or she can confess all present sins, asking for forgiveness and cleansing. He or she should practice thanking God for taking away the sin and guilt, remembering that God takes away all our sins.

6. Suggest finding a Bible-teaching church and identifying with it. Here he or she can fellowship regularly with God's forgiven people, and hear and study God's Word.

7. Pray with the inquirer personally for deliverance and heartfelt peace: "He Himself is our peace" (Ephesians 2:14).

8. If your inquirer seems unable to respond immediately to your sharing Christ, and if he or she continues to struggle with guilt, encourage finding the pastor of a Bible-teaching church for further help. It may be that in time he or she will be able to respond. Stress that he or she should take the initiative in finding such a pastor.

For the Christian:

For the Christian who admits to recurring problems with guilt, proceed as follows:

1. Reassure him or her of God's love and forgiveness. God can cleanse all our guilt! If God has forgiven the inquirer, he or she must practice self-forgiveness. A Christian has the right to claim with confidence the truth of 1 John 1:9. Christ, our Savior, removes all our sins—past, present, and future—through His finished work on the cross.

2. Encourage getting into the Bible, reading, studying, and reflecting at length on such passages as Psalm 103:1–6; Psalm 51; Isaiah 53; and John 18–19. Suggest writing down the references of these passages so that he or she can find them in the Bible. Relief from guilt will surely come as he or she appropriates Christ's sacrifice and promised forgiveness and cleansing.

3. Suggest that the caller pray specifically and faithfully for a "conscience without offense toward God and men" (Acts 24:16). He or she should continue praying until peace comes.

4. Recommend that he or she get in touch with a pastor for further help.

Scripture

"I have blotted out, like a thick cloud, your transgressions, and like a cloud, your sins. Return to Me, for I have redeemed you" (Isaiah 44:22).

"Therefore if the Son makes you free, you shall be free indeed" (John 8:36).

"I know I am rotten through and through so far as my old sinful nature is concerned. No matter which way I turn I can't make myself do right. I want to but I can't. . . . So you see how it is: my new life tells me to do right, but the old nature that is still inside me loves to sin. Oh, what a terrible predicament I'm in! Who will free me from my slavery to this deadly lower nature? Thank God! It has been done by Jesus Christ our Lord. He has set me free" (Romans 7:18, 23–25, TLB).

"There is therefore now no condemnation to those who are in Christ Jesus" (Romans 8:1).

"One thing I do, forgetting those things which are behind and reaching forward to those things which are ahead, I press toward the goal for the prize of the upward call of God in Christ Jesus" (Philippians 3:13–14).

HEALING

Background

The biblical concept of healing means far more than relief from a set of physical symptoms. It means wholeness of body and spirit. The words *healthy, whole,* and *holy* all derive from the same Old English root word. Jesus asked the man in John 5:6, "Wilt thou be made whole?" (KJV). Many sicknesses are the result of the individual's attitude or lifestyle:

- Medical scientists maintain that much of our sickness has emotional causes: tensions, fear, sorrow, envy, resentment, hatred, and the like. Physical pains and problems may be real enough, but their causes are rooted in the emotions.

- Lifestyle choices such as smoking, drinking, and overeating cause much illness. The lifelong smoker may develop problems such as emphysema, cancer, or high blood pressure.

Alcohol consumption can have devastating consequences, both emotional and physical. Many of these are irreversible because of an ulcerated digestive tract, a destroyed liver, or a damaged brain.

Overeating or chronic nutritional deficiency will also cause bad health.

However, many illnesses are not the result of abuses, dissipation, or emotional problems. Many people are just ill! Jesus, referring to the man born blind, said, "Neither this man nor his parents sinned, but that the works of God should be revealed in him" (John 9:3). Among these purely organic diseases are such things as birth defects or genetic illnesses, injuries, and viral or bacterial infections.

Sadly, many people suffer physically from the bad choices of others, such as the victims of violence or of environmental hazards such as chemical waste or second-hand smoke.

God offers healing in at least three ways:

God Heals Through the New Birth

When a person becomes a "new creation" in Christ (2 Corinthians 5:17), he or she finds that Jesus can meet every need. Many testify that when they made things right spiritually, and began to live in proper perspective and relationship with God, their illnesses were taken away. The hymn writer William B. Bradbury refers to this new perspective:

"Just as I am, poor, wretched, blind;

Sight, riches, healing of the mind,
Yea, all I need, in Thee I find. . . . "

Illnesses that result from the anxiety or depression caused by true guilt can be alleviated when true repentance and forgiveness occurs.

God Heals Through the Confession of Sin

Many Christians live miserable, weakened, and often sickly lives because of disobedience and unconfessed sin. Such people can become completely well if they will deal with the sin. The psalmist spoke of God as the one "who forgives all your iniquities, who heals all your diseases, who redeems your life from destruction, who crowns you with lovingkindness and tender mercies" (Psalm 103:3–4). As with the healing that can follow initial conversion to Christ, this healing relates to illnesses caused by mental or emotional dysfunction.

God Heals Miraculously, in Keeping with His Sovereign Will

The Bible contains many examples of God actually healing people of organic diseases—those with no psychosomatic cause. There is present-day evidence of this as well. However, God does not heal all who call on Him or who are prayed for by others. "God shows no partiality" (Acts 10:34), but He heals some and not others with a divine selectivity which reflects His own eternal wisdom and will. His ways are higher than our ways (Isaiah 55:8).

This divine selectivity may be seen in the example of Paul, who prayed long for the removal of an affliction (2 Corinthians 12:8–10). God didn't heal Paul. He did, however, provide grace and strength in the situation. God is trying to teach us that "the excellence of the power may be of God and not of us" (2 Corinthians 4:7). The glorious will and ways of God came into focus in Paul's life when he learned that "when I am weak, then I am strong" (2 Corinthians 12:10).

None of this, however, should discourage or hinder us from praying in faith for the sick. God may answer our prayer of faith in ways that will amaze us. "Pray without ceasing" (1 Thessalonians 5:17) is His command. You should be cautious, however, not to promise physical healing as a result of your prayer or the inquirer's prayer.

Helping Strategy

1. Reassure the inquirer of God's love and of His ability to meet all our

needs, and that you are happy to share and pray with him or her.

NOTE: Some people tend to describe their ailments at great length. You should be sympathetic and caring, but at an appropriate opportunity take command of the conversation.

2. After the inquirer has explained the problem, say that you would be glad to speak about the matter but you would first like to ask a very important question directly related to the issue: Has he or she ever received Jesus Christ as Savior and Lord? If not, explain "Steps to Peace with God," page 11, followed by "Assurance," page 15, and the chapter on "Assurance of Salvation."

3. Now, redirect the conversation to the emotional or physical problem. Is it due, possibly, to habits or excesses such as those mentioned in the "Background"? Some discussion may follow at this point. Help the person to realize that these habits, if involved, might be directly related to the problems. Encourage asking God for help in getting his or her lifestyle under control.

4. Pray with the inquirer for victory over the contributing excesses, if any, as well as for complete restoration to health.

5. If the caller is a Christian, try to determine if the illness is in any way related to a lack of harmony with God's will and plan for his or her life. Gently ask if there is any anger, bitterness, resentment, or some other unconfessed sin. If so, share "Restoration," page 17. Emphasize 1 John 1:9 and 2:1.

   Encourage the inquirer to live in fellowship with Christ, seeking always to glorify Him (1 Corinthians 10:31). Following this, pray earnestly and in faith for healing, according to Matthew 18:19.

6. If the inquirer is a Christian who feels that he or she has been walking in God's will, go immediately to prayer, claiming God's promise according to the prayer of faith.

7. Following your handling of any of the above cases, always speak of the peace and completeness which can be experienced as we learn to depend on God's Word and prayer. These will provide the greatest encouragement in the face of illness or adversity. Offer to send *Living in Christ*, which will help get him or her started in Bible reading and study.

8. Recommend that he or she get involved with a Bible-teaching church. The fellowship, care, and prayers of God's people are a great strength. And counsel and encouragement from the pastor may be a definite asset.

Scripture

"If I regard iniquity in my heart, the Lord will not hear" (Psalm 66:18).

"And lest I [Paul] should be exalted above measure by the abundance of the revelations, a thorn in the flesh was given to me, a messenger of Satan to buffet me, lest I be exalted above measure. Concerning this thing I pleaded with the Lord three times that it might depart from me. And He said to me, 'My grace is sufficient for you, for My strength is made perfect in weakness.' Therefore most gladly I will rather boast in my infirmities, that the power of Christ may rest upon me" (2 Corinthians 12:7–9).

"But let him ask in faith, with no doubting, for he who doubts is like a wave of the sea driven and tossed by the wind" (James 1:6).

"Is anyone among you suffering? Let him pray. Is anyone cheerful? Let him sing psalms. Is anyone among you sick? Let him call for the elders of the church, and let them pray over him, anointing him with oil in the name of the Lord. And the prayer of faith will save the sick, and the Lord will raise him up. And if he has committed sins, he will be forgiven. Confess your trespasses to one another, and pray for one another, that you may be healed. The effective, fervent prayer of a righteous man avails much" (James 5:13–16).

HEAVEN

Background

Heaven is a prepared place for a redeemed people (John 14:1–6). As hell is the final abode of all who live and die in their sins, so heaven is the final abode of all who are redeemed by the blood of Christ and regenerated by the Holy Spirit. It is a known, permanent place, which is said to be:

- *The place where God dwells:* "Hear in heaven Your dwelling place; and when You hear, forgive" (1 Kings 8:30).

- *The city of God:* "But you have come to Mount Zion, to the heavenly Jerusalem, the city of the living God" (Hebrews 12:22, NIV).

- *God's house:* "In My Father's house are many mansions" (John 14:2).

- *Where Christ is in God's presence:* "For Christ did not enter a man-made sanctuary that was only a copy of the true one; he entered heaven itself, now to appear for us in God's presence" (Hebrews 9:24, NIV).

- *The dwelling place of angels and saints:* "See that you do not look down on one of these little ones. For I tell you that their angels in heaven always see the face of my Father in heaven" (Matthew 18:10, NIV). "Likewise, I say to you, there is joy in the presence of the angels of God over one sinner who repents" (Luke 15:10).

- *The eternal home of all believers:* "We are confident, yes, well pleased rather to be absent from the body and to be present with the Lord" (2 Corinthians 5:8). "Then we who are alive and remain shall be caught up together with them in the clouds to meet the Lord in the air. And thus we shall always be with the Lord" (1 Thessalonians 4:17).

- *A state of perfect love and perfect rest.* Heaven is entirely separated from earth's impurities, imperfections, and deceptions. Heaven is a place of worship, praise, and service where the redeemed will be forever relieved of sinfulness by Him who will be our unending joy.

- *A perfect place from which unredeemed sinners will be excluded:* "But there shall by no means enter it anything that defiles, or causes an abomination or a lie, but only those who are written in the Lamb's Book of Life" (Revelation 21:27; see also Revelation 5:9–13).

- *A place where we will see Christ and become more like Him:* "Beloved, now we are children of God; and it has not yet been revealed what we shall be, but we know that when He is revealed, we shall be like Him, for we shall see Him as He is" (1 John 3:2).

- *We will recognize our loved ones who died in Christ, and also fellowship with the great Bible saints:* "And behold, Moses and Elijah appeared to them, talking with Him. Then Peter answered and said to Jesus, 'Lord, it is good for us to be here; if You wish, let us make here three tabernacles: one for You, one for Moses, and one for Elijah'" (Matthew 17:3–4).

- *Heaven's completeness and glories are indescribable:* "But we speak the wisdom of God in a mystery, the hidden wisdom which God ordained before the ages for our glory. . . . But as it is written: 'Eye has not seen, nor ear heard, nor have entered into the heart of man the things which God has prepared for those who love Him'" (1 Corinthians 2:7, 9).

Billy Graham comments: "Heaven will be a place in which its inhabitants will be freed from the fears and insecurities that plague and haunt us in the present life. . . . We will be free from the economic and financial pressures that burden us down here, free from the fear of personal and physical harm. . . . There will be no fear of personal failure. . . . Our relationship with Him will be intimate and direct. I'm looking forward to that glorious day of going to heaven."

Helping Strategy

1. For the Christian who wants to be reassured about heaven and the future life, share the material in the "Background." Perhaps he or she has lost a loved one; be sympathetic and sensitive to the Holy Spirit as you try to encourage and comfort: "Therefore comfort one another with these words" (1 Thessalonians 4:18). Make sure your inquirer is a Christian and is ready for heaven. If needed, refer to "Steps to Peace with God," page 11.

2. For the non-Christian with questions about future events and heaven, share the material in the "Background," turning, if indicated, to the chapter on "Prophecy" for additional help. Share "Steps to Peace with God," page 11.

Scripture

"For to me, to live is Christ, and to die is gain. But if I live on in the flesh, this will mean fruit from my labor; yet what I shall choose I cannot tell.

For I am hard pressed between the two, having a desire to depart and be with Christ, which is far better" (Philippians 1:21–23).

"And God will wipe away every tear from their eyes; there shall be no more death, nor sorrow, nor crying; and there shall be no more pain, for the former things have passed away" (Revelation 21:4).

Other suggested Scriptures:

John 14:1–6

HELL

Background

Hell is not the kingdom of Satan where he will reign over demons and all who are bad. Nor is there anything in Scripture to indicate that hell will be some sort of fellowship of sinners, where life will continue pretty much as it was on earth. The pathetic jokes about plans for "living it up" in hell demonstrate ignorance of its purpose and nature.

There are three Greek words translated *hell* in our English Bible:

- The word *tartaros* is found only once in the Bible: "God did not spare the angels who sinned, but cast them down to hell [tartaros] and delivered them into chains of darkness, to be reserved for judgment" (2 Peter 2:4). The angels mentioned here refer to those "who did not keep their proper domain, but left their own habitation [in rebellion]" (Jude 6). Tartaros, then, is a place of confinement for the rebellious angels until the time of their judgment.

- The word *hades* is found ten times in the New Testament (Matthew 11:23; 16:18; Luke 10:15; 16:23; Acts 2:27, 31; Revelation 1:18; 6:8; 20:13–14). Hades is not the final destiny of those who die without accepting Christ, but rather a place of torment until they are resurrected to stand before God at the Great White Throne Judgment (Revelation 20:13–15). Hades is a place of separation from God and of no escape: "Between us and you there is a great gulf fixed, so that those who want to pass from here to you cannot, nor can those from there pass to us" (Luke 16:26).

- The word *geenna* (transliterated "gehenna") is translated "hell" twelve times (Matthew 5:22, 29–30; 10:28; 18:9; Mark 9:43, 45, 47; Luke 12:5; James 3:6). Eleven of the twelve references are from the lips of Jesus Himself. Geenna refers to the valley of Hinnom, a place outside the southern wall of Jerusalem where children were once sacrificed to the god Molech (2 Chronicles 33:1–6). In later days, it was a convenient place for residents to throw their rubbish; even dead bodies of animals and criminals were disposed there. This "city dump" was a place of decomposition and continuous fire (Mark 9:44) and was used by Jesus to teach about the eventual abode of those who reject Him as Savior.

  Geenna is also called the lake of fire: "Anyone not found written in the Book of Life was cast into the lake of fire" (Revelation 20:15).

NOTE: Purgatory, the imagined place of remedial suffering, has no
   scriptural foundation.

There will be no appeal after the passing of sentence at the Great White
Throne Judgment. All who have rejected Christ will be present: "The sea
gave up the dead who were in it, and Death and Hades delivered up the
dead who were in them. . . . Then Death and Hades were cast into the lake
of fire. This is the second death" (Revelation 20:13–14).

---

*Billy Graham writes: "No matter how excruciating or how literal the fire of hell may or
may not be, the thirst of a lost soul for the Living Water will be more painful. . . . Hell,
essentially and basically, is banishment from the presence of God for deliberately
rejecting Jesus Christ as Lord and Savior."*

Helping Strategy

1. If the inquirer is fearful of hell and the possibility of going there, stress
   the need for certainty about his or her eternal salvation. Explain "Steps to
   Peace with God," page 11. In Christ, he or she need not fear hell: "There
   is therefore now no condemnation to those who are in Christ Jesus"
   (Romans 8:1).

2. If the inquirer denies the existence of hell, share material from the
   "Background."

3. If the inquirer accuses God of being unjust in condemning people to hell,
   point out that "the everlasting fire," according to Matthew 25:41, was
   prepared for the devil and his angels, not for mankind. If a person goes
   to hell, it will be because of his willful sin in rejecting Jesus Christ as
   Lord and Savior (John 3:16–18; John 5:24). Point out that God will forgive
   and save the person if he or she will receive Jesus Christ. Share "Steps to
   Peace with God," page 11.

4. If the inquirer accuses God of being unjust for condemning those who
   have never had an opportunity to hear the Gospel, remind him or her
   that God has condemned no one to hell, but that those who end up there
   will have condemned themselves (John 3:16–18). In the case of those who
   have never heard, trust God to do the right thing! We can be assured that
   He will be fair and merciful. There are degrees of rewards to be given at
   the judgment seat of Christ (Luke 12:47–48; 1 Corinthians 3:12–14). One
   may logically conclude that there will also be degrees of reckoning for
   those deprived of hearing the Gospel.

Scripture

Matthew 11:23
Matthew 16:18
Luke 10:15
Luke 12:5
Acts 2:17, 31

THE HOLY SPIRIT

Background

The Holy Spirit is one of the three persons of the Trinity. He is equal to the other two in position and power, possessing all the essential aspects of deity. He shares all the attributes of the Godhead: He is eternal, having neither beginning nor end (Hebrews 9:14); omnipotent, having all power (Luke 1:35); omnipresent, being everywhere present at the same time (Psalm 139:7); and omniscient, or all knowing (1 Corinthians 2:10–11).

The Holy Spirit possesses all the characteristics of personality. He is not an "it" (Romans 8:16, 26, NIV).

The Holy Spirit has intellect, emotions, and will. He speaks (Acts 13:2); intercedes (Romans 8:26); testifies (John 15:26); guides (John 16:13); commands (Acts 16:6–7); appoints (Acts 20:28); leads (Romans 8:14); and reproves and convicts of sin (John 16:8). He can be lied to and tested (Acts 5:3–4, 9); resisted (Acts 7:51); grieved (Ephesians 4:30); and blasphemed (Matthew 12:31).

Each Christian must understand his or her own relationship with the Holy Spirit:

That which has been realized:

- We are born of the Holy Spirit (John 3:6, 8).
- God has given us the Holy Spirit (John 14:16; 16:7).
- We are baptized by the Holy Spirit (1 Corinthians 12:13).
- We are the temple of the Holy Spirit (1 Corinthians 6:19–20).
- We are sealed by the Holy Spirit (Ephesians 1:13).

That which is potential reality:

Each Christian has the Holy Spirit, but not every Christian is *filled* with the Holy Spirit. We ought to desire this fullness because God commands it: "Be filled with the Spirit" (Ephesians 5:18).

Billy Graham writes: "I believe the Bible teaches that there is one baptism in the Spirit—when we come to faith in Christ. The Bible teaches, however, that there are many fillings—in fact, we are to be continually filled by the Holy Spirit. One baptism, many fillings. When we are filled with the Spirit, it is not a question of there being more of Him, as though His work in us is quantitative. It is not how much of the Spirit we have, but how much the Spirit has of us. . . . As we come to understand more and more of Christ's leadership, we surrender and yield more to Him. So, in seeking the fullness of the Spirit, we receive and enjoy His filling and His fullness more and more."

Helping Strategy

1. If a question is asked about the Holy Spirit, try to answer it from material in the "Background."

2. If a question is asked or desire expressed about the fullness of the Holy Spirit, share the following points:

    A. God has given Christians His Holy Spirit and He dwells within us. See Scriptures in the "Background."

    B. God commands us to be filled with the Holy Spirit (Ephesians 5:18).

    C. Before we can receive the fullness of the Spirit, we must deal honestly with every known sin in our life. This involves repentance and confession to God.

    D. We must clearly and completely turn over the control of our life to the Lord in a definite act of commitment. We must renounce our own way and seek above all else to continuously submit to Christ as Lord, being ruled by Him in every area of life. This obedience demands a daily yielding of ourselves to God so that we may learn the secrets of walking in faith.

    When we are yielded to God and His will, we are filled with the Holy Spirit. The Holy Spirit controls and dominates us. Now we are to act on this truth, and walk or live with full assurance that God has already filled us and that we are under His control.

3. Pray with the inquirer about the application of these truths to his or her life, and pray that he or she may be filled with the Spirit.

Scripture

"And I will pray the Father, and He will give you another Helper, that He may abide with you forever, even the Spirit of truth, whom the world cannot receive, because it neither sees Him nor knows Him; but you know Him, for He dwells with you and will be in you" (John 14:16–17).

"Nevertheless I tell you the truth. It is to your advantage that I go away; for if I do not go away, the Helper will not come to you; but if I depart, I will send Him to you. And when He has come, He will convict the world of sin, and of righteousness, and of judgment: of sin, because they do not believe in Me; of righteousness, because I go to My Father and you see Me no more; of judgment, because the ruler of this world is judged" (John 16:7–11).

"But you shall receive power when the Holy Spirit has come upon you; and you shall be witnesses to Me in Jerusalem, and in all Judea and Samaria, and to the end of the earth" (Acts 1:8).

Other suggested Scriptures:

John 3:6–8
John 16:13–14
Romans 8:14–16
1 Corinthians 6:19–20
1 Corinthians 12:13
Ephesians 1:13

See also Fruit of *and* Gifts of Holy Spirit

HOLY SPIRIT, FRUIT OF

Background

The filling of the Holy Spirit (previous chapter) includes two areas: evidence of the fruit of the Holy Spirit (this chapter), and the gifts of the Spirit (following chapter).

To be filled with the Spirit means that the believer will demonstrate the fruit of the Spirit in his or her life. The New Testament pattern for living is set in Matthew 7:16: "You will know them by their fruits." The first evidence of being filled with the Spirit is godly living. God wants mature Christians, who manifest the fruits of the Spirit listed in Galatians 5:22–23: "love, joy, peace, patience, kindness, goodness, faithfulness, gentleness and self-control" (NIV).

"The fruit of the Spirit is God's expectation in our lives," says Billy Graham: "Unlike the gifts of the Spirit, the fruit of the Spirit is not divided among believers. Instead, all Christians should be marked by all the fruit of the Spirit. Put in the simplest terms, the Bible tells us we need the Spirit to bring fruit into our lives because we cannot produce godliness apart from the Spirit. In our own selves we are filled with all kinds of self-centered and self-seeking desires which are opposed to God's will for our lives."

Practically, how do we begin to work this fruit of the Spirit into our lives?

We must consciously surrender ourselves to the Holy Spirit (1 Corinthians 6:19–20; Romans 12:1–2). Ask yourself, have you ever realized that you belong to God, that your body is the actual residence of the Holy Spirit? Have you ever offered your body (life), to God as Romans 12:1 demands?

Next, we must see ourselves as having died to sin but having become alive to Christ (Romans 6:11). Paul said in Galatians 2:20, "I have been crucified with Christ; it is no longer I who live, but Christ lives in me; and the life which I now live in the flesh I live by faith in the Son of God, who loved me and gave Himself for me." You are dead to sin in the sense that it no longer has control over you (Romans 6:12–13).

Then, we determine by faith to bring ourselves under the lordship of Christ. This happens progressively as we bring our minds under His control. Our actions respond to the Spirit's control over our thoughts: "And do not be conformed to this world, but be transformed by the renewing of your mind, that you may prove what is that good and acceptable and perfect will of God" (Romans 12:2).

We work on one "fruit" at a time, praying in faith and trusting God that the love, joy, peace, and patience spoken of in Galatians 5:22–23 might become a reality in our lives.

Helping Strategy

1. If the inquirer expresses concern about having the fruit of the Spirit in his or her life, you may review the appropriate information from the "Background."

2. Sometimes questions reveal where the focus is needed. Ask:

   - Is there any unconfessed sin in your life which is keeping you from a close walk with God?
   - Do you know of any lack of personal discipline?
   - Is there a broken relationship that needs healing?
   - Are you consciously abiding in Christ?
   - Are you reading and studying your Bible daily?
   - Are you praying about your relationship with Christ, asking Him to develop the fruit of the Spirit in you?

3. Pray with the inquirer that his or her desires for the fullness of the Spirit and the fruit of the Spirit may be fulfilled.

Scripture

"Likewise you also, reckon yourselves to be dead indeed to sin, but alive to God in Christ Jesus our Lord. Therefore do not let sin reign in your mortal body, that you should obey it in its lusts. And do not present your members as instruments of unrighteousness to sin, but present yourselves to God as being alive from the dead, and your members as instruments of righteousness to God" (Romans 6:11–13).

"Therefore, I urge you, brothers, in view of God's mercy, to offer your bodies as living sacrifices, holy and pleasing to God—which is your spiritual act of worship. Do not conform any longer to the pattern of this world, but be transformed by the renewing of your mind. Then you will be able to test and approve what God's will is—his good, pleasing and perfect will" (Romans 12:1–2, NIV).

"Or do you not know that your body is the temple of the Holy Spirit who is in you, whom you have from God, and you are not your own? For you were bought at a price; therefore glorify God in your body and in your spirit, which are God's" (1 Corinthians 6:19–20).

Other suggested Scriptures:
Galatians 5:22–23

HOLY SPIRIT, GIFTS OF

Background

The truly committed Christian will want to appropriate all that God has in reserve for his or her life. We have received God's grace through the person and work of the Lord Jesus Christ. Now we should be open to receiving the gifts of the Holy Spirit; we should "earnestly desire" them (1 Corinthians 12:31).

We need to be careful, however, not to be presumptuous in claiming any gifts, but rather trust the sovereign Holy Spirit to give "to each one individually as He wills" (1 Corinthians 12:11). Many people claim to be possessors of certain gifts, but their lives and ministry do not give evidence of such possession. Spiritual gifts are not to be thought of as making any one believer or group of believers any more holy or more spiritually advanced than others. Spiritual pride can nullify the effectiveness of any gift.

Some Christians obviously possess the more "public" gifts, such as preaching, teaching, or evangelizing. This does not mean that they are "super-Christians." They are merely exercising the gifts God has given them. The Christian who exercises the quiet gift of faith is just as important to God and to the building up of the body. Nowhere in the Scripture is it indicated that we are to seek the same gifts. All gifts are not the same, but they all have the same goal: They are all meant to contribute toward the uniting and building up of Christ's body, the church (Ephesians 4:12–16).

Two Scripture portions enumerate the gifts of the Holy Spirit:

"To one there is given through the Spirit the message of wisdom, to another the message of knowledge by means of the same Spirit, to another faith by the same Spirit, to another gifts of healing by that one Spirit, to another miraculous powers, to another prophecy, to another distinguishing between spirits, to another speaking in different kinds of tongues, and to still another the interpretation of tongues. All these are the work of one and the same Spirit, and he gives them to each one, just as he determines" (1 Corinthians 12:8–11, NIV).

"It was he who gave some to be apostles, some to be prophets, some to be evangelists, and some to be pastors and teachers, to prepare God's people for works of service, so that the body of Christ may be built up" (Ephesians 4:11–12, NIV).

Billy Graham's comments on this important subject are helpful: "These gifts come to us from the Holy Spirit. He chooses who gets which gifts, and He dispenses them at His good pleasure. While we are held accountable for the use of any gifts He gives us, we have no responsibility for gifts we have not been given. Nor are we to covet what someone else has or be envious of that person. We may wish to have certain gifts and even ask for them, but if it is not the will of the Holy Spirit, we will not get what we ask for. And if we are dissatisfied because the Holy Spirit does not give us the gifts we want, we sin."

Helping Strategy

1. Stay within the guidelines of the above "Background" when discussing the area of the gifts of the Spirit. It is possible to be diverted by some who would make the gifts something they were never meant to be.

2. Make it clear that one must be a born-again Christian in order to appropriate the gifts of the Spirit. Contrary to the insistence of some, this order cannot be reversed. Ask the inquirer if he or she has received the Lord Jesus Christ as Lord and Savior. If not, share "Steps to Peace with God," page 11.

3. If your inquirer is a believer who is sincerely seeking the fullness of the Holy Spirit and identification of a gift, encourage prolonged and careful study of the Scriptures that deal with the gifts, including the book of Acts and the epistles of Paul, where we see the gifts being exercised. Careful and thoughtful prayer should accompany such study, as spiritual discernment and wisdom will come to guide the seeker away from excesses.

4. Advise him or her not to be unduly influenced by people or groups who insist on a kind of standardized approach for the receiving and exercising of any gift or gifts, or who insist that all believers must possess certain gifts. Each one must trust the Holy Spirit to distribute as He wills (John 3:8; 1 Corinthians 12:11).

A comment by Billy Graham helps put this into perspective: "I believe that a person who is Spirit-filled—constantly submitting to the lordship of Christ—will come to discover his or her gifts with some degree of ease. He or she wants God's guidance, and that is the kind of person God stands ready to bless, revealing the gifts that the Holy Spirit has bestowed on him or her."

5. Remind the inquirer that along with the gifts of the Spirit we should constantly seek to demonstrate the fruit of the Spirit: "But the fruit of the Spirit is love, joy, peace, patience, kindness, goodness, faithfulness, gentleness and self-control. Against such things there is no law" (Galatians 5:22–23, NIV). Fruit and gifts must go hand in hand. We are known by our fruit (Matthew 7:16, 20).

6. Pray with the inquirer for a demonstration of the fruit of the Spirit in his or her life, and for increased and effective service to the body of Christ and to the world through the exercise of his or her gifts.

Scripture

Study 1 Corinthians 13 in relation to other Scriptures for perspective on the gifts of the Holy Spirit.

"As each one has received a gift, minister it to one another, as good stewards of the manifold grace of God" (1 Peter 4:10).

THE HOME

(Conflicts Between Parents and Teenagers)

Background

In our fast-moving electronic age, kids grow up quicker and want to be free earlier in life than their parents did. Parents often find it difficult to keep pace with the lightning changes in their children, and as a result, conflicts come.

It seems that one day a child is in the parents' arms and the next day he or she is beginning school, bringing friends home, helping around the house, starting Little League or Brownies—in general, a pretty good kid. Then, suddenly, the roof caves in! He or she begins to talk back, question and break rules, and become at times sullen and noncommunicative. The teen years have arrived, catching the parents completely off guard.

There can be many areas of conflict: their friends (many of whom the parents don't approve), choices related to clothing and personal grooming, dating and other social activities, chores around the home, allowance, use of the family car, school and homework, discipline.

Because of such conflicts, a communication barrier may develop. Parents find it difficult to talk things over with their children. They delay explanations of crucial physical and mental changes, especially in the areas of sex and reproduction. Controls are tightened by the parents and the teenager fights even harder for independence. The gap widens; they become antagonists—and the battle goes on.

Billy Graham writes: "Rebellion, waywardness, lack of discipline, confusion, and conflict prevent happy relationships within the home. But God is interested in your family, your marriage, your children. He shows us the ideals and the goals for the family. He's willing to help us. . . . Have you sought God's will? Have you gotten on your knees and committed your children to the Lord? Do you gather them for family devotions? The answer is in surrendering your heart and life to Jesus Christ so that every member of the home knows Jesus Christ and loves the Word of God."

Helping Strategy

When talking with parents in conflict with their children, urge them to put their house in order spiritually. Read Billy Graham's paragraph in the "Background," then:

1. Advise them that in order to have the peace of God in the home, they must have the peace of God in their hearts. This comes through a personal relationship with Jesus Christ. Explain "Steps to Peace with God," page 11.

2. Encourage parents to take a firm stand for Christ in the spirit of Joshua, who said, "Choose for yourselves this day whom you will serve. . . . But as for me and my house, we will serve the Lord" (Joshua 24:15). They must determine to have a home that exalts Christ.

3. Suggest that they learn to rely on God's resources, available through prayer. They should covenant with God for the wisdom He offers (James 1:5) and claim His help for the proper spiritual development for their children (Philippians 4:6). They must learn to pray *with* their children as well as for them.

4. Urge parents to build the life of the family around the Word of God, helping each member to understand the issues of life from its viewpoint. Encourage them to:

    A. Seek each one's conversion to Christ.

    B. Center family activities around a Bible-teaching church.

    C. Be willing to deal patiently with the children's spiritual doubts.

5. Parents must establish rules governing the home which are equitable, reasonable, and "keepable." Respect is learned through responding to authority. Be as flexible as you can where the children's identity, independence, and self-esteem are concerned. Teenagers need a lot of support and encouragement. Conflicts are never resolved by argument or fighting.

6. Parental example and stability influence children greatly. A good, happy marriage will do more to prepare young people for life than rules and surveillance. A consistent demonstration of Christian virtues such as love, patience, understanding, encouragement, and trust will provide the anchor the teenager needs in stressful and changing times. The beliefs of the parents should always be reflected in actions, especially in the home.

7. Consistent communication with the teenager will do much to avoid conflict. This includes not only meaningful conversation, but time spent in other meaningful activities with each teen, individually. This personal attention will help create a positive self-image and will fortify family solidarity. Don't be afraid to show physical affection. A fatherly hug or a motherly kiss will help the child feel accepted and loved.

Scripture

"Be careful to obey all these regulations I am giving you, so that it may always go well with you and your children after you, because you will be doing what is good and right in the eyes of the Lord your God" (Deuteronomy 12:28, NIV).

"The righteous man leads a blameless life; blessed are his children after him" (Proverbs 20:7, NIV).

"Train up a child in the way he should go, and when he is old he will not depart from it" (Proverbs 22:6).

"Children, obey your parents in the Lord, for this is right. 'Honor your father and mother'—which is the first commandment with a promise—'that it may go well with you and that you may enjoy long life on the earth.' Fathers, do not exasperate your children; instead, bring them up in the training and instruction of the Lord" (Ephesians 6:1–4, NIV).

"Fathers, do not embitter your children, or they will become discouraged" (Colossians 3:21, NIV).

THE HOME

(Raising and Disciplining Children)

Background

A recurrent theme in the Bible is the training of children through teaching and example. The book of Deuteronomy explicitly states that children should be taught the ways of God:

"And these words which I command you today shall be in your heart; you shall teach them diligently to your children, and shall talk of them when you sit in your house, when you walk by the way, when you lie down, and when you rise up" (Deuteronomy 6:6–7).

The book of Proverbs is a compendium of the wisdom of God's people. The family and the nurturing of children in the faith is one of its strong emphases: "Train up a child in the way he should go, and when he is old he will not depart from it" (Proverbs 22:6).

Timothy had been taught the Scriptures from infancy, according to God's command and Jewish custom: "From childhood you have known the Holy Scriptures, which are able to make you wise for salvation through faith which is in Christ Jesus" (2 Timothy 3:15).

Paul speaks of the necessity for continuity in how we train and discipline our children: ". . . when I call to remembrance the genuine faith that is in you, which dwelt first in your grandmother Lois and your mother Eunice, and I am persuaded is in you also" (2 Timothy 1:5).

The Bible teaches that parents have the responsibility of training and disciplining their children so that they might be brought up knowing the Bible and honoring the Lord.

Billy Graham cautions: "The basic reason for unhappiness in the home is that we have disregarded God and the principles He has given us. We have refused to acknowledge His plan for the family. The members of the home have refused to accept their particular responsibilities as given in the Bible. It is well known that obedience doesn't come naturally. It must be taught and learned. Children must be taught obedience just as much as they need to be taught to read and write."

Helping Strategy

1. Encourage parents to provide the kind of home that is conducive to solid spiritual and mental development:

   A. A stable, peaceful, and loving home.

   B. A family-centered home where there is a sense of solidarity, mutual respect, and encouragement; a home where the family does things together, especially when children are younger.

   C. A God-centered home where each member has the right to respond to God's love in Christ and to be taught how to live from a spiritual perspective (Proverbs 22:6). (This would be an appropriate time to ask the parent if he or she has ever received Jesus Christ as Lord and Savior. As appropriate, present "Steps to Peace with God," page 11.)

   D. A church-oriented home. It is much easier to raise children when their lives and those of their families and friends are centered in the church.

   E. Parents should introduce their children to the world of the mind by example and practice. If parents are readers, children are likely to read also. Good books and magazines on the child's level should be introduced into the home. Music lessons, hobbies, and sports should be introduced while children are at grade school level. This will be a safeguard against conflicts as the teen years come.

2. Encourage parents to recognize that their child has certain rights, but that these rights integrate with those affecting all members of the family. Children have a right to:

   A. Be loved and accepted.

   B. Receive the kind of reinforcement which leads to self-respect and a sense of security and significance.

   C. See their parents demonstrate genuine affection and respect for each other. Examples of mature Christian behavior are needed in order that children may see how the parents handle problems and stress.

   D. Be disciplined and punished with fairness and consistency:

      (1) Do not expect more from a child than he or she can deliver.

      (2) Be fair and just in administering punishment. Excessive demands and harsh physical punishment lead quickly to resentment and rebellion. Parents should be flexible and not demand the "letter of the law."

(3) Never punish in anger or on the spur of the moment.

(4) Always give an explanation to the child so that he or she knows the reason for the punishment.

3. Encourage the parent to keep the lines of communication open at all costs. They must:

A. Take time to be an attentive listener and take the initiative in encouraging dialogue. There must be frank discussion in regard to sex, drugs, alcohol, dating, and the like.

B. Share experiences from his or her own childhood and teen years, including mistakes and failures.

C. Permit children to question their standards and beliefs. This gives the opportunity to explain and defend those beliefs. Through this, children will formulate their own standards of beliefs and values. They can be challenged and helped in setting goals for the moment and for life.

Scripture

"My son, do not despise the Lord's discipline and do not resent his rebuke, because the Lord disciplines those he loves, as a father the son he delights in" (Proverbs 3:11–12, NIV).

"The righteous man walks in his integrity; His children are blessed after him" (Proverbs 20:7).

"Children, obey your parents in the Lord, for this is right. 'Honor your father and mother'—which is the first commandment with a promise—'that it may go well with you and that you may enjoy long life on the earth.' Fathers, do not exasperate your children; instead, bring them up in the training and instruction of the Lord" (Ephesians 6:1–4, NIV).

"Fathers, do not provoke your children, lest they become discouraged" (Colossians 3:21).

Other suggested Scriptures:
Deuteronomy 12:28
Proverbs 30:11
Proverbs 31:10, 26–28

THE HOME

(Winning Parents to Christ)

Background

Paul, writing to Timothy, advised:

"Don't let anyone look down on you because you are young, but set an example for the believers in speech, in life, in love, in faith and in purity. . . . Watch your life and doctrine closely. Persevere in them, because if you do, you will save both yourself and your hearers" (1 Timothy 4:12, 16, NIV).

Though this advice was given nearly 2,000 years ago, it is still timely for the young person who has received Christ and is deeply concerned for a parent's spiritual welfare.

Recently a pastor said that when teenagers are converted and want to know how to witness, he advises them to go home, straighten up their room, mind their parents, smile, listen to other people, and wait until they ask what has happened before telling them about Christ!

NOTE: Christian teenagers are not the only ones with unsaved parents. Some Christian adults also have non-Christian parents—and some of them are getting on in years!

In Billy Graham Answers Your Questions, *Mr. Graham offers this advice: "First of all, I suggest patience with your parents. They will want to be sure that your experience with Christ is not just a passing fancy. Second, let Christ so possess you that they see a difference in you. Third, pray for them. They may seem to be turning a deaf ear to you, but they are hearing more than you think. This won't happen in a week, in a month, or perhaps even in a year, but God's Spirit is always at work. Remember, the Bible says, 'Let us not grow weary while doing good, for in due season we shall reap if we do not lose heart' (Galatians 6:9)."*

Helping Strategy

1. Commend the person seeking advice about witnessing to parents. It is an indication of a more-than-average spiritual concern.

2. Read Billy Graham's advice from the "Background," then emphasize the following:

A. In 1 Timothy 4:12, 16, the key word is example. In the home, this would be best demonstrated by respect, obedience, and acts of love and kindness. Remember the old saying, "What you do speaks so loudly that I can't hear what you are saying."

B. Make sure you are being consistent in Christian living, that you are not up one day and down the next.

3. Recommend giving attention to spiritual development by reading and studying God's Word, by prayer (with parents' names at the top of the prayer list!), by being a good student at school, and by becoming involved in Christian activities with other young people.

4. Suggest praying patiently for opportunities to witness. This may be done personally or by inviting the family to a special Christian function or to church.

5. Pray with the person that Paul's advice to Timothy (1 Timothy 4:12, 16) might become a reality in his or her life. The witnessing methods outlined may not sound very exciting, but experience has indicated that it is the best method.

Scripture

"You shall receive power when the Holy Spirit has come upon you; and you shall be witnesses to Me in Jerusalem, and in all Judea and Samaria, and to the end of the earth" (Acts 1:8).

"Therefore put on the full armor of God, so that when the day of evil comes, you may be able to stand your ground, and after you have done everything, to stand" (Ephesians 6:13, NIV).

"Do not be anxious about anything, but in everything, by prayer and petition, with thanksgiving, present your requests to God. And the peace of God, which transcends all understanding, will guard your hearts and your minds in Christ Jesus" (Philippians 4:6–7, NIV).

"Don't let anyone look down on you because you are young, but set an example for the believers in speech, in life, in love, in faith and in purity. . . . Be diligent in these matters; give yourself wholly to them, so that everyone may see your progress. Watch your life and doctrine closely. Persevere in them, because if you do, you will save both yourself and your hearers" (1 Timothy 4:12, 15–16, NIV).

HOMOSEXUALITY

Background

Homosexuals are people who are sexually attracted to those of their own sex. While the term *gay* commonly refers to homosexuals of both genders, female homosexuals are often referred to as "lesbians."

Homosexuality is a very complex problem and one that is greatly misunderstood by a large segment of society. Homosexuals defy stereotyping; not all homosexuals are effeminate men or masculine women, although some do manifest such characteristics. Homosexuality is practiced at all levels of society. A significant number of homosexuals are found among those who hold responsible positions in business, industry, the professions, and government.

Although there is increasing militancy among homosexuals, resulting in an open defense of their lifestyle and the formation of gay organizations and campaigns for gay rights, millions among them still live a double life due to societal pressure and intolerance. Fear of discovery becomes an obsession and a heavy load of guilt may be carried by those who realize the moral implications of the practice.

The serious student of the Bible cannot dismiss homosexual behavior simply as an alternate lifestyle. Nor can it be argued that homosexuals were "born this way" or that such behavior is an illness. While God does not love the homosexual any less than He does anyone else, such behavior is a departure from the natural order of His creation. Though most homosexuals feel that they have not chosen their sexual orientation, the fact remains that many have responded improperly to this orientation; it is this *response* which must be dealt with in the light of Scripture.

The Bible speaks clearly of what constitutes a proper sexual relationship:

> "Therefore a man shall leave his father and mother and be joined to his wife, and they shall become one flesh" (Genesis 2:24).

> "As for you, be fruitful and multiply; bring forth abundantly in the earth and multiply in it" (Genesis 9:7).

> "The husband should fulfill his marital duty to his wife, and likewise the wife to her husband. The wife's body does not belong to her alone but also to her husband. In the same way, the husband's body does not belong to him alone but also to his wife" (1 Corinthians 7:3–4, NIV).

These Scriptures show the dual purpose of the sexual relationship: It seals the marriage bond between a man and a woman, and it perpetuates the human race. The family, consisting of father, mother, and children, is at the very heart of God's established order. It is the basis for society, and families are the greatest strength of any society. (One should not assume, however, that every person is going to marry and reproduce. Celibacy and singleness also have a part in God's order.)

There are also many Scriptures that show God's disapproval of homosexual behavior (see "Scripture," below). The Bible includes homosexual behavior in lists of sins along with such things as adultery, fornication, prostitution, and lust. It is not to be singled out as a "special sin," especially offensive to God beyond any other sin. God deals with all sin through the cross. On the other hand, however, homosexual behavior should not be singled out for special leniency either. It is only as we are willing to confess our sin that God is able to deal with it.

Billy Graham comments: "No matter how we may rationalize the practice [of homosexuality] as a viable alternative to heterosexual relationships, Romans 1 makes it clearly the product of a reprobate mind. By making this statement, I am not exonerating all heterosexual activity. As Dr. Harold Lindsell has put it, 'The immoral heterosexual is neither better nor worse than the practicing homosexual. Both come under divine judgment.' . . . When we come to Christ, we are called upon to repent of our sins and no longer to practice the ungodly patterns of living we may have enjoyed before."

The church cannot condone the lifestyle of homosexuals nor encourage their involvement as unrepentant sinners in the life of the church. On the other hand, however, it should not try to pretend that the problem does not exist. It should address the problem honestly and realistically, in love and understanding. It is not God's will that anyone should be bound by homosexuality. His grace is sufficient to bring victory to those who are willing to submit this area to Him. The church needs to take the initiative in encouraging the homosexual with this message.

It is a source of encouragement that many homosexuals report being transformed through the power of the Gospel, even though some of them may never be completely free from homosexual tendencies or temptation. Paul, in writing to people who had been involved in homosexual behavior and many other types of sin, says, "There was a time when some of you were just like that but now your sins are washed away, and you are set apart for God, and he has accepted you because of what the Lord Jesus Christ and the Spirit of our God have done for you" (1 Corinthians 6:11, TLB).

Paul's words should give us confidence in dealing with homosexuals. The only real cure for this problem, as for any type of sinful behavior, is a personal, intimate, continuous relationship with Jesus Christ. This relationship is an ongoing process of growth and change. Sometimes it can be a painful process, punctuated by relapses and discouragement. Such setbacks should not lead to a sense of despair or to the thought that it is not worth the effort. The Christian's fellowship with Christ is maintained on the basis of 1 John 1:9, with confession of sin resulting in immediate renewal of our ongoing relationship with Him.

Helping Strategy

In anticipation of witnessing in this delicate area, you should examine your attitudes toward the problem. If you are not objectively and genuinely able to offer God's love and grace to the homosexual, you should refer the inquirer to another Christian.

Three situations are likely to arise:

- The family member who has just learned that a loved one is a practicing homosexual and asks, "How can I live with this? What should I do?"

- An individual who admits to being a practicing homosexual and seeks help. Frequently a homosexual will want to talk without revealing the problem, or will try to cover up. Sometimes the subject will be obliquely approached, such as, "I have this friend . . ."

- A Christian who struggles with homosexual feelings and temptations, but who does not engage in homosexual behavior.

If the Family Is Facing This Problem:

If the caller is trying to deal with the homosexuality of a loved one, advise him or her to:

1. Not panic, but ask God for the grace to accept the situation, however difficult.

2. Keep the "love lines" open. We must love as God loves us all—in spite of what we struggle with.

3. Avoid condemning or putting down. This only results in antagonism and loss of communication.

4. On the other hand, don't condone the homosexual practice or rationalize it. Don't reinterpret the Bible in accommodation.

5. Take a firm but loving stand with Scripture as he or she firmly and gently witnesses to the person involved, using the Bible as a sword, not a club.

6. Commit the loved one to God in faith (Proverbs 3:5–6). God sometimes permits us to live through a crisis situation in order to sharpen our dependence on Him.

7. Try not to live with bottled-up emotions. He or she might want to confide in a Christian friend and learn to share concerns and disappointments. A Christian prayer partner is a great resource.

8. Be prepared to persevere with hope if the situation doesn't change immediately.

If the Inquirer Is a Practicing Homosexual:

1. The attitude of the helper must be tempered by love and understanding. Often you will be speaking to one who feels lonely, guilt-ridden, and rejected. Demonstrate a sympathetic, caring attitude without being patronizing. Be prepared to dispel the "smoke screens" the inquirer may throw up to hide the real reason for making contact. Do not be intimidated by accusations that "You don't know what it's like." Do not begin your conversation by confronting the individual concerning the sinfulness of homosexual behavior. Opportunities for such discussion will emerge more naturally as you share "Steps to Peace with God" and various Scriptures.

2. Try to win confidence by encouraging the inquirer: "I am glad to talk with you and will share anything I can to help."

3. At some convenient point in the conversation, even if you must suggest that other things be temporarily set aside, ask the inquirer if he or she has ever received Jesus Christ as Lord and Savior. Proceed with "Steps to Peace with God," page 11. Reassure the individual that, as in the case of anyone without Christ, the transforming experience of the new birth is the first step to spiritual health: "He restores my soul" (Psalm 23:3).

4. If he or she responds affirmatively, pray for deliverance from bondage and for a renewal of mind through the Gospel. Encourage being willing to let God change some things in his or her life, whatever the inconvenience and discomfort.

5. Stress the importance of reading and studying God's Word. It is the source of our knowledge of God and His ways with us. No one can learn to think God's thoughts apart from the Bible.

6. Encourage the inquirer to establish new relationships after breaking with former associations. This can best be done by becoming part of a Bible-teaching church where friendships can be established with committed

Christians. Sometimes a singles group is available.

7. For ongoing help, encourage the inquirer to seek professional counseling with a Christian psychologist or a qualified pastor.

If the Inquirer Claims to Be a Christian:

We must realize that many Christians struggle with homosexual attractions, and some yield to temptation.

1. An attitude of love and compassion is needed. Determine to be a patient listener until you have the inquirer's story.

2. If indicated, share "Steps to Peace with God" in order to determine if the person has ever truly received Christ as personal Savior and Lord.

3. If you encounter resistance, or if the person tries to justify his or her lifestyle, patiently but firmly present the teaching of Scripture on the subject. Ask how he or she can reconcile homosexual behavior with Bible teaching. No amount of rationalization will change the fact that Scripture condemns such behavior (see "Scripture," below). He or she must recognize it as wrong and as sin. Confessing it as such before God and turning from its practice offers the only real hope for rehabilitation.

4. Encourage reading and studying the Bible. Assimilating God's Word will result in a "renewing of the mind." As thought patterns change, behavior and lifestyle will follow suit.

5. Help him or her distinguish between *sexual orientation* (unchosen feelings/attractions) and *sinful behavior* (willful lusts/acts). Many homosexuals feel condemned by God simply for their feelings and temptations.

6. Recommend identifying with a dynamic Bible-teaching church for Christian fellowship, studying the Bible, learning to pray, and worshiping and witnessing.

7. Encourage seeking additional help from a Christian professional counselor or pastor.

NOTE: Encourage homosexuals and their families to also contact Exodus International, a worldwide network of Christian organizations which minister to all those impacted by homosexuality.

Scripture

Homosexual Behavior Is Sin:

"Therefore God gave them over in the sinful desires of their hearts to sexual impurity for the degrading of their bodies with one another. They exchanged the truth of God for a lie, and worshiped . . . created things rather than the Creator—who is forever praised. Amen. Because of this, God gave them over to shameful lusts. Even their women exchanged natural relations for unnatural ones. In the same way the men also abandoned natural relations with women and were inflamed with lust for one another. Men committed indecent acts with other men, and received in themselves the due penalty for their perversion" (Romans 1:24–27, NIV).

"Yes, these laws are made to identify as sinners all who are immoral and impure: homosexuals, kidnappers, liars, and all others who do things that contradict the glorious Good News of our blessed God, whose messenger I am" (1 Timothy 1:10–11, TLB).

Homosexual Behavior Will Be Judged by God:

Genesis 18–19 (The story of Sodom and Gomorrah; read as background.)

"Do you not know that the wicked will not inherit the kingdom of God? Do not be deceived: Neither the sexually immoral nor idolaters nor adulterers nor male prostitutes nor homosexual offenders nor thieves nor the greedy nor drunkards nor slanderers nor swindlers will inherit the kingdom of God" (1 Corinthians 6:9–10, NIV).

The Power of the Gospel to Deliver:

"The Spirit of the Lord is upon Me, because He has anointed Me to preach the gospel to the poor. He has sent Me to heal the brokenhearted, to preach deliverance to the captives and recovery of sight to the blind, to set at liberty those who are oppressed, to preach the acceptable year of the Lord" (Luke 4:18–19).

"But as many as received Him, to them He gave the right to become children of God, even to those who believe in His name" (John 1:12).

"For I am not ashamed of the gospel of Christ, for it is the power of God to salvation for everyone who believes" (Romans 1:16).

"There was a time when some of you were just like that but now your sins are washed away, and you are set apart for God, and he has accepted you because of what the Lord Jesus Christ and the Spirit of our God have done for you" (1 Corinthians 6:11, TLB).

"When someone becomes a Christian he becomes a brand new person inside. He is not the same any more. A new life has begun!" (2 Corinthians 5:17, TLB).

Temptation Can Be Overcome:

"But remember this—the wrong desires that come into your life aren't anything new and different. Many others have faced exactly the same problems before you. And no temptation is irresistible. You can trust God to keep the temptation from becoming so strong that you can't stand up against it, for he has promised this and will do what he says. He will show you how to escape temptation's power so that you can bear up patiently against it" (1 Corinthians 10:13, TLB).

"For since he himself has now been through suffering and temptation, he knows what it is like when we suffer and are tempted, and he is wonderfully able to help us" (Hebrews 2:18, TLB).

"But Jesus the Son of God is our great High Priest who has gone to heaven itself to help us; therefore let us never stop trusting him. This High Priest of ours understands our weaknesses, since he had the same temptations we do, though he never once gave way to them and sinned. So let us come boldly to the very throne of God and stay there to receive his mercy and to find grace to help us in our times of need" (Hebrews 4:14–16, TLB).

A Renewed Mind:

"You will keep him in perfect peace, whose mind is stayed on You, because he trusts in You" (Isaiah 26:3).

"Therefore, I urge you, brothers, in view of God's mercy, to offer your bodies as living sacrifices, holy and pleasing to God—which is your spiritual act of worship. Do not conform any longer to the pattern of this world, but be transformed by the renewing of your mind. Then you will be able to test and approve what God's will is—his good, pleasing and perfect will" (Romans 12:1–2, NIV).

"These weapons can break down every proud argument against God and every wall that can be built to keep men from finding him. With these weapons I can capture rebels and bring them back to God, and change them into men whose hearts' desire is obedience to Christ" (2 Corinthians 10:5, TLB).

"You were taught, with regard to your former way of life, to put off your old self, which is being corrupted by its deceitful desires; to be made new in the attitude of your minds; and to put on the new self, created to be like God in true righteousness and holiness" (Ephesians 4:22–24, NIV).

INCEST

Background

Incest is defined as sexual relations between people in the same family. The person reporting this problem will most likely be a young female who reports sexual contact (not always intercourse) with her father or another male in her family. Young boys may also be victims of incest.

A news telecast called incest the "hidden shame," and the "least reported devastating crime in America." It is feared that from 100,000 to 1,000,000 youngsters are sexually abused by a family member each year.

Incest is very destructive to a child, and often the damage cannot be undone. A U.S. district judge recently observed: "Abused children have suffered unspeakable injuries to body and soul." Because of shame, fright, or a feeling that they have done something terribly wrong or that they are being punished, the victims of incest rarely report their involvement. Being trapped in such a situation leads to confusion and a "learned helplessness."

Sexually abused children have a low self-image, are depressed, and often harbor thoughts of self-destruction. Many run away from home and frequently get involved in drugs, alcohol, and further deviant sexual behavior such as prostitution and homosexuality. Unable to concentrate on learning, they may do poorly in school. Chances of a successful adulthood are poor, because many do not recover from the effects of the relationship and many commit suicide.

There is little hope of freeing the victim of incest from her (or his) helpless situation unless the offender is stopped. The person guilty of incest is unlikely to change unless faced with the legal implications of the crime. Once the situation is called to the attention of the courts, authorities will intervene, removing the victim from her surroundings. Eventually, both the parents and the victim will need counseling, both separately and together, if any solutions are to be found. Hopefully such services exist in the victim's community.

Often the victim will be intimidated by family members not to press charges or testify against the offender because of the shame if the "family secret" becomes known. In such situations, the pastor may be the only one able to intervene.

Helping Strategy

1. Victims of incest demand a special sympathy and tenderness. Try to project all the love you can.

2. Assure the inquirer that she (or he) has done the right thing in sharing the problem, and that we want to help.

3. Assure her that, though there may be feelings of defilement, she is not bad or vile. She has been forced or tricked into something degrading, and may feel confused, but that does not imply any kind of mental imbalance. What has happened is very wrong, but the victim is not responsible for it. Though abused, she no longer needs to feel intimidated or filled with feelings of helplessness, self-pity, and self-doubt. We want to help solve the terrible problem.

4. Assure the caller of God's love. To God, she is special and just as worthy as anyone. God loved her so much that He sent His Son, Jesus Christ, to die for her sins. Explain "Steps to Peace with God," page 11.

5. Suggest reading the Bible. Offer to send *Living in Christ*, which has recommended Bible readings and studies.

6. Strongly recommend immediately contacting a pastor, in order to relate what has been happening. Also recommend reporting the incident to the school or guidance counselor. This will be difficult and embarrassing, but it must be done.

7. Pray with the inquirer, committing the problem to the Lord. After praying, reassure her of your concern and prayers.

Scripture

"You will keep in perfect peace him whose mind is steadfast, because he trusts in you. Trust in the Lord forever, for the Lord, the Lord, is the Rock eternal" (Isaiah 26:3–4, NIV).

"Trust in the Lord with all your heart, and lean not on your own understanding; in all your ways acknowledge Him, and He shall direct your paths" (Proverbs 3:5–6).

"Come to Me, all you who labor and are heavy laden, and I will give you rest. Take My yoke upon you and learn from Me, for I am gentle and lowly in heart, and you will find rest for your souls" (Matthew 11:28–29).

"Jesus said, 'Let the little children come to me, and do not hinder them, for the kingdom of heaven belongs to such as these'" (Matthew 19:14, NIV).

"Do not be anxious about anything, but in everything, by prayer and petition, with thanksgiving, present your requests to God. And the peace of God, which transcends all understanding, will guard your hearts and your minds in Christ Jesus" (Philippians 4:6–7, NIV).

"Let him have all your worries and cares, for he is always thinking about you and watching everything that concerns you" (1 Peter 5:7, TLB).

JESUS CHRIST

Background

The Christian worker will sometimes encounter those who acclaim Jesus as the greatest religious leader who ever lived, as the most influential person in our planet's history, but who nonetheless refuse to accept Him as Savior and Lord.

The person and work of Jesus Christ is the predominant theme of the Bible: He is God. He became a human being, died by crucifixion, was buried, and rose again from the dead. He is the only and the all-sufficient Savior of the world.

The following outline should provide structure for a discussion as you help the inquirer better understand what the Bible reveals about Christ.

Jesus Christ Is God

Deity is the only possible explanation for all that Christ was and all that He did:

1. He was preexistent with God the Father: "He was in the beginning with God. All things were made through Him, and without Him nothing was made that was made" (John 1:2–3; see also John 17:5; Colossians 1:17).

2. He is the Son of God:

   - His enemies observed: "He . . . said that God was His Father, making Himself equal with God" (John 5:18).

   - Peter confessed: "Also we have come to believe and know that You are the Christ, the Son of the living God" (John 6:69).

   - Jesus affirmed: "I and My Father are one" (John 10:30).

3. He was sinless, as only God can be:

   - Jesus challenged His enemies: "Which of you convicts Me of sin?" (John 8:46).

   - Peter testified: "Christ also suffered for us, leaving us an example, that you should follow His steps: 'Who committed no sin, nor was guile found in His mouth'" (1 Peter 2:21–22).

   - Paul stated: "For He made Him who knew no sin to be sin for us, that we might become the righteousness of God in Him" (2 Corinthians 5:21).

4. He forgives sin, as only God can:

- The scribes said: "Who can forgive sins but God alone?" (Mark 2:7).

- Jesus said: ". . . but that you may know that the Son of Man has power on earth to forgive sins" (Matthew 9:6; see also John 8:11).

- Peter wrote: ". . . who Himself bore our sins in His own body on the tree, that we, having died to sins, might live for righteousness—by whose stripes you were healed" (1 Peter 2:24).

5. He performed miraculous works:

- He healed the sick (Matthew 8:9–13; Luke 4:31–41; 5:12–15; John 4:43 to 5:16; and other references).

- He fed the hungry (Mark 8; John 6).

- He raised the dead (Luke 7:11–18; John 11:1–46).

Jesus Christ, Who Is God, Became a Man

"And the Word became flesh and dwelt among us . . . full of grace and truth" (John 1:14; see also Philippians 2:7–8).

1. His miraculous birth was prophesied 800 years before His coming: "Behold, the virgin shall conceive and bear a Son, and shall call His name Immanuel" (Isaiah 7:14).

2. The prophecy was fulfilled to the letter: "Do not be afraid, Mary, for you have found favor with God. And behold, you will conceive in your womb and bring forth a Son, and shall call His name Jesus" (Luke 1:30–31).

3. While on earth as a man, Jesus demonstrated human characteristics: He became tired (John 4:6), He thirsted (John 19:28), He ate food (Luke 24:40–43), He showed feelings (Mark 6:34; John 11:35), He knew temptation (Hebrews 4:15), and He died (John 19:30).

Jesus Christ Accomplished the Work His Father Had Sent Him to Earth to Accomplish:

1. He died on the cross. This is the fundamental theme of the Gospel:

A. The fact of His death: One-fourth of the material in the four gospels relates to Christ's death and resurrection:

(1) The cross was the purpose for which He came into the world (John 12:27).

(2) His death was prophesied hundreds of years before He came (Isaiah 53:3–8).

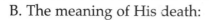

B. The meaning of His death:

(1) It was a ransom for sin (Matthew 20:28; Romans 3:24; 1 Peter 1:18).

(2) It was to pay the penalty for sin (Romans 3:24; 1 John 2:2; 4:10). Mankind is the object of God's wrath because of rebellion and sin, but God took the initiative in satisfying His wrath by sending His own Son to Calvary.

(3) It is a reconciliation. Because of Christ's death, the enmity between us and God has ended (Romans 5:10) and we are restored to fellowship with God (2 Corinthians 5:18–19).

(4) It is a substitution: He died in our place (2 Corinthians 5:21; 1 Peter 3:18).

(5) In summary, the problem of sin has been completely dealt with by Christ's death (Hebrews 9:26; 10:12; 1 Peter 2:24)

2. He was resurrected from the dead: This event was unique in human history and is fundamental to Christianity:

A. The reality of the Resurrection (John 20:1–10; 1 Corinthians 15:4).

B. The credibility of the Resurrection:

(1) Jesus predicted it (Matthew 20:18–19; Luke 24:1–7).

(2) The tomb was empty (John 20:11–13).

(3) Many witnesses saw Him alive: the women (Luke 23:55–56); Mary Magdalene (John 20:1–2, 11–18); Peter and the other disciples (John 20:3–9, 19–20, 24–31; 21:1–14).

The Results of His Work

1. He ascended to His Father (Luke 24:49–53; Acts 1:6–11).

2. He is our eternal mediator (1 Timothy 2:5; Hebrews 8:6; 1 John 2:1).

3. He is our Savior: "You shall call His name Jesus, for He will save His people from their sins" (Matthew 1:21). "Him God has exalted to His right hand to be Prince and Savior, to give repentance to Israel and forgiveness of sins" (Acts 5:31):

A. He is the only Savior: "Salvation is found in no one else, for there is no other name under heaven given to men by which we must be saved" (Acts 4:12, NIV).

B. He is a complete Savior: "Therefore He is also able to save to the uttermost those who come to God through Him, since He ever lives to make intercession for them" (Hebrews 7:25).

C. He is a personal Savior: "If you confess with your mouth the Lord Jesus and believe in your heart that God has raised Him from the dead, you will be saved. For with the heart one believes to righteousness, and with the mouth confession is made to salvation" (Romans 10:9–10).

The Consummation of His Work

1. He shall return again to this earth (John 14:3; Acts 1:11; Hebrews 10:37).

2. Believers in Christ shall be physically resurrected to begin a new, everlasting life (1 Corinthians 15:51–58; 1 Thessalonians 4:17–18).

3. He will reign as King of kings and Lord of lords over His new creation (2 Peter 3:10–13; Revelation 22:3–5).

Helping Strategy

The greatest response we can make to Jesus Christ and His claims is to:

1. Receive Him as Lord and Savior. Ask the inquirer if he or she has done this. Share "Steps to Peace with God," page 11.

2. Enthrone Him as Lord of our life: "These people honor me with their lips, but their hearts are far from me" (Matthew 15:8, NIV). "Therefore, I urge you, brothers, in view of God's mercy, to offer your bodies as living sacrifices, holy and pleasing to God—this is your spiritual act of worship. Do not conform any longer to the pattern of this world, but be transformed by the renewing of your mind. Then you will be able to test and approve what God's will is—his good, pleasing and perfect will" (Romans 12:1–2, NIV).

3. Witness for Him as He commands: "That which we have seen and heard we declare to you, that you also may have fellowship with us; and truly our fellowship is with the Father and with His Son Jesus Christ" (1 John 1:3). "You shall receive power when the Holy Spirit has come upon you; and you shall be witnesses to Me in Jerusalem, and in all Judea and Samaria, and to the end of the earth" (Acts 1:8).

Scripture

His Deity:

John 1:1–3; 8:56–59; 10:30–33; 17:5; Philippians 2:6–11; Colossians 1:15–19; 2:8–9; Revelation 5:12–14.

His Humanity:

Matthew 1:18; Mark 6:34; Luke 1:30–33; 24:40–43; John 1:14; 10:30; 11:35; 19:28; Philippians 2:5–8; Hebrews 4:15.

His Death:

Isaiah 53; Matthew 27:32–56; Mark 15:20–47; Luke 23:26–49; John 19:1–42; 1 Corinthians 15:24; 2 Corinthians 5:21; 1 Peter 1:18–19; 2:22–24; 1 John 3:5–8.

His Resurrection:

Matthew 28; Mark 16; Luke 24; John 20–21; Acts 2:24–36; Romans 10:9–10; 1 Corinthians 15; Galatians 2:20; 1 Thessalonians 1:10; 1 Peter 1:19–21.

His Second Coming:

Matthew 24:30, 42–44; John 14:1–6; 21:23; Acts 1:11; 1 Corinthians 15:51–57; 1 Thessalonians 4:13–18; 2 Thessalonians 2:1–11; 1 John 3:2–3; Revelation 1:7.

JUDGMENT

Background

The biblical doctrine of a future day of judgment is one of the most misunderstood subjects among Christians. The idea of one general judgment, when all the people of all ages will stand before God, has always been erroneously prevalent.

All people who have ever lived—both saints and sinners—will be judged, but not at the same time. The judgments differ as to subjects, time, place, and results. This discussion will deal only with the aspects of the future judgments which the helper will most likely need to address.

There are three judgments for the believer in Christ:

1. The believer has already been judged for his or her sins, by the death of Christ at Calvary:

   > "For He made Him who knew no sin to be sin for us, that we might become the righteousness of God in Him" (2 Corinthians 5:21).

   > ". . . who Himself bore our sins in His own body on the tree, that we, having died to sins, might live for righteousness—by whose stripes you were healed" (1 Peter 2:24).

   When He died on the cross, Jesus bore the full thrust of God's righteous judgment against sin. The believer receives Christ as his or her sin-bearer, meaning that he or she trusts fully in the redemption accomplished at Calvary and is freed from sin and guilt. Believers will never again be judged for their sins.

2. The believer will someday stand before the judgment seat of Christ to be judged for how he or she lived as a Christian:

   > "For we must all appear before the judgment seat of Christ, that each one may receive the things done in the body, according to what he has done, whether good or bad" (2 Corinthians 5:10).

   This judgment will bring rewards to some and loss to others. Some will have no profitable works to lay at the Master's feet, while others will be called "good and profitable servants" and will be asked to enter into the joy of their Lord. This judgment will immediately follow the "rapture" of believers, both alive and dead, as recorded in 1 Thessalonians 4:15–17 (see "Scripture" on the following pages).

3. There is also the daily self-judgment of the believer:

"Search me, O God, and know my heart; try me, and know my anxieties; and see if there is any wicked way in me, and lead me in the way everlasting" (Psalm 139:23–24).

"Keeping short accounts" with God is the only way to spiritual maturity. This judgment of self results in confession and forgiveness:

> "He who covers his sins will not prosper, but whoever confesses and forsakes them will have mercy" (Proverbs 28:13).

> "If we confess our sins, He is faithful and just to forgive us our sins and to cleanse us from all unrighteousness" (1 John 1:9).

There will be a judgment of unbelievers, known as the Great White Throne Judgment (Revelation 20:11–15—see "Scripture" on the following pages):

All people who find themselves in hell will be there because they have rejected God's salvation and have chosen instead to serve Satan. Scripture indicates clearly that all such people must appear before the Great White Throne Judgment and that they will be judged on the basis of the light they had and rejected while on earth.

This judgment follows God's final judgment of the devil (Revelation 20:10) and the rebellious angels (Jude 6), and comes after the millennial reign. The lost of all ages will stand before God for this most terrible of all judgments (Matthew 12:36).

Helping Strategy
For Those Fearful of the Coming Judgment and Its Consequences:

1. Assure the person that God is reaching out in love and is "not willing that any should perish but that all should come to repentance" (2 Peter 3:9). "For God did not send His Son into the world to condemn the world, but that the world through Him might be saved" (John 3:17).

2. Invite him or her to receive Jesus Christ as Savior and Lord, sharing "Steps to Peace with God," page 11.

3. Challenge him or her to take a firm stand for Jesus Christ, to stand up and be counted. He or she should begin reading and studying the Bible on a daily basis. (Offer to send *Living in Christ*.)

4. Advise seeking fellowship, worship, and opportunities for service in a local Bible-teaching church.

5. Pray that the inquirer might know the reality of Christ in his or her life.

For Those Unaware of Biblical Teaching on Judgment:

1. Explain the material in the "Background." Note: Most cults have unbiblical views of this subject.

2. Invite him or her to receive Christ, if this is indicated in the conversation.

3. Follow the suggestions on the previous page in numbers 3, 4, and 5.

Scripture

"There is therefore now no condemnation to those who are in Christ Jesus, who do not walk according to the flesh, but according to the Spirit" (Romans 8:1).

"For no other foundation can anyone lay than that which is laid, which is Jesus Christ. Now if anyone builds on this foundation with gold, silver, precious stones, wood, hay, straw, each one's work will become manifest; for the Day will declare it, because it will be revealed by fire; and the fire will test each one's work, of what sort it is. If anyone's work which he has built on it endures, he will receive a reward. If anyone's work is burned, he will suffer loss; but he himself will be saved, yet so as through fire" (1 Corinthians 3:11–15).

"Then I saw a great white throne and Him who sat on it, from whose face the earth and the heaven fled away. And there was found no place for them. And I saw the dead, small and great, standing before God, and books were opened. And another book was opened, which is the Book of Life. And the dead were judged according to their works, by the things which were written in the books. The sea gave up the dead who were in it, and Death and Hades delivered up the dead who were in them. And they were judged, each one according to his works" (Revelation 20:11–13).

LONELINESS

Background

Loneliness is the painful realization that we lack meaningful and close relationships with others. This lack leads to emptiness, melancholy, isolation, and even despair. A sense of rejection and a low self-image are present because we can't relate, or we feel left out and unwanted, no matter how hard we try to belong.

The kind of society we live in can contribute to loneliness. It is difficult for some to maintain a strong identity and meaningful relationships amid what seems to be a jungle of bureaucracy, specialization, regimentation, and competition. Mobility and constant change tend to make some individuals feel rootless and disconnected.

Loneliness can be self-inflicted. Some people find it difficult to communicate with others or lack confidence because they have a poor self-image. Others yearn for togetherness, yet their demand for privacy and independence inhibits the development of meaningful ties with others. The fear of exposure of their inner selves results in a kind of social paralysis.

In many of his messages, Billy Graham has referred to that "cosmic loneliness" of the person who is separated from God and feels that life has little meaning. He says, "There are thousands of lonely people who carry heavy and difficult burdens of grief, anxiety, pain, and disappointment; but the loneliest of all is one whose life is steeped in sin."

One of the results of the Fall is that humankind became alienated from God. This alienation caused Adam and Eve to hide from God and to try to cover up their sin. It is only as we find forgiveness in Christ that we are relieved of the loneliness resulting from this alienation from God. The psalmist exulted in God's work in his life by writing, "He restores my soul" (Psalm 23:3). This restoration removes the causes of our alienation: "Once you were alienated from God and were enemies in your minds because of your evil behavior. But now he has reconciled you by Christ's physical body through death to present you holy in his sight, without blemish and free from accusation" (Colossians 1:21–22, NIV).

Our restoration to fellowship with God also involves our being indwelt by God's Holy Spirit: "Do you not know that your body is a temple of the Holy Spirit, who is in you, whom you have received from God?"

(1 Corinthians 6:19, NIV). Thus, we are complete in Him: "And you are complete in Him, who is the head of all principality and power" (Colossians 2:10).

Helping Strategy

Only when our fellowship with God has been restored can we experience full fellowship with our fellow humans. Whether dealing with Christians or nonbelievers, the helper must approach the problem of loneliness from this perspective.

For the Lonely Non-Christian:

1. Offer a word of encouragement. In sharing his or her problem of loneliness, the inquirer is admitting a need. This is important in solving any problem in life. Offer reassurance that this first important step can lead to a satisfactory solution.

2. Try to determine the causes of the person's loneliness. If not enough information is forthcoming, ask relevant questions: Where does the caller live? Who are his or her neighbors? Where does he or she work? Is the job satisfactory? What about hobbies, friendships, church, etc.?

3. Determine whether the caller has ever received Christ as Savior. Explain "Steps to Peace with God," page 11. The first step in God's plan for the person's life can be realized only by receiving Christ, and that first step should also take care of much of the alienation he or she feels. He or she will be at peace with God (Romans 5:1) and will have Christ as a constant friend: "There is a friend who sticks closer than a brother" (Proverbs 18:24).

4. Suggest seeking spiritual growth by reading and studying the Bible and learning to pray. Offer to send *Living in Christ* for initial help with Bible study. The daily exercise of prayer will do much to diminish lingering feelings of aloneness, as it provides immediate access to God, who is "a very present help in trouble" (Psalm 46:1).

5. Recommend seeking a relationship with a Bible-teaching church where warmth of fellowship and opportunities for worship and service can be found. Advise that he or she must not expect too much too quickly. Meaningful relationships do not develop overnight; they must be cultivated, and this takes time. The more the lonely person gives, the more he or she will receive from others: "A man who has friends must himself be friendly" (Proverbs 18:24). Explain that some churches have a singles fellowship, if this should be of interest.

6. Advise the person to strengthen any home ties that may not be all they should be. Communication with other members of the family will do much to develop mutual respect and caring. Now that he or she knows Christ, the salvation of family members should be a primary concern.

7. Pray for spiritual growth and the development of meaningful relationships with both Christian and non-Christian friends.

For the Lonely Christian:

1. Encourage the inquirer to develop a daily quiet time. A sense of God's never-failing presence will help diminish feelings of loneliness.

Billy Graham offers his own experience for encouragement: "I will give you a little recipe I have found for conquering loneliness. First, I am never lonely when I am praying, for this brings me into companionship with the greatest friend of all—Jesus Christ. He said, 'I call you not servants, but friends' (see John 15:15). Then, I am never lonely when I am reading the Bible. I read it every day—whole chapters of it. Nothing dissolves loneliness like a session with God's Word."

As we grow in this devotional relationship with God, we begin to change. The attitudes of loving and caring which gradually develop become the basis for contacts with others and for the deepening of friendships.

2. Recommend seeking a meaningful place of service in an active Bible-teaching church. Focusing on the needs of others will put our problems into perspective and make them seem a little less important. Service helps us cultivate relationships with other Christians who serve, and tends to increase our self-esteem as we become a part of the group.

Billy Graham says about service, "I am never lonely when I am sharing Him with others. There is a great exhilaration in talking to others about Christ. This is something we can all do."

3. Suggest strengthening family ties. Lonely people often have some "loose ends" in regard to family relationships. Constant efforts to communicate with our own family—learning to share, to respect and care, to become a part of each other—will do much to prevent loneliness. Improved relationships at home will always lead to improvement elsewhere.

4. Encourage the inquirer to seek counsel from a local pastor, preferably his or her own. A pastor can help the person develop relationships and can recommend areas of service through the church.

Scripture

"I waited patiently for the Lord; and He inclined to me, and heard my cry. He also brought me up out of a horrible pit, out of the miry clay, and set my feet upon a rock, and established my steps. He has put a new song in my mouth—Praise to our God; many will see it and fear, and will trust in the Lord. Blessed is that man who makes the Lord his trust, and does not respect the proud, nor such as turn aside to lies. Many, O Lord my God, are Your wonderful works which You have done; and Your thoughts which are toward us cannot be recounted to You in order; if I would declare and speak of them, they are more than can be numbered" (Psalm 40:1–5).

"Come to Me, all you who labor and are heavy laden, and I will give you rest. Take My yoke upon you and learn from Me, for I am gentle and lowly in heart, and you will find rest for your souls. For My yoke is easy and My burden is light" (Matthew 11:28–30).

"Lo, I am with you always, even to the end of the age" (Matthew 28:20).

"God is faithful, by whom you were called into the fellowship of His Son, Jesus Christ our Lord" (1 Corinthians 1:9).

"He Himself has said, 'I will never leave you nor forsake you.' So we may boldly say: 'The Lord is my helper; I will not fear. What can man do to me?'" (Hebrews 13:5–6).

Other suggested Scriptures:

Proverbs 3:5–6

LOVE

Background

Until the Good News of Jesus Christ burst onto the human scene, the word *love* was understood mostly in terms of seeking one's own advantage. Loving the unlovely was incomprehensible. A loving God reaching down to sinful humans was unthinkable.

The New Testament writers chose a little-used Greek word for love, *agape*, to express what God wanted to reveal about Himself in Christ and how He wanted Christians to relate to each other: "By this we know love, because He laid down His life for us. And we also ought to lay down our lives for the brethren" (1 John 3:16).

This new love bond was given its fullest expression at Calvary. Those redeemed by Christ's death would be able to reach out to God and to each other in a dimension never before understood or experienced. Agape would now be the "more excellent way" of living (1 Corinthians 12:31). This new kind of love quickly became the identifying characteristic of the early church. Jesus had said: "A new commandment I give to you . . . as I have loved you, that you also love one another. By this all will know that you are My disciples, if you have love for one another" (John 13:34–35).

But as the years passed, much of the true force of agape faded. The church of today is in the position of having to rediscover its meaning. Agape is not mere sentiment; love that is dormant is powerless. Love is dynamic only when it actively loves God, even as He loved us; only when it is surging, unconstrained—loving brothers, sisters, neighbors, and the world for which Christ died (1 John 4:10–12; 2 Corinthians 5:14).

On the human plane, as on the divine, love says: "I respect you. I care for you. I am responsible for you":

I respect you: I see you as you are, a unique individual—as we are all unique. I accept you as you are and will permit you to develop as God purposes for you. I will not exploit you for my own benefit. I will try to know you as well as I can, because I know that increased communication and knowledge will enhance my respect for you.

I care for you: What happens to you matters to me. I am concerned for your life and growth. I desire to promote your interests, even if it means sacrificing my own.

I am responsible for you: I will respond to you, not out of a sense of duty, but voluntarily. Your spiritual needs will motivate me to pray for you. I will protect you, but will guard against overprotection. I will correct you in love, but will try not to overcorrect. I will find no pleasure in your weaknesses or failures, and will keep no record of either. By God's grace, I will be patient and will not fail you (1 Corinthians 13).

We understand God's love only as we respond to it in Christ. The most important point in the life of any individual is the moment of decision to receive this unmerited, unearned love through which we learn to love Him and to pass this love on to others.

"God is love. This is how God showed his love among us: He sent his one and only Son into the world that we might live through him. This is love: not that we loved God, but that he loved us" (1 John 4:8–10, NIV).

Helping Strategy
For the Non-Christian:

If the inquirer has never experienced God's forgiving love, share "Steps to Peace with God," page 11, emphasizing John 3:16.

For the Christian:

1. If the inquirer is a Christian expressing the desire to love God more, offer commendation and encouragement, for this is also God's highest will for us: "Jesus said to him, 'You shall love the Lord your God with all your heart, with all your soul, and with all your mind'" (Matthew 22:37):

   A. We are to love God because He first loved us (1 John 4:10).

   B. We are to love Him "because the love of God has been poured out in our hearts by the Holy Spirit who was given to us" (Romans 5:5). "But the fruit of the Spirit is love" (Galatians 5:22).

   C. We are to love Him through obedience: "Jesus replied, 'If anyone loves me, he will obey my teaching. My Father will love him, and we will come to him and make our home with him. He who does not love me will not obey my teaching'" (John 14:23–24, NIV).

   D. We demonstrate our love through devotion to Him: "I delight to do Your will, O my God, and Your law is within my heart" (Psalm 40:8):

   (1) We seek Him through His Word: "But his delight is in the law of the Lord, and in His law he meditates day and night" (Psalm 1:2).

(2) We seek Him through prayer: "'Then you will call upon me and come and pray to me, and I will listen to you. You will seek me and find me when you seek me with all your heart. I will be found by you,' declares the Lord" (Jeremiah 29:12–14, NIV).

(3) We seek to serve Him: "Always give yourselves fully to the work of the Lord, because you know that your labor in the Lord is not in vain" (1 Corinthians 15:58, NIV). "He will not forget your work and the love you have shown him as you have helped his people and continue to help them" (Hebrews 6:10, NIV).

Agape love is the greatest motivation to become involved in evangelism and missions, as we seek to share God's love with a lost world.

2. If the inquirer is a Christian who has problems in loving a fellow Christian, point out that we only begin to understand God's love as we reach out in love to each other:

A. It is a command of God to love our fellow Christians: "Be devoted to one another in brotherly love. Honor one another above yourselves" (Romans 12:10, NIV).

B. Because God has loved us, we should be able to love regardless of the worthiness of the object of our love: ". . . because the love of God has been poured out in our hearts by the Holy Spirit who was given to us" (Romans 5:5). Share the outline in the "Background" on the dimensions of agape love: respect, care, and responsibility.

Billy Graham says: "The fruit of the Spirit is love. I cannot love on my own, I cannot have joy, peace, patience, gentleness, goodness, faith, meekness, and temperance by myself. There is no one who has the ability to really love . . . until he really comes to Christ. Until the Holy Spirit has control of one's life, he doesn't have the power to love."

C. Point out that love doesn't demonstrate itself automatically: it is a learned, practiced behavior. The more we love, and the more deeply we love, the more love is perfected in us:

(1) Prayer for others stimulates a deeper love for them.

(2) Acts of kindness, service, and sacrifice add the dynamic dimension to love. "Be kindly affectionate to one another with brotherly love, in honor giving preference to one another" (Romans 12:10). "Love is patient, love is kind. It does not envy, it does not boast, it is not

proud. It is not rude, it is not self-seeking, it is not easily angered, it keeps no record of wrongs. Love does not delight in evil but rejoices with the truth. It always protects, always trusts, always hopes, always perseveres. Love never fails" (1 Corinthians 13:4–8, NIV).

Scripture

"For God so loved the world that He gave His only begotten Son, that whoever believes in Him should not perish but have everlasting life" (John 3:16).

"Greater love has no one than this, that he lay down his life for his friends" (John 15:13, NIV).

"Let us have no imitation Christian love. Let us have a genuine hatred for evil and a real devotion to good. Let us have real warm affection for one another as between brothers, and a willingness to let the other man have the credit" (Romans 12:9–10, PHILLIPS).

"But because of his great love for us, God, who is rich in mercy, made us alive with Christ even when we were dead in transgressions—it is by grace you have been saved" (Ephesians 2:4–5, NIV).

"How great is the love the Father has lavished on us, that we should be called children of God! And that is what we are! The reason the world does not know us is that it did not know him" (1 John 3:1, NIV).

"No one has ever seen God; but if we love one another, God lives in us and his love is made complete in us" (1 John 4:12, NIV).

Other suggested Scriptures:

Matthew 22:37, NIV

MARRIAGE, ANTICIPATING

Background

Marriage is the most serious long-term contract a couple will make in their lifetime, but many enter into it with a lack of maturity and knowledge. The growing number of divorces shows how imperative it is that young people be adequately prepared for marriage.

Here are a few helpful principles for prospective marriage partners:

- A good marriage is not "made in heaven," but on earth. Love is a fragile commodity which needs to be cultivated and nourished constantly. Of course, those intending to marry should look to God for His guidance, but the success of the marriage will be largely dependent on the couple and their efforts in response to God's leading.

- A good marriage is not based on idealism, but on reality. The Cinderella syndrome where every girl finds a prince and "lives happily ever after" is usually just a fairy tale. Far too many marry with unrealistically high expectations, and then spend years suffering and adjusting—if they stay together at all.

- A good marriage is based on respect for oneself and for the partner. A poor self-image, inherited from a stressful home background or the product of immaturity, can lead to stormy seas. A solid relationship with Jesus Christ and an understanding of oneself in the light of that relationship are very important.

A poor understanding of each other can also lead to misunderstanding and conflict. It doesn't take too much discernment to realize that males and females are different physically, but how many anticipate that their partner-to-be is just as different emotionally and mentally? Each partner must realize this and be prepared to make the necessary allowances and adjustments. "He created them male and female, and blessed them" (Genesis 5:2).

- A marriage where there are similarities in the partners has a better chance to succeed. This means:

  * The same religious background

  * Similar cultural and social backgrounds

  * Comparable economic levels

  * Equal educational advantages

* A stable home situation

- Marriage was never intended to be a reform school! One who marries another with the hope of "correcting" problem behavior is courting a disastrous future. What could not be changed before marriage is not likely to change at all. This should especially be taken seriously in those instances where alcohol, drugs, or immorality are involved.

- Couples who marry "in the Lord" (1 Corinthians 7:39) have the potential for a much better relationship than those outside of Christ.

Billy Graham advises: "The home only fulfills its true purpose when it is God-controlled. Leave Jesus Christ out of your home and it loses its meaning. But take Christ into your heart and the life of your family, and He will transform your home."

Helping Strategy

1. Commend the inquirer for seeking advice about a forthcoming marriage. Share the following Scriptures: "And the Lord God said, 'It is not good that man should be alone; I will make him a helper comparable to him'" (Genesis 2:18). "He who finds a wife finds a good thing, and obtains favor from the Lord" (Proverbs 18:22).

2. Advise that in order to have God's presence and guidance in life and marriage, one must commit one's life to Jesus Christ. Share "Steps to Peace with God," page 11.

3. Encourage the inquirer to take a firm stand for Jesus Christ, whether previously a Christian or having just received Christ. He or she should also begin to read and study God's Word, to pray about all matters, and to become involved in a Bible-teaching church. All these things will deeply enrich life, enabling the prospective bride or groom to offer much more to the marriage.

4. When the individual marries, be sure that it is "in the Lord" (1 Corinthians 7:39). "Do not be unequally yoked together with unbelievers. For what fellowship has righteousness with lawlessness? And what communion has light with darkness?" (2 Corinthians 6:14).

5. Before the marriage, the inquirer can improve its chances of success by:

   A. Seeking God's blessing and control over his or her own life and that of the partner.

B. Assimilating all the knowledge possible about a Christ-centered home and marriage:

- Search the Bible for passages on marriage and the home.

- Read books by Christian counselors and pastors. Such materials are available at Christian bookstores and in church libraries.

- Take advantage of seminars, courses, and films prepared for this purpose.

- Seek counseling from a qualified pastor, marriage counselor, or Christian psychologist. Such counseling should include a comprehensive approach to marriage, including personal, spiritual, financial, and sexual matters.

6. After marriage, practice the following:

- Become involved in a Bible-teaching church where the marriage will be able to flourish spiritually, and where the future family can be received and nurtured in eternal things.

- Resolve to communicate freely and honestly with the partner on all levels of life: mental, emotional, and physical. Such a practice will help greatly in problem solving as issues arise in the marriage.

7. Pray with the inquirer for God's blessing, presence, and leading in his or her life and approaching marriage.

Scripture

"By wisdom a house is built, and through understanding it is established; through knowledge its rooms are filled with rare and beautiful treasures" (Proverbs 24:3–4, NIV).

"Do two walk together unless they have agreed to do so?" (Amos 3:3, NIV).

"Submit to one another out of reverence for Christ. Wives, submit to your husbands as to the Lord. . . . In this same way, husbands ought to love their wives as their own bodies. He who loves his wife loves himself" (Ephesians 5:21–22, 28, NIV).

"Likewise you husbands, dwell with them with understanding, giving honor to the wife, as to the weaker vessel, and as being heirs together of the grace of life, that your prayers may not be hindered" (1 Peter 3:7).

Other suggested Scriptures:

2 Corinthians 6:14–15, NIV

MARRIAGE

(Pressure to Do Wrong from an Unbelieving Spouse)

Background

When a Christian is married to a nonbeliever, he or she may at times feel pressured by the mate to do things that are either clearly contrary to Scripture or that simply give the believer an uneasy conscience—perhaps something involving worldly involvements or sexual practices. This can lead to unhappiness and conflict in the marriage.

The Bible commands mutual love and respect between husband and wife (Ephesians 5:22, 28). Neither has the right to order the other to do something that is contrary to the Bible or that offends the partner's conscience. When one partner is not a believer, and therefore perhaps not willing to abide by biblical principles, special wisdom and sensitivity are needed to resolve the conflict.

Helping Strategy

1. Commend the inquirer for being sensitive to the leading of the Holy Spirit in his or her life, and for wanting to do right.

2. Encourage a firm stand for Christ (Romans 12:1–2).

3. Urge the individual to keep the lines of communication open with his or her mate, in order to discuss freely and fully the problems involved and the reasons why it is not possible to agree to such requests. The Christian partner should not be critical or judgmental. "We catch more flies with honey than with vinegar." If one is not careful at this point, the point of no return could quickly be reached, bringing conflict and hostility.

4. Love covers a multitude of sins. Encourage the Christian partner to love sincerely, demonstrating it through word and action. As much as possible, express appreciation, admiration, and praise for the unbelieving spouse in those areas where it is due.

5. Encourage the inquirer to pray, first for wisdom and guidance in the situation (James 1:5), then for the unbelieving partner's obedience to the Word of God and commitment to personal faith in Christ.

   CAUTION: One should not be too aggressive in trying to win a husband or wife to Christ. See the chapter on "Marriage (Winning One's Mate to Christ)."

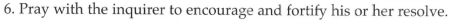
6. Pray with the inquirer to encourage and fortify his or her resolve.

Billy Graham comments: "Complete fulfillment in marriage can never be realized outside the life in Christ. It is written in the Bible that Christ came into the world to destroy the works of the devil. Christ's power over the devil is available to the Christian, and the destroyer of the ideal home can only be put to flight through the power of Christ."

Scripture

"We must obey God rather than men!" (Acts 5:29, NIV).

"How much more, then, will the blood of Christ, who through the eternal Spirit offered himself unblemished to God, cleanse our consciences from acts that lead to death, so that we may serve the living God!" (Hebrews 9:14, NIV).

"Wives, in the same way be submissive to your husbands so that, if any of them do not believe the word, they may be won over without words by the behavior of their wives, when they see the purity and reverence of your lives. . . . For this is the way the holy women of the past who put their hope in God used to make themselves beautiful. . . . Husbands, in the same way be considerate as you live with your wives, and treat them with respect as the weaker partner and as heirs with you of the gracious gift of life, so that nothing will hinder your prayers. Finally, all of you, live in harmony with one another; be sympathetic, love as brothers, be compassionate and humble. . . . But in your hearts set apart Christ as Lord. Always be prepared to give an answer to everyone who asks you to give the reason for the hope that you have. But do this with gentleness and respect, keeping a clear conscience, so that those who speak maliciously against your good behavior in Christ may be ashamed of their slander" (1 Peter 3:1–2, 5, 7–8, 15–16, NIV).

MARRIAGE PROBLEMS

Background

When two lives are bonded together in a long-term intimate relationship, there is bound to be an occasional problem. Many couples go into marriage with very little preparation. Sometimes they lack the emotional maturity, stability, or flexibility which a successful union must have.

What are the components of a good marriage?

- *Mutual respect.* Respect means that each partner accepts the other partner as he or she is, not trying to manipulate but unselfishly nourishing the partner in such a way that he or she may become the person God intended. Respect distinguishes between the ideal and the real, and does not demand too much: "Each one of you also must love his wife as he loves himself, and the wife must respect her husband" (Ephesians 5:33, NIV).

- *Genuine commitment.* The marriage vow says, "Forsaking all others." The Bible says, "For this reason a man shall leave his father and mother and be joined to his wife, and the two shall become one flesh" (Matthew 19:5). Time and experience in marriage reveal that being "one flesh" does not mean an abdication of personality or personal rights. Rather, it is a fulfillment of those things.

- *Good communication.* For genuine communication, there must be an understanding of the emotional, mental, and physical differences between men and women. There must be companionship. "I'd rather be with my spouse than with anyone else." There must be conversation, not only a discussion of differences when such arise, but a meaningful exchange on the intellectual and emotional levels.

- *Time and effort.* Love must be given the opportunity to mature. The climate for this is set in God's Word. When the going gets rough, a couple doesn't just "fall out of love"; they stay together and work things out. They do not consider themselves as martyrs of a "bad bargain," but "heirs together of the grace of life" (1 Peter 3:7). "Each one of you also must love his wife as he loves himself, and the wife must respect her husband" (Ephesians 5:33, NIV).

Problems and differences are resolved through forgiveness: "Be kind and compassionate to one another, forgiving each other, just as in Christ God forgave you" (Ephesians 4:32, NIV).

Cliff Barrows often gives a message to Christian couples which he calls, "Ten Words that Will Safeguard a Marriage." They are:

I was wrong.   Forgive me.

I'm sorry.   I love you.

This same formula will work to safeguard one's spiritual life as well. Couples need to learn to clean up issues as soon as they develop and to erase the slate every day. See Ephesians 4:26.

- *Spiritual unity.* Understanding the spiritual dimension in marriage has profound implications. Paul compared marriage—the union of husband and wife—to the eternal relationship between Christ and the church (Ephesians 5:22–33).

Billy Graham writes: "The perfect marriage is a uniting of three persons—a man, a woman, and God! That is what makes marriage holy. Faith in Christ is the most important of all principles in the building of a happy marriage and a happy home."

Helping Strategy

1. Be supportive and encouraging. Listen carefully, with understanding. Don't judge. Don't take sides. Sometimes the *inquirer* is at fault.

2. Try to discover the reasons for the disagreements and problems. Ask questions, if necessary. Does the inquirer feel that he or she has any responsibility in any of the negative developments? Ask how the inquirer would rate the marriage in the light of the "Background." How has he or she fallen short? What might be done to improve the relationship? In humility, the caller could ask forgiveness for insensitivities, hurts, and offenses. It may take time, but it is worth the effort.

3. Ask if God has ever been brought into their life and marriage. Share "Steps to Peace with God," page 11.

4. Where does the individual go from here? Share follow-up steps:

   A. Get into the Bible—reading, studying, and applying it to his or her life and marriage.

   B. Learn to pray daily. Pray for each other. Pray about existing or potential problem areas: "Cast all your anxiety on him because he cares for you" (1 Peter 5:7, NIV). Better attitudes lead to a deeper sensitivity as to the needs of one's mate, producing better relationships. This is one of the values of Bible study and prayer: It will help us anticipate problems as it makes us more spiritually sensitive.

C. Become involved with spouse and family in a Bible-teaching church. Active participation in a dynamic church can revolutionize a marriage and family. Spiritual resources and support can be found in fellowship with committed Christians and in consultation with a committed pastor.

D. Should further counseling be needed—and it often is in troubled marriages—help could be found through contacting a qualified pastor or Christian psychologist or marriage counselor.

If the inquirer is a Christian, encourage serious counseling with a Christian marriage service or qualified pastor. Often many concessions and adjustments have to be made on the part of each partner, requiring prolonged professional sessions. The important thing is for them to honestly and sincerely face their situation in the light of God's Word. A good place to start might be an application of the Cliff Barrows formula from the "Background."

Scripture

"Let the husband render to his wife the affection due her, and likewise also the wife to her husband. The wife does not have authority over her own body, but the husband does. And likewise the husband does not have authority over his own body, but the wife does" (1 Corinthians 7:3–4).

"Let nothing be done through selfish ambition or conceit, but in lowliness of mind let each esteem others better than himself. Let each of you look out not only for his own interests, but also for the interests of others. Let this mind be in you which was also in Christ Jesus" (Philippians 2:3–5).

"Likewise you husbands, dwell with them with understanding, giving honor to the wife, as to the weaker vessel, and as being heirs together of the grace of life, that your prayers may not be hindered" (1 Peter 3:7).

Other suggested Scriptures:
Ephesians 5:22–33

MARRIAGE

(Winning One's Mate to Christ)

Background

On a certain occasion, Jesus startled His disciples with a paradox: "Do not suppose that I have come to bring peace to the earth. I did not come to bring peace, but a sword. For I have come to turn a 'man against his father, a daughter against her mother, a daughter-in-law against her mother-in-law—a man's enemies will be the members of his own household'" (Matthew 10:34–36, NIV). Nowhere is the cost of discipleship more evident than in a marriage where one partner is a Christian and the other is not. Life becomes complicated as interests, activities, and goals are at variance. The conversion to Christ of one's mate should receive the highest priority, but extreme caution should be exercised as to methods followed in pursuit of this goal. Many marriages end in divorce because of the insensitivity and overzealous evangelizing of the Christian partner.

Helping Strategy

1. Commend the inquirer for his or her concern in wanting to share the Gospel with the unbelieving spouse. He or she must be aware, however, of the "sword" Jesus referred to in the above quote: The Christian faith can unite people, but it can also divide them.

2. Encourage the individual not to try to "play God." He or she cannot force the mate to accept Christ. Those who try to take things into their own hands may be headed for disaster.

3. Recommend not coming on too strong but maintaining a humble attitude rather than a judgmental one. Attitude is extremely important.

4. Encourage the development of personal spiritual maturity through reading and studying God's Word and through faithfully practicing a life of prayer. Prayer is of great value. Commit the mate to the Lord and by faith claim conversion. Trust God. He has a wonderful way of working things out. (It would probably be best not to tell the unbelieving mate that he or she is the object of prayer!)

5. Example is powerful! Let the mate see Jesus in the believer's attitudes and actions. Let love overflow. True love cannot be counterfeited. Paul says: "Love is patient, love is kind. . . . Love never fails" (1 Corinthians 13:4, 8, NIV). Try to demonstrate that "the love of God has been poured out in our hearts" (Romans 5:5).

6. Never try to win the mate through argument or sermonizing. This will usually produce antagonism and deepen resistance. Peaceful coexistence is a method suggested by Paul (1 Corinthians 7:12–15).

Billy Graham says: "The apostle Peter had something to say about this. He said: 'Likewise you wives, be submissive to your own husbands, that even if some do not obey the word, they, without a word, may be won by the conduct of their wives' (1 Peter 3:1). This is no easy assignment, but the responsibility is on you, not on your husband, to live a life that will challenge him to make his own decision. This cannot be done by nagging or lecturing, but by the manifestation of a spirit of meekness and submission that he or she had not discovered in you before. Whether it is the husband or the wife who is the Christian, as a Christian he or she must always accept and expect some ridicule and even mistreatment for the faith. Just bear this in mind: No one is in a better relationship to win the other to Christ than a life partner."

---

7. Do not insist that the mate attend church or special Christian services unless there seems to be a disposition to do so. An alternative to church would be introducing Christian friends into the home on social occasions. The husband or wife is bound to see the difference in their lives. The opportune moment for sharing Christ will come.

8. Pray with the inquirer for the perception, wisdom, and patience to await the right moment for openly witnessing, while putting into practice all the above suggestions.

Scripture

"Do not be anxious about anything, but in everything, by prayer and petition, with thanksgiving, present your requests to God. And the peace of God, which transcends all understanding, will guard your hearts and your minds in Christ Jesus" (Philippians 4:6–7, NIV).

"If any of you lacks wisdom, let him ask of God, who gives to all liberally and without reproach, and it will be given to him" (James 1:5).

"But the wisdom that is from above is first pure, then peaceable, gentle, willing to yield, full of mercy and good fruits, without partiality and without hypocrisy" (James 3:17).

"Wives, in the same way be submissive to your husbands so that, if any of them do not believe the word, they may be won over without words by the behavior of their wives, when they see the purity and reverence of your lives. Your beauty should not come from outward adornment, such as braided hair and the wearing of gold jewelry and fine clothes. Instead, it should be that of your inner self, the unfading beauty of a gentle and quiet spirit, which is of great worth in God's sight" (1 Peter 3:1–4, NIV).

MENTAL ILLNESS

Background

Mental illness is a general term commonly used to cover a wide range of psychoneurological disorders. There are those who are truly ill, suffering some type of malfunction due to a brain injury, an inherited illness, or a glandular or chemical imbalance. Such cases should be referred to appropriate trained professionals.

There are, however, many behaviors often classified as mental illness which are the result of unresolved sinful attitudes or conduct. Those affected may display the symptoms of illness, but many times these symptoms are stress-related and due to spiritual problems. At times such people are feigning illness rather than facing the reality of their situation. They will blame other people and circumstances for their problems in order to divert attention from themselves: "Then the man and his wife heard the sound of the Lord God as he was walking in the garden in the cool of the day, and they hid from the Lord God. . . . The man said, 'The woman you put here with me— she gave me some fruit from the tree, and I ate it.' The woman said, 'The serpent deceived me, and I ate'" (Genesis 3:8, 12–13, NIV).

It would be a disservice merely to treat the symptoms or excuse such a person just "because of the way he is." The fact is that he or she will never feel good until he or she corrects the problem. The first step in recovery is to assume personal responsibility for wrong attitudes and actions: "Everything is uncovered and laid bare before the eyes of him to whom we must give account" (Hebrews 4:13, NIV). "So then, each of us will give an account of himself to God" (Romans 14:12, NIV).

Change is possible, if such an individual will face reality and:

- Lay bare his or her life before God.

- Repent of what is wrong in attitudes and actions.

- Confess it to God with the intention of abandoning it in favor of newness of life in Christ Jesus.

Many lives have been redirected through receiving Jesus Christ as Lord and Savior. The power of the Word of God and the ministry of the Holy Spirit, unleashed in a life, have positive effects.

In his "My Answer" column, Billy Graham calls attention to the "multitudes of people who, through God's Word, have become thoroughly integrated persons. Writing to Timothy, the apostle Paul once said: 'For God has not given us the spirit of fear, but of power and of love and of a sound mind' (2 Timothy 1:7)."

Helping Strategy

1. Encourage the inquirer by saying that he or she has called the right place and that you are glad to talk with him or her and to help if you can.

2. Be prepared to listen if the inquirer is willing to talk. Ask questions as needed to stimulate the conversation, hoping that something will emerge to give you the opportunity to suggest a spiritual solution.

3. When you feel the time is opportune, ask if he or she has ever received Christ as Lord and Savior. Share "Steps to Peace with God," page 11. His or her commitment may initiate a new awareness and a new perception which will provide the desire and the motivation for facing the "mental illness" with reality and determination.

4. Encourage Bible reading and study. Offer *Living in Christ,* to help him or her begin study. This discipline will help direct his or her thoughts toward the Lord, which will bring an inner peace (Isaiah 26:3).

5. Encourage daily prayer.

6. Recommend becoming involved in a Bible-teaching church where he or she can worship, enjoy Christian fellowship, and serve Christ.

7. Pray with the inquirer personally that a commitment to Christ might redirect his or her attitudes and actions and produce a life that is pleasing to God. Read Romans 12:1–2, pointing out that by following these principles, he or she can become a whole person.

8. Recommend seeking further counseling with a Christian pastor or psychologist, so that there will be a continuity in the treatment of the problems in the light of Scripture.

If the inquirer is a Christian with unresolved personal problems, share "Restoration," page 17, and then the "Follow-Up Steps."

Scripture

"Oh, the joys of those who do not follow evil men's advice, who do not hang around with sinners, scoffing at the things of God: but they delight in doing everything God wants them to, and day and night are always meditating on his laws and thinking about ways to follow him more closely. For the Lord watches over all the plans and paths of godly men, but the paths of the godless lead to doom" (Psalm 1:1–2, 6, TLB).

"You will keep him in perfect peace, whose mind is stayed on You, because he trusts in You" (Isaiah 26:3).

"The Spirit of the Lord is upon Me, because He has anointed Me to preach the gospel to the poor. He has sent Me to heal the brokenhearted, to proclaim deliverance to the captives and recovery of sight to the blind, to set at liberty those who are oppressed, to preach the acceptable year of the Lord" (Luke 4:18–19).

"Therefore, I urge you, brothers, in view of God's mercy, to offer your bodies as living sacrifices, holy and pleasing to God—this is your spiritual act of worship. Do not conform any longer to the pattern of this world, but be transformed by the renewing of your mind. Then you will be able to test and approve what God's will is—his good, pleasing and perfect will" (Romans 12:1–2, NIV).

"Let this mind be in you which was also in Christ Jesus" (Philippians 2:5).

THE NEW AGE MOVEMENT

Background

Because of its complex and individualistic nature, the New Age Movement is difficult to define. It is not a single organization but a spiritual, political and social network brought together through common interests in occult and pagan beliefs. Though Eastern religions are especially favored by New Agers, all religions are accepted as equal except for Christianity, which teaches only one way to God. New Agers may be involved in such pursuits as extrasensory perception, telepathy, clairvoyance, astral projection, psychokinesis, channeling, astrology, psychic healing, transcendental meditation, and yoga.

To the New Age follower, God is merely an impersonal consciousness or force, a divine essence that is inseparable from the earth and universe. Indeed New Agers see themselves as a part of God, and they seek altered states of consciousness through meditation or hypnosis in order to more fully experience their divine nature.

There is nothing new in the New Age Movement! It is merely the latest expression of humankind's age-old sinful desire to be a god while rejecting "the true God," and Jesus Christ whom He has sent (John 17:3). It is the religion Satan was practicing when he tried to exalt himself to be "like the Most High" (Isaiah 14:12–14, NIV). It is the religion Adam and Eve accepted when Satan convinced them that they, too, could "be like God" (Genesis 3:4–5, NIV).

Needless to say, the New Age Movement is both alien and hostile to Christianity.

Various New Age Beliefs

- *Truth.* Previous ways of thinking are obsolete. New ways of thought are needed to face and resolve the problems of today's world. Truth is strictly subjective, intuitive, and relative. Experience alone is the test of spiritual realities. There is no such thing as verbal or written revelation; because the Bible claims to have God's revealed truth, it is a barrier to spiritual awareness.

New Agers see themselves as open-minded, tolerant, and progressive, while Christians are narrow-minded, intolerant, and repressive. (Of course, the New Ager may be intolerant of Christianity!)

- *Salvation.* The human problem is the inability to experience true identity in cosmic terms. True identity can be reached only through meditation and/or hypnosis when, suddenly, one experiences divinity in a burst of cosmic consciousness.

To the New Ager, sin and death are mere illusions. Consequently, there is no need for the redemptive act of God in Christ. At this point, however, there is a blatant contradiction in the New Age belief system: Some New Agers accept the Hindu doctrines of karma and reincarnation. Karma is the belief that whatever a person does in this life, good or bad, must return to him or her in exact proportions of good or bad. Since most people are unable to "experience" all their bad karma in one lifetime, they are compelled to return in repeated reincarnations until all the bad is overcome by the good. This is an admission of evil in humankind and of the need to resolve it.

(Understood in Christian terms, belief in karma and reincarnation amounts to a belief in salvation by works.)

Through reincarnation, the soul continues to be reborn until "oneness with God" is experienced. This may require millions of reincarnations. It is, of course, incompatible with the biblical teaching that we have only one lifetime to settle accounts with God (Hebrews 9:27).

- *World problems and social concerns.* Many New Age followers seem to be genuinely desirous of coming to grips with the world's vexing problems: inequality, poverty, hunger, crime, disease, the ecology, and the like. Some see the movement as a revolt against the secularism which has left a great spiritual void in our culture.

New Agers generally see pantheism (the belief that God is one with His creation) as the way to "solve" the world's problems: We need to enter a state of "God consciousness" and usher in the "New Age" of enlightenment which will bring prosperity, peace, and harmony to all.

NOTE: In speaking with a New Age follower, the point needs to be made that the true Christian is also interested in the world, and that the church with all its flaws does more than any other entity to alleviate suffering, through its annual gifts of billions of dollars and through its relief agencies which minister worldwide.

Things to Remember in Talking with a New Age Adherent

- Don't underestimate the New Ager by thinking that he or she is ignorant or is living on the fringes of society. Many New Agers are well educated, successful people who believe that there has to be an alternative to the secularism of our times.

- Do not attack with biblical texts or by condemning practices which are at the heart of their beliefs. Your goal is to positively and patiently witness for Jesus Christ and the Gospel.

- Do not assume that the New Ager will understand the meaning of your Christian vocabulary. You may use evangelical words such as *saved, new birth, sin,* or *judgment,* but be prepared to illustrate and explain such terms. Be sure that you also know something about *their* beliefs.

- Don't try to match spiritual experiences with them, such as conversion stories, healings, and the like.

- Seek to make an *objective* presentation of God's truth from the biblical perspective. Though your antagonist will have repudiated the Judeo-Christian concepts as no longer serving our culture, you have no other authority than the Bible. Tolerant people (as New Agers claim to be) owe you a hearing.

- Be patient and prayerful, depending on the Holy Spirit.

Helping Strategy

1. Present God as a person. He is not an essence, a force, or a mere cosmic energy:

    A. He exists: "He who comes to God must believe that He is, and that He is a rewarder of those who diligently seek Him" (Hebrews 11:6).

    B. He exists eternally: "Have you not known? Have you not heard? The everlasting God, the Lord, the Creator of the ends of the earth, neither faints nor is weary. There is no searching of His understanding" (Isaiah 40:28).

    C. He possesses the qualities of a person: He loves (John 3:16; 1 John 4:8), He speaks (Genesis 28:15; 1 Samuel 3:9), He has wisdom and knowledge (Romans 11:33), He acts (Deuteronomy 11:7; Psalm 145:4, 6, 12).

2. Present God as Creator. The New Ager holds a spiritualized concept of evolution, in which only "consciousness," not matter, is of any consequence. State clearly your belief that:

    A. An all-knowing, all-powerful, ever-present God created the universe (Acts 17:24).

    B. He objectively planned and executed His creation as an act independent of Himself. God and the universe are *not* one and the same (Genesis 1:26–27, 31).

C. He independently sustains His creation (Colossians 1:17).

3. Present truth as an objective reality. God reveals Himself to humans in three ways:

A. Through His creation (Genesis 1:1; Romans 1:20).

B. Through the written Word (Romans 10:17; 2 Timothy 3:16; Hebrews 4:12).

C. Through Jesus Christ, His Son (Galatians 4:4; Hebrews 1:1–2).

4. Present salvation as an act of God, who intervened in space and time to redeem us. Show both the human need for salvation, and the fact that it is offered through Jesus Christ:

A. Sin is everything which is against—or fails to conform to—the character of God (Romans 3:9–18; 2 Timothy 3:2–5; 1 John 1:5–6, 10):

(1) Our conduct reveals sin. We do not live up to God's standards (Ecclesiastes 7:20; Romans 3:23).

(2) Our conscience reveals sin (Romans 1:21–23).

(3) God's written Word clarifies for us the true nature of sin (Romans 1:18–19; 3:20; 1 Timothy 1:8–10).

B. Because of sin, judgment and death are inevitable (Acts 17:31; Romans 5:18; Hebrews 9:27). The New Ager may pretend that sin, death, and judgment do not exist; they may make "new rules" in order to avoid fear and guilt, but this doesn't change reality:

(1) If the New Ager denies the concept of "right or wrong" or "good or evil," ask him or her about the New Age acceptance of the Hindu doctrine of karma, which tries to balance the good and evil deeds of one's life.

(2) If there is no sin, how does one explain all the evil in the world?

C. Objectively, it would be impossible to be a participant in a "New Age" or "New World Order" without experiencing a "new life." Something special must transpire in an individual before he or she can pretend to offer a "New Age" for others. Only in the Gospel of Jesus Christ can we find personal transformation, reconciliation with the God-Creator of the universe, and the fulfillment of all those noble goals that we fail to achieve because of our fallen nature (John 3:3; 2 Corinthians 5:17):

(1) Jesus Christ, the Son of God, became incarnate, thus making God *accessible* (John 1:14). Accessibility also makes God

approachable. Because He is approachable, we can enter into a *new relationship* with Him (John 14:6).

(2) Jesus Christ died on the cross, satisfying God's demands for righteousness (2 Corinthians 5:17; 1 Peter 3:18) and reconciling us to God in spite of our broken relationship with Him (2 Corinthians 5:18; Colossians 1:21).

(3) An unconditional commitment to Jesus Christ must be made in order to bring about this new relationship (John 1:12; 5:24; 2 Corinthians 5:17).

(4) At the moment of salvation we are fully restored to God's image, thus satisfying one of mankind's deepest longings:

(a) We were made in God's image (Genesis 1:26; 5:1).

(b) We lost something of that image through the Fall (Genesis 3:1–7; Romans 3:23; 5:12–14; 1 Corinthians 15:22).

(c) We shall be restored in God's image (Psalm 17:15; 1 John 3:1–2).

(5) The Christian message is one of love toward God and others (Matthew 22:37–39; John 15:12, 17; 1 John 4:7–11). Christ has set the example for such unselfish love through His death on the cross.

5. Discuss the bodily resurrection of Jesus Christ as the cornerstone of the Christian faith. He rose physically *never to die again.* He ascended into God the Father's presence and is now the object of our faith:

A. An objective and measurable experience of new life in Christ is possible because of the Resurrection. All of Christianity can be defended because its truth is based on historical events. All we ask of any opponent of the Christian message is to hear and evaluate it as he or she would any serious evidence. Secular records, as well as biblical facts, substantiate the fact that Jesus Christ is alive (Romans 4:25; 6:7–9, 11; 1 Corinthians 15:20)!

B. Christ's death and resurrection not only assure eternal spiritual redemption, but also our own future bodily resurrection (John 14:19; 1 Corinthians 15:19; 2 Corinthians 4:14). The Bible makes no mention of reincarnation.

6. Present God's future kingdom as the legitimate coming "New Age": God is preparing a genuine new age, a perfect world where injustice, selfishness, crime, disease, war, and other forms of inhumanity will be no more. It will be a reign of peace, love, equality, and prosperity to be enjoyed by all the redeemed. It will be a theocracy where Jesus Christ

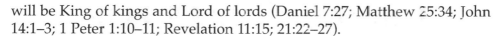

will be King of kings and Lord of lords (Daniel 7:27; Matthew 25:34; John 14:1–3; 1 Peter 1:10–11; Revelation 11:15; 21:22–27).

7. Present "Steps to Peace with God," page 11.

8. Use the "Follow-Up Steps" as indicated.

See also Cults, Demons, The Occult, A Comparison of Christianity with Major Religions and Cults

OBEDIENCE, DESIRE FOR

Background

Each Christian is responsible to determine the will of God for his or her life and then to do it. It is often easier for us to do anything *other than* what we know to be the will of God, deviating from essentials and substituting frenetic activity. But "to obey is better than sacrifice" (1 Samuel 15:22). "My food," said Jesus, "is to do the will of Him who sent Me, and to finish His work" (John 4:34).

> *Billy Graham says: "Only by a life of obedience to the voice of the Spirit, by a daily denying of self, by full dedication to Christ, and by constant fellowship with Him are we enabled to live a godly life and an influential life in this present ungodly world."*

The first step toward a life of obedience is to commit ourselves, once and for all, to obeying God. Joshua said: "As for me and my house, we will serve the Lord" (Joshua 24:15). This once-for-all commitment then leads to a daily presenting of ourselves to the Lord: "Present your bodies a living sacrifice . . . to God, which is your reasonable service" (Romans 12:1).

As we mature in Christ and in the knowledge of His Word, God expects from us an ever-deepening obedience. Even the sufferings and hardships we face should be seen as opportunities to learn greater obedience; Jesus "learned obedience by the things which He suffered" (Hebrews 5:8). As we understand new demands, we must respond immediately and irrevocably so that God can reveal yet deeper levels of His will for our lives. He desires that we bring "every thought into captivity to the obedience of Christ" (2 Corinthians 10:5).

Helping Strategy

1. A person who asks questions about the will of God is a maturing Christian, one who is interested in a deeper walk with God. Commend his or her desire, offering your assurance that God wants to take the person just as far as he or she is willing to obey.

2. Take time to listen to concerns and desires. It may be helpful to refer to some aspect of the "Background" to encourage and guide the person further.

3. Encourage the inquirer to repent of any disobedience or vacillation. Only

as we confess all known sin can we aspire to a deeper commitment.

4. Encourage getting into the Bible. There are no shortcuts in the life of obedience. Our minds must be set always to seek the will of the Lord. Following the progressive discipline revealed through the Bible will result in a walk of obedience to God. We must "hunger and thirst for righteousness" (Matthew 5:6).

5. Pray with the inquirer for the fulfillment of his or her desire to obey God's will.

6. Recommend cultivating fellowship with spiritually minded Christians in a Bible-teaching church, where he or she can learn more of the will and ways of God.

Scripture

"See, I am setting before you today a blessing and a curse—the blessing if you obey the commands of the Lord your God that I am giving you today; the curse if you disobey the commands of the Lord your God and turn from the way that I command you today by following other gods, which you have not known" (Deuteronomy 11:26–28, NIV).

"Has the Lord as great delight in burnt offerings and sacrifices, as in obeying the voice of the Lord? Behold, to obey is better than sacrifice, and to heed than the fat of rams" (1 Samuel 15:22).

"Why do you call Me 'Lord, Lord,' and do not do the things which I say?" (Luke 6:46).

"If you love me, you will obey what I command. . . . Whoever has my commands and obeys them, he is the one who loves me. He who loves me will be loved by my Father, and I too will love him and show myself to him" (John 14:15, 21, NIV).

"But if anyone obeys his word, God's love is truly made complete in him. This is how we know we are in him" (1 John 2:5, NIV).

Other suggested Scriptures:
1 Peter 2:13–16

THE OCCULT

Background

A national newspaper reported that occultism is the most rapidly growing religion in our country. When a spiritual vacuum exists, those who are empty, curious, and gullible are going to fill it with something. Occultism is a disturbing sign of the accelerating disintegration of our culture.

The primary meaning of the word *occult* is "hidden or concealed." The specifically religious definition of the word is somewhat ambiguous, covering a wide range of mystical phenomena. In general, the following religious practices are identified as occult:

Spiritism: The belief that people can make contact with the dead through a medium in order to receive revelations from the spirit world.

Clairvoyance: The belief that certain people possess "extrasensory" powers—the ability to see what cannot be seen by the ordinary five senses.

Fortune-telling: The claim of ability to predict the future by reading tea leaves, palms, tarot cards, and the like.

Astrology: The belief that the future can be foretold by studying the relative positions of the sun, moon, stars, and planets. The "horoscopes" found in local newspapers and other media offer advice based on astrological calculations.

Witchcraft: A "witch" could be defined as a person claiming the ability to contact and utilize powers from the unseen world.

The Bible Forbids Involvement in the Occult

"Let no one be found among you . . . who practices divination or sorcery, interprets omens, engages in witchcraft, or casts spells, or who is a medium or spiritist or who consults the dead. Anyone who does these things is detestable to the Lord" (Deuteronomy 18:10–12, NIV).

"The acts of the sinful nature are obvious: sexual immorality, impurity and debauchery; idolatry and witchcraft; hatred, discord, jealousy, fits of rage, selfish ambition, dissensions, factions and envy; drunkenness, orgies, and the like. I warn you, as I did before, that those who live like this will not inherit the kingdom of God" (Galatians 5:19, NIV).

God was displeased when Saul sought the help of a medium: "Saul died because he was unfaithful to the Lord; he did not keep the word of the

Lord and even consulted a medium for guidance, and did not inquire of the Lord. So the Lord put him to death and turned the kingdom over to David son of Jesse" (1 Chronicles 10:13–14, NIV).

Revelation 21:8 condemns those who practice magic arts. In pronouncing judgment against Babylon in Isaiah 47:11–15, the Lord enumerates a long list of the occult practices of that nation.

From the Scriptural evidence available, we deduce that anything which seeks to detract from an all-knowing, all-powerful, and all-loving God and His purposes for human life is to be rejected.

Helping Strategy
For the Non-Christian:

1. Commend his or her evident desire to know the truth. God's Word has an answer to the occult.

2. Strongly emphasize that any involvement with the occult is displeasing to God (see "Background").

3. Invite him or her to receive Jesus Christ as Lord and Savior. Share "Steps to Peace with God," page 11.

4. Encourage the inquirer to sever all ties with people involved in the occult and to get rid of any literature and paraphernalia on magic and the occult, including horoscopes and Ouija boards.

5. Encourage reading and studying the Bible. Offer *Living in Christ,* explaining its purpose.

6. Encourage seeking fellowship with committed Christians in a Bible-teaching church for worship, Bible study, prayer, and Christian service. Development of new relationships will be a big help in erasing the past.

7. Pray for complete deliverance from the former interest in occult practices and for full commitment to Christ.

For the Christian:

1. Explain that any involvement in the occult displeases God (see "Background").

2. If the inquirer is anxious because of the uncertainties of life, wanting to know the future, offer the assurance that God has promised to "never leave you nor forsake you" (Hebrews 13:5). We are to "seek first the kingdom of God and His righteousness, and all these things shall be added to you" (Matthew 6:33). The Bible tells us that, "No good thing

will He withhold from those who walk uprightly" (Psalm 84:11). We can leave it all with Him (Philippians 4:6)!

3. Encourage the Christian to seek God's forgiveness for his or her involvement. Go over "Restoration," page 17. Also share "Assurance," page 15.

4. Suggest praying especially about the involvement in the occult so that he or she never becomes entangled with it again. Encourage a serious commitment to Bible study. This is a way of redeeming the misspent hours of occult involvement: ". . . redeeming the time, because the days are evil" (Ephesians 5:16). Offer to send *Living in Christ*, which is a great help for Bible study.

5. Encourage the inquirer to seek fellowship with committed Christians and to get involved with a Bible-teaching church for worship, Bible study, prayer, and witnessing. As he or she seeks this new identity, all relationships with friends involved in the occult should be severed, and any books on the occult in his or her possession should be destroyed.

6. Pray with the inquirer for complete deliverance and restoration to the Lord.

Scripture

See "Background." Paul, writing to Timothy, offers understanding about the "spirit of the age" in which we live and advice on how to counteract it:

"But you must realize that in the last days the times will be full of danger. Men will become utterly self-centered, greedy for money, full of big words. They will be proud and abusive, without any regard for what their parents taught them. They will be utterly lacking in gratitude, reverence and normal human affections. They will be remorseless, scandal-mongers, uncontrolled and violent and haters of all that is good. They will be treacherous, reckless and arrogant, loving what gives them pleasure instead of loving God. They will maintain a facade of 'religion' but their life denies truth. Keep clear of people like that. . . . . Their minds are distorted, and they are traitors to the faith. . . . Remember from whom your knowledge has come, and how from early childhood your mind has been familiar with the holy scriptures, which can open the mind to the salvation which comes through believing in Christ Jesus. All scripture is inspired by God and is useful for teaching the faith and correcting error, for resetting the direction of a man's life and training him in good living. The scriptures are the comprehensive equipment of the man of God, and fit him fully for all branches of his work" (2 Timothy 3:1–5, 8, 14–17, PHILLIPS).

PATIENCE, LACK OF

Background

Patience is an admirable character quality that few people, including Christians, seem to possess. According to the Bible, our lives are to be characterized by patience, for it is important in developing the mature, stable character which God wants to produce in His people: "Love is patient, love is kind . . . it is not easily angered" (1 Corinthians 13:4–5, NIV).

Patience is the ability to absorb strain and stress without complaint, to be left undisturbed by obstacles, delays, or failures. God allows difficulties, inconveniences, trials, and even suffering to come our way for a specific purpose: They help develop the right attitude for the growth of patience. As the Christian sees these trials producing beneficial, character-building results, the stage is set for the development of a patient spirit. God the Holy Spirit will then be able to produce the fruit of patience in his or her life: "But the fruit of the Spirit is love, joy, peace, patience . . ." (Galatians 5:22, NIV).

Billy Graham comments on the lack of patience which characterizes our generation: "This is a high-strung, neurotic, impatient age. We hurry when there is no reason to hurry, just to be hurrying. This fast-paced age has produced more problems and less morality than previous generations, and it has given us jangled nerves. Impatience has produced a crop of broken homes, ulcers, and has set the stage for more world wars."

A bit of introspection and analysis with regard to impatience may be revealing and helpful. What makes me impatient?

- Am I immature? Am I petty?

  "But solid food is for the mature, who by constant use have trained themselves to distinguish good from evil" (Hebrews 5:14, NIV).

- Am I selfish, legalistic, or demanding? Am I able to make allowances for the mistakes and imperfections in others, remembering that God is still working on me, too?

  "Be patient with all. See that no one renders evil for evil to anyone, but always pursue what is good both for yourselves and for all" (1 Thessalonians 5:14–15).

- Am I easily irked because "someone is getting away with something"?

"Do not fret because of evildoers" (Psalm 37:1).

- Am I envious or jealous?

"Be patient and stand firm. . . . Don't grumble against each other, brothers, or you will be judged" (James 5:8–9, NIV).

- Am I materialistic? Am I dominated by the spirit of this world?

"If then you were raised with Christ, seek those things which are above" (Colossians 3:1).

- Have I really dealt with the "secular mentality"?

"For I have learned to be content whatever the circumstances" (Philippians 4:11, NIV).

- Do I realize that God permits adverse circumstances, irritations, and stress to buffet me in order that through His grace I might learn to transcend self and grow in love and spiritual stature?

"My brethren, count it all joy when you fall into various trials, knowing that the testing of your faith produces patience. But let patience have its perfect work, that you may be perfect and complete, lacking nothing" (James 1:2–4).

Helping Strategy

1. Tactfully ask the inquirer if he or she has ever received Jesus Christ as Lord and Savior. Explain "Steps to Peace with God," page 11.

2. Encourage the impatient person to:

   A. Admit having a problem. Impatience is sin and should be dealt with.

   B. Identify the areas of impatience and the circumstances that trigger this negative response.

   C. Pray about these circumstances daily:

      (1) Confess the impatience as sin, asking God's forgiveness (1 John 1:9).

      (2) Ask God for sensitivity to this area of failure and for help in bringing it under control.

   D. Resolve to work on the problem:

      (1) Because impatient people seem to be dominated by a mind-set which causes them to respond negatively to irritations, stresses, and provocations, the inquirer should be willing to let God work

in him or her to produce patience. He or she must resolve to bring "every thought into captivity to the obedience of Christ" (2 Corinthians 10:5).

(2) Because impatience is a characteristic of the "old nature" (Colossians 3:9–10), the "put off—put on" principle should be practiced. Impatience is a response that must be "unlearned." Paul says, "But I see another law at work . . . waging war against the law of my mind and making me a prisoner of the law of sin. . . . What a wretched man I am! Who will rescue me from this body of death? Thanks be to God—through Jesus Christ our Lord!" (Romans 7:23–25, NIV). Thus:

- I must renounce my impatience—"put off."

- I must surrender a little more each day as I claim His power in faith—"put off" + "put on" (Galatians 2:20; 2 Timothy 1:7).

- I then claim His victory, His love, and His patience as the fruit of the Spirit—"put on" (1 Corinthians 13:4–5; Galatians 5:22).

E. Request the help of another Christian to monitor your patient vs. impatient responses, recording both victories or failures.

F. Develop the discipline of daily Bible reading and study, Scripture memorization, and prayer.

G. Seek out other Christians of like mind in a Bible-teaching church for fellowship and Bible study.

Scripture

"Rest in the Lord, and wait patiently for Him; do not fret because of him who prospers in his way, because of the man who brings wicked schemes to pass" (Psalm 37:7).

"We also glory in tribulations, knowing that tribulation produces perseverance; and perseverance, character; and character, hope. Now hope does not disappoint . . ." (Romans 5:3–5).

"Love is patient, love is kind. It does not envy, it does not boast, it is not proud. It is not rude, it is not self-seeking, it is not easily angered, it keeps no record of wrongs" (1 Corinthians 13:4–5, NIV).

"I have been crucified with Christ; it is no longer I who live, but Christ lives in me; and the life which I now live in the flesh I live by faith in the Son of God, who loved me and gave Himself for me" (Galatians 2:20).

"But the fruit of the Spirit is love, joy, peace, longsuffering, kindness, goodness, faithfulness, gentleness, self-control. Against such there is no law" (Galatians 5:22–23).

"Be patient, then, brothers, until the Lord's coming. See how the farmer waits for the land to yield its valuable crop and how patient he is for the autumn and spring rains. You too, be patient and stand firm, because the Lord's coming is near. Don't grumble against each other, brothers, or you will be judged. The Judge is standing at the door!" (James 5:7–8, NIV).

Other suggested Scriptures:

Colossians 3:9–10
2 Peter 1:5–9, NIV

PEACE

Background

In our restless age there is a worldwide longing for peace. The book *Peace with God* by Billy Graham has sold millions of copies in many languages, an indication of this longing. In some languages, such as Arabic and Hebrew, the standard greeting is "peace." But only as Jesus Christ possesses our hearts can we know true peace. In this section, we shall deal with two aspects of peace.

Peace with God:

Peace with God comes to us in the forgiveness of sin through the merit and suffering of Jesus Christ.

Peace with God means a cessation of our hostility toward Him. When a person confesses his or her sinful pride, admits defeat, and submits to God, the war with Him is over: "Therefore, having been justified by faith, we have peace with God through our Lord Jesus Christ" (Romans 5:1).

Peace with God means reconciliation with Him. We are no longer alienated: "And you, who once were alienated and enemies in your mind by wicked works, yet now He has reconciled in the body of His flesh through death, to present you holy, and blameless, and irreproachable in His sight" (Colossians 1:21–22).

". . . to reconcile all things to Himself, by Him, whether things on earth or things in heaven, having made peace through the blood of His cross" (Colossians 1:20).

"That God was reconciling the world to himself in Christ, not counting men's sins against them" (2 Corinthians 5:19, NIV).

Peace with God brings a sense of well-being and confidence: "May the God of hope fill you with all joy and peace as you trust in him, so that you may overflow with hope by the power of the Holy Spirit" (Romans 15:13, NIV).

The Peace of God:

The peace of God is the legacy of Christian believers and comes as we walk in obedience to His will for our lives. Many Christians have peace with God but have never gone on to experience the peace *of* God in their lives. They are torn with anxieties and fears that destroy their spiritual stability and joy. Peace is a gift from God and the rightful legacy of all believers, but far too many do not enjoy it. The peace of God flows from a full, unhindered fellowship with Him who is our peace.

Here is a simple formula from the Bible for enjoying the peace of God:

Psalm 37:1–5 tells us:

1. Do not fret (verse 1)

2. Trust in the Lord (verse 3)

3. Delight yourself in the Lord (verse 4)

Philippians 4:6–7 tells us:

1. Be anxious for nothing (verse 6)

2. Be prayerful in everything (verse 6)

3. Be thankful for anything (verse 6)

4. And you will have peace (verse 7)

Helping Strategy

For the Non-Christian:

1. Explain "Steps to Peace with God," page 11.

2. Encourage the caller to take a firm stand for Christ and to get into the Bible by reading and studying it daily. Offer to send *Living in Christ*.

3. Encourage becoming involved in a Bible-teaching church for fellowship, worship, Bible study, and prayer.

4. Pray with the inquirer that the peace of God may be generously experienced.

For the Christian:

Probe gently for unconfessed sin, worry, or emotional problems. Then:

1. Encourage confessing any known sin, wrong, irritation, anger, or bitterness that might be blocking a full experience of the peace of God.

2. Share thoughts from the "Background" on the peace of God.

3. Suggest developing a daily devotional life as a means of "delighting in the Lord" and experiencing His peace. The person should:

A. Read and study the Bible daily. Offer to send *Living in Christ*.

    B. Pray about everything, trusting God to work according to Romans 8:28.

    C. Daily commit his or her life into God's hands in the spirit of Proverbs 3:5–6.

4. Recommend that the inquirer get involved in a Bible-teaching church for fellowship, worship, prayer, Bible study, and opportunities for service.

5. Pray with the inquirer for God's peace, victory, and joy.

Scripture

Psalm 34:14
Isaiah 26:3
John 14:27
John 16:33
Romans 8:6, NIV

PORNOGRAPHY

Background

Pornography can be described as visual images, writing, or speech that is used for the purpose of arousing lustful sexual desires. The term derives from two Greek words: *porne* ("prostitute") and *graphein* ("to write"). Pornographic material comes not only in various media but in varying degrees of "taste," from titillating photos and writings to the most grotesquely immoral and perverted materials.

Pornography is both a symptom and a cause of the widespread immorality and corruption of modern society. It reaches people of all age levels through a multibillion-dollar industry including movies, books and magazines, videos for home use or for viewing in hotel rooms, and phone messages available to children as well as adults. The subject matter of these pornographic media include every imaginable perversion: homosexuality, rape, incest, sadism, bestiality, bisexuality, and the sexual exploitation of children.

The Real Problem with Pornography:

It Is Deceptive.

The vivid descriptions and the airbrushed photos and movies of naked women and men are a fantasy. Pornography purposely diverts sex from its intended meaning; it does not enhance natural sexual appetites or satisfaction, but rather desensitizes them. It is often an attempt by the user to heal wounds caused by loneliness, rejection, isolation, and the pain of being unable to measure up to expectations.

It Is Corrupting.

Pornography leads inevitably to lust, which warps an individual's perception of self and sexuality. Respect and self-esteem plunge while guilt escalates. Normal marital relationships often dissolve through disinterest or conflict. For some users, pornography leads to deviant sexual behavior and sex crimes.

It Leads to Addiction.

What begins as a simple incursion into the fantasy world of sex can lead to obsession. As in drugs and alcohol, prolonged and uncontrolled use will have a degenerative and progressive effect on the mind and morals of the user. One's goals become reduced to sexual gratification by whatever means. The user becomes dependent upon increasingly racy material to satisfy mental and physical demands.

It Is Spiritually Deadening.

Pornography desensitizes and corrupts moral and spiritual values; pornography and spirituality cannot coexist:

> "For the flesh lusts against the Spirit, and the Spirit against the flesh; and these are *contrary* to one another, so that you do not do the things that you wish" (Galatians 5:17).

Lust alienates from God.

> "For to be carnally minded is death, but to be spiritually minded is life and peace" (Romans 8:6).

> "Do you not know that the unrighteous will not inherit the kingdom of God? Do not be deceived. . . . Now the body is not for sexual immorality but for the Lord, and the Lord for the body. . . . Flee sexual immorality. Every sin that a man does is outside the body, but he who commits sexual immorality sins against his own body" (1 Corinthians 6:9, 13, 18).

Lust must be avoided.

> "Do not let sin reign in your mortal body, that you should obey it in its lusts" (Romans 6:12).

> "Flee sexual immorality" (1 Corinthians 6:18).

Lust ends in spiritual death.

> "For if you live according to the flesh you will die; but if by the Spirit you put to death the deeds of the body, you will live" (Romans 8:13).

> "Then, when desire has conceived, it gives birth to sin; and sin, when it is full-grown, brings forth death" (James 1:15).

Helping Strategy

1. Commend the person for seeking help in matters beyond his or her control. Express your willingness to encourage and help as you can.

2. Because pornography is mainly a spiritual and moral problem, the inquirer must seek deliverance from personal sins and immoral sexual behaviors:

A. If the person is not a Christian, invite him or her to receive Jesus Christ as Lord and Savior. Share "Steps to Peace with God," page 11.

Explain that involvement in lust through pornography is often an attempt on the part of the user to solve his or her problems of loneliness, isolation, pain, or guilt. It is an attempt to play God, creating his or her own world through fantasy. Jesus bore our sins and our sorrows. We must cast all our anxieties and cares on Him (1 Peter 5:7).

B. It is surprising to discover just how many Christians, including pastors and leaders, are involved in some phase of pornography and its consequences. Providing help and healing for your inquirer will depend on the type of addiction and the level of involvement.

The person may have been agonizing over the addiction for years. Assure the person of our sympathy and desire to encourage and be of help. We do not sit in judgment and will prayerfully suggest a possible procedure.

3. The individual must accept the full weight of the problem:

A. Frankly face the truth of addiction to lust through pornography.

B. Boldly confront the problem with the Lord's help—without denial, rationalizations, or minimizing.

C. Take responsibility for immediate action. This means to stop feeding the addiction:

(1) Destroy all pornographic materials.

(2) Immediately stop visits to all places of temptation, such as pornographic movies, adult bookstores, or video rental stores.

(3) Sever any relationships that have encouraged the addiction.

4. Begin a serious effort to build or rebuild a godly life. Full and ultimate freedom and restoration will demand a sincere commitment to seeking God:

"As the deer pants for the water brooks, so pants my soul for You, O God. My soul thirsts for God, for the living God" (Psalm 42:1–2).

"And you will seek Me and find Me, when you search for Me with all your heart" (Jeremiah 29:13) (see also Mark 9:29; Philippians 3:7–17).

Godliness can be found as one submits to Christ's lordship through the disciplines of:

A. Prayer:

(1) Daily confession of all known sin (1 John 1:7, 9). Until truly experiencing deliverance from the lust and addiction to pornography, special attention should be given to confession (Psalm 51; Mark 7:20–22; 1 John 1:7).

(2) Daily renunciation of conformity to the world in all its forms (Romans 12:2; 6:13–14).

(3) Cultivation of an intimate relationship with Christ (John 10:10; 15:5–7; Ephesians 3:14–19; Philippians 3:10–14).

(4) A daily offering up of one's body as a "living sacrifice" to God (Romans 12:1; 1 Corinthians 6:19–20).

(5) Worship and praise in prayer (John 4:23–24; Philippians 3:3; Revelation 4:8–11).

(6) Thanksgiving (Philippians 4:6–7; Colossians 4:2).

(7) Supplication or petition (Philippians 4:6–7; Hebrews 4:16).

B. The Word of God:

In a battle to gain renewal and transformation of the mind, one must commit oneself to the reading, study, and memorization of the Bible (Romans 8:7; 12:2; 2 Corinthians 10:3–6).

C. Dependence on the Holy Spirit (Romans 8:26–27; 1 Corinthians 6:19–20).

D. Seeking fellowship with God (Philippians 3:10–14).

5. Establish fellowship links with spiritually minded Christians, which will mean:

A. Becoming actively involved in a Christ-centered church.

B. Burning bridges or links to the past—the surrender of all previous relationships and the cultivation of new ones.

6. Set up a network of accountability, making oneself subject to a mature Christian (not always a pastor) or group of Christians to whom the person can report on a regular basis so that spiritual progress may be monitored. Interfacing with such a person or group will supply encouragement and spiritual guidance. NOTE: It is at this point that spiritual pride, renewed denial, and rationalization are likely to be a problem.

7. It might be advisable to recommend that your inquirer seek the professional help of a Christian psychologist or psychiatrist who follows biblical principles of counseling. The addiction to lust and pornography may have its roots in the pain of a wounded childhood or dysfunctional family. A more in-depth treatment may be indicated in order to rebuild communication and relationships with a spouse or family.

PRAYER

Background

Prayer has a place of highest priority in the Bible. Some of the Scriptures' most transcendent passages deal with prayers expressing praise, worship, thanksgiving, confession, and supplication. The lives of the outstanding people of God of both the Old and New Testaments, and down through the history of the church, were characterized by much prayer. All the recorded revivals of history had their beginnings in prayer. Anything of value in the kingdom of God is initiated in and dependent on prayer.

The Bible reveals our ignorance of prayer:

> "We do not know what we should pray for as we ought, but the Spirit Himself makes intercession for us with groanings which cannot be uttered" (Romans 8:26).

> "When you pray, do not use vain repetitions as the heathen do. For they think that they will be heard for their many words" (Matthew 6:7).

The Bible invites us, actually commands us, to pray:

> "In everything by prayer and supplication, with thanksgiving, let your requests be made known to God" (Philippians 4:6).

> "Let us therefore come boldly to the throne of grace, that we may obtain mercy and find grace to help in time of need" (Hebrews 4:16).

> "Pray without ceasing" (1 Thessalonians 5:17).

The Bible offers many guidelines for praying:

1. Through individual promises (there are hundreds of recorded promises in the Bible):

> "But you, when you pray, go into your room, and when you have shut your door, pray to your Father who is in the secret place; and your Father who sees in secret will reward you openly" (Matthew 6:6).

> "Ask, and you will receive, that your joy may be full" (John 16:24).

> "If you abide in Me, and My words abide in you, you will ask what you desire, and it shall be done for you" (John 15:7).

> "And my God shall supply all your need according to His riches in glory by Christ Jesus" (Philippians 4:19).

2. Through the prayers of Christ:

- The Lord's Prayer (Matthew 6:6–14; Luke 11:1–4)

- His prayer for His own (John 17)

- His prayer at Lazarus' tomb (John 11:41–45)

- His prayer at His Transfiguration (Luke 9:28–36)

- His prayer in the Garden of Gethsemane (Matthew 26:36–46)

- His prayers from the cross (Matthew 27:46; Luke 23:34, 46)

3. Through the prayers of the great spiritual leaders of the Bible:

- Abraham's servant's prayer and God's answer (Genesis 24:12–66)

- Jacob's prayer for deliverance from Esau and God's answer (Genesis 32:9–33:16)

- Moses' prayer for God's presence and glory (Exodus 33:12–23)

- Joshua's prayer of despair and God's answer (Joshua 7:6–26)

- Hannah's prayer and vow, and God's answer (1 Samuel 1:1–28)

- Elijah's prayer and God's answer (1 Kings 18:41–46; see James 5:17–18)

- Hezekiah's prayer and God's answer (2 Kings 19:14–37)

- David's thanksgiving and prayer for his people and for his son (1 Chronicles 29:10–19)

- Solomon's prayer at the temple dedication and God's answer (2 Chronicles 6:12–42)

- David's prayer of repentance and confession (Psalm 51)

- Other prayers, thanksgiving, and praise in the book of Psalms

- Paul's prayer for knowledge and wisdom (Ephesians 1:15–23)

- Paul's prayer for believers (Ephesians 3:14–21)

- Paul's exhortation to Timothy (1 Timothy 2:1–8)

Billy Graham emphasizes prayer: "The Bible says, 'Pray without ceasing!'
(1 Thessalonians 5:17). This means that we must be always ready to pray. Prayer is like
a child's communion with a father. Because the Christian is one who has been born into

the family of God, it is as natural to pray as it is for an earthly child to ask his or her father for the things he or she needs. We are living in dangerous times; and if there was ever a time when we needed to pray, it's now. Because more can be done by prayer than anything else, prayer is our greatest weapon."

Helping Strategy

Many people ask for prayer because they have specific concerns but do not know how to pray and what language to use in approaching God. We should be ready to offer encouragement and to pray with them about their requests. Reassure them that you are delighted to share their concerns, because God knows about them. He cares and has promised to answer prayer.

1. One prayer that delights God's heart is the sinner's prayer: "God be merciful to me a sinner!" (Luke 18:13). Do not assume that because the caller has requested prayer that he or she is a Christian. Assure the individual that you are concerned and are happy to take his or her request to God. However, before doing so, you would like to ask if he or she has ever received Jesus Christ as Savior and Lord. If appropriate, present "Steps to Peace with God," page 11, and then the "Follow-Up Steps."

2. Just before praying for the expressed need, encourage the individual by reading these two prayer promises from the Bible:

    "And all things, whatever you ask in prayer, believing, you will receive" (Matthew 21:22).

    "If two of you agree on earth concerning anything that they ask, it will be done for them by My Father in heaven" (Matthew 18:19). (Suggest that the person write down the references for later reading.)

3. Pray the fervent prayer of faith, and then thank God for the answer.

4. Sometimes a Christian will complain that God does not seem to answer his or her prayers. Encourage such a person to continue praying in faith, being persistent like the woman in Luke 18:1–5. Also, advise being sure that the motives for the prayer are pure, according to James 4:3.

Billy Graham offers some suggestions for Christians with unanswered prayers:

"1. Prayer is for God's children.

2. *Effectual prayer is offered in faith. The Bible says, 'Therefore I say to you, whatever things you ask when you pray, believe that you receive them, and you will have them' (Mark 11:24).*

3. *Dynamic prayer emanates from an obedient heart. The Bible says whatever we ask, we receive of him.*

4. *We are to pray in Christ's name. Jesus said, 'And whatever you ask in My name, that I will do, that the Father may be glorified in the Son' (John 14:13). We are not worthy to approach the holy throne of God except through our advocate, Jesus Christ.*

5. *We must desire the will of God. Even our Lord, contrary to His own wish at the moment, said, 'O My Father, if this cup cannot pass away from Me unless I drink it, Your will be done' (Matthew 26:42).*

6. *Our prayer must be for God's glory. The model prayer which Jesus has given to us concludes with, 'Yours is the kingdom and the power and the glory' (Matthew 6:13). If we are to have our prayers answered, we must give God the glory."*

Scripture
Encouragement to Pray:

"When you pray, go into your room, close the door and pray to your Father, who is unseen. Then your Father, who sees what is done in secret, will reward you. And when you pray, do not keep on babbling like pagans, for they think they will be heard because of their many words. Do not be like them, for your Father knows what you need before you ask him" (Matthew 6:6–8, NIV).

"And pray in the Spirit on all occasions with all kinds of prayers and requests. With this in mind, be alert and always keep on praying for all the saints" (Ephesians 6:18, NIV).

"Let us therefore come boldly to the throne of grace, that we may obtain mercy and find grace to help in time of need" (Hebrews 4:16).

Prayer Promises:

"Ask, and it will be given to you; seek, and you will find; knock, and it will be opened to you. For everyone who asks receives, and he who seeks finds, and to him who knocks it will be opened" (Luke 11:9–10).

"And I will do whatever you ask in my name, so that the Son may bring glory to the Father. You may ask me for anything in my name, and I will do it" (John 14:13–14, NIV).

"If you abide in Me, and My words abide in you, you will ask what you desire, and it shall be done for you" (John 15:7).

"In him and through faith in him we may approach God with freedom and confidence" (Ephesians 3:12, NIV).

How to Pray:

"This, then, is how you should pray: 'Our Father in heaven, hallowed be your name, your kingdom come, your will be done on earth as it is in heaven. Give us today our daily bread. Forgive us our debts, as we also have forgiven our debtors. And lead us not into temptation, but deliver us from the evil one'" (Matthew 6:9–13, NIV).

"I want men everywhere to lift up holy hands in prayer, without anger or disputing" (1 Timothy 2:8, NIV).

PROPHECY

Background

Prophecy, the prediction of future events, plays a key role in the Bible. Its pages record both the giving of prophecies and their fulfillment. Many prophecies given in Old Testament times were fulfilled in New Testament times in the life and work of Christ. As someone has said, "The New is in the Old concealed; the Old is in the New revealed."

Bible prophets often accurately predicted events decades or even centuries before they occurred. Much of the prophecy in the Bible has already been fulfilled. Other prophecies are being fulfilled even in our day.

Peter declares the Bible's prophets to be divinely inspired: "We also have the prophetic word made more sure, which you do well to heed as a light that shines in a dark place, until the day dawns and the morning star rises in your hearts; knowing this first, that no prophecy of Scripture is of any private interpretation, for prophecy never came by the will of man, but holy men of God spoke as they were moved by the Holy Spirit" (2 Peter 1:19–21).

Prophets foretell future events. The Bible also describes as prophets those who "forth tell" or boldly declare God's will to His people. Nathan the prophet confronted David about his sin (2 Samuel 12). Prophets, along with evangelists and pastors, have a role of edification in the church (Ephesians 4:11).

Prophecy Fulfilled

The most convincing evidence of fulfilled prophecy concerns the person and work of Jesus Christ, as recorded in the four gospels. Lack of space precludes the listing of all such prophecies. The following, however, constitute powerful evidence:

- Christ would be descended from King David's family (Psalm 89:3–4; Isaiah 9:6–7; 11:1; see Mark 12:36; John 7:42).
- He would be born of a virgin (Isaiah 7:14; see Matthew 1:23).
- He would be born in Bethlehem (Micah 5:2; see John 7:42).
- He would make a triumphant entry into Jerusalem (Zechariah 9:9; see Matthew 21:5).
- The soldiers would cast lots for His garments (Psalm 22:18; see Matthew 27:35).

- His dying words were foretold (Psalm 22:1; see Matthew 27:46).

- He would die with criminals (Isaiah 53:9, 12; see Luke 22:37).

- His death would be for the salvation of mankind (Isaiah 53:6; see 1 Corinthians 15:3).

- He would rise from the dead the third day (Psalm 16:10). Jesus confirmed the Resurrection by referring to past Scriptures (Luke 24:46); Peter confirmed it by quoting David's prophecy (Acts 2:25–32).

Prophecy to Be Fulfilled

The prophecies yet to be fulfilled largely concern the return of Jesus Christ. "This hope," says the writer of Hebrews, "we have as an anchor of the soul, both sure and steadfast" (Hebrews 6:19).

Billy Graham writes: "The importance of the hope of Christ's return is established by the frequency, extent, and intensity of its mention in the Bible. It is mentioned in all but four books of the New Testament. Christ referred constantly to His return, not only to His disciples, but to others as well. He said to the high priest, 'Hereafter you will see the Son of Man sitting at the right hand of the Power, and coming on the clouds of heaven' (Matthew 26:64).

"One out of every thirty verses in the Bible mentions this subject. There are 318 references to it in 216 chapters of the New Testament. One-twentieth of the entire New Testament deals with this subject. It was predicted by most of the Old Testament writers: by Moses (Deuteronomy 33:2), by Job (Job 19:25), by David (Psalm 102:16), by Isaiah (Isaiah 59:20), by Jeremiah (Jeremiah 23:5), by Daniel (Daniel 7:13–14), by Zechariah (Zechariah 14:4), and by many others."

There are differing views concerning future prophecies. Instead of arguing about them, let us remember that "no prophecy of Scripture is of any private interpretation" (2 Peter 1:20). We believe, however, that the so-called "premillennial" view offers the most comprehensive explanation of coming events. According to this view:

1. Christ's coming is imminent: It could occur at any time (Matthew 24:42–44; 1 Corinthians 15:52; Revelation 22:12).

2. The first stage of His coming is known as the "Rapture": "We believe that Jesus died and rose again and so we believe that God will bring with Jesus those who have fallen asleep in him. . . . For the Lord himself will come down from heaven, with a loud command, with the voice of the archangel and with the trumpet call of God, and the dead in Christ will

rise first. After that, we who are still alive and are left will be caught up together with them in the clouds to meet the Lord in the air. And so we will be with the Lord forever" (1 Thessalonians 4:14, 16–17, NIV; see also Titus 2:13). This is the first resurrection (1 Corinthians 15:52–57; 2 Corinthians 5:4; 1 John 3:2).

3. Next comes the judgment seat of Christ for believers (2 Corinthians 5:10). Believers will be judged for their faithfulness in life and service (1 Corinthians 3:11–15; 4:1–5). But they will not be judged for their sins. That was taken care of at Calvary (2 Corinthians 5:21).

4. The Great Tribulation period comes next (Daniel 12:1; Matthew 24:21, 29; Revelation 7:14); and the "man of sin" (Antichrist) will be manifested (2 Thessalonians 2:3, 4, 8; Revelation 13:1–10).

5. Christ returns (second stage) as King of kings and Lord of lords (Revelation 19:11–16). The decisive Battle of Armageddon takes place (Joel 3:12; Revelation 16:16; 19:17–21).

6. The Millennium (Christ's thousand-year reign) will follow (Revelation 20:4–6).

7. A second resurrection will bring together all who have rejected Christ throughout the ages. They will be judged "according to their works, by the things which [are] written in the books" (Revelation 20:12), at the Great White Throne judgment, "And anyone not found written in the Book of Life [will be] cast into the lake of fire" (Revelation 20:15).

8. Finally, those who have been redeemed through faith in Christ will begin their everlasting life in the "new heaven and new earth" (Revelation 21–22).

Helping Strategy
For One Fearful of Future Events:

The only way to be confident and secure about the future is to commit our life to Him who holds the future: "This hope we have as an anchor of the soul, both sure and steadfast" (Hebrews 6:19). Explain "Steps to Peace with God," page 11.

For the Christian Uncertain About Christ's Coming:

1. Reassure the believer that we can be enlightened and certain about both the present and the future. Paul said, "Brothers, we do not want you to be ignorant about those who fall asleep, or to grieve like the rest of men,

who have no hope" (1 Thessalonians 4:13, NIV).

2. Share "Assurance," page 15, also emphasizing 1 John 5:13.

3. Encourage the inquirer to get into Bible reading and study and to become involved with a Bible-teaching church where he or she can learn about "rightly dividing the word of truth" (2 Timothy 2:15). Suggest purchasing good books about the Christian life and witnessing, as well as Bible studies on prophecy.

For the Christian Concerned About His or Her Standing Before God:

1. Ask questions concerning where he or she went astray.

2. Invite him or her back to Calvary for confession and forgiveness on the basis of 1 John 1:9 and 2:1. Share "Restoration," page 17.

3. Encourage taking a firm stand for the Lord by:

- Getting involved in Bible reading and study

- Seeking fellowship in a Bible-teaching church

- Actively witnessing both by word and by example

Taking these steps should give the insecure Christian a greater assurance in Christ and a better understanding of God's will for his or her life.

Scripture

The First Stage of His Coming, The Rapture:

"Brothers, we do not want you to be ignorant about those who fall asleep, or to grieve like the rest of men, who have no hope. We believe that Jesus died and rose again and so we believe that God will bring with Jesus those who have fallen asleep in him. According to the Lord's own word, we tell you that we who are still alive, who are left till the coming of the Lord, will certainly not precede those who have fallen asleep. For the Lord himself will come down from heaven, with a loud command, with the voice of the archangel and with the trumpet call of God, and the dead in Christ will rise first. After that, we who are still alive and are left will be caught up together with them in the clouds to meet the Lord in the air. And so we will be with the Lord forever. Therefore encourage each other with these words" (1 Thessalonians 4:13–17, NIV).

"Dear friends, now we are children of God, and what we will be has not yet been made known. But we know that when he appears, we shall be like him, for we shall see him as he is. Everyone who has this hope in him purifies himself, just as he is pure" (1 John 3:2, NIV).

The Second Stage of His Coming, The Day of the Lord:

"In my vision at night I looked, and there before me was one like a son of man, coming with the clouds of heaven. He approached the Ancient of Days and was led into his presence. He was given authority, glory and sovereign power; all peoples, nations and men of every language worshiped him. His dominion is an everlasting dominion that will not pass away, and his kingdom is one that will never be destroyed" (Daniel 7:13–14, NIV).

"But the day of the Lord will come like a thief. The heavens will disappear with a roar; the elements will be destroyed by fire, and the earth and everything in it will be laid bare. . . . But in keeping with his promise we are looking forward to a new heaven and a new earth, the home of righteousness" (2 Peter 3:10, 13, NIV).

The Attitude of the Believer in Light of His Coming:

"Whoever is ashamed of Me and My words in this adulterous and sinful generation, of him the Son of Man also will be ashamed when He comes in the glory of His Father with the holy angels" (Mark 8:38).

"Preach the Word; be prepared in season and out of season; correct, rebuke and encourage—with great patience and careful instruction. For the time will come when men will not put up with sound doctrine. Instead, to suit their own desires, they will gather around them a great number of teachers to say what their itching ears want to hear. They will turn their ears away from the truth and turn aside to myths. But you, keep your head in all situations, endure hardship, do the work of an evangelist, discharge all the duties of your ministry" (2 Timothy 4:2–5, NIV).

"These have come so that your faith—of greater worth than gold, which perishes even though refined by fire—may be proved genuine and may result in praise, glory and honor when Jesus Christ is revealed. . . . Therefore prepare your minds for action; be self-controlled; set your hope fully on the grace to be given you when Jesus Christ is revealed" (1 Peter 1:7, 13, NIV).

"The end of all things is near. Therefore be clear minded and self-controlled so that you can pray. Above all, love each other deeply, because love covers

over a multitude of sins. Offer hospitality to one another without grumbling. Each one should use whatever gift he has received to serve others, faithfully administering God's grace in its various forms" (1 Peter 4:7–8, NIV).

PROSPERITY OF THE UNRIGHTEOUS

Background

More than 3,000 years ago, a humble but envious singer-priest of Israel went into God's sanctuary deeply troubled over the apparent prosperity, freedom from care, arrogance, indifference, and power of his unrighteous neighbors. "Why do I even bother to seek after righteousness?" Asaph wondered. "Why do I bother to keep my heart pure? It hardly seems worth the effort, when they prosper and I don't!" (See Psalm 73.)

In answer to his questions, the Lord showed Asaph that appearances are often deceiving, and that God has truly reserved the best for those who are faithful to Him. The prosperous wicked have their rewards, such as they are, during this lifetime; but they will perish in their unfaithfulness.

Some Christians are bothered by observing the apparent prosperity and success of non-Christians while they themselves face all kinds of hardships.

Helping Strategy

After patiently listening to the inquirer who registers this sort of complaint, reassure him or her of your interest and concern. This is an area that troubles many of the Lord's people. Express that you are glad to share what you can, and hope it will be an encouragement. Discuss the following considerations:

1. Prosperity doesn't necessarily indicate God's blessing. Wealth is in many cases ill-gotten and amassed at the expense of others. There are, however, many wealthy Christians who are thoroughly committed to Christ and attribute their wealth to the blessing of God. They joyfully support the Lord's work as faithful stewards, while many wealthy nonbelievers are simply enjoying "the passing pleasures of sin" (Hebrews 11:25).

2. The inquirer is not accountable to God for the excesses of the rich, so he or she shouldn't assume this responsibility. God will deal with them in His own time and in His own way. Remember, God keeps the records, both theirs and ours!

3. Encourage him or her to avoid being envious or bitter, not coveting what another has. He or she must not become immersed in self-pity. Such thoughts are displeasing to God and will destroy a person's spiritual life. Remember that most of the world's Christians are poor—if the inquirer is

a poor Christian, he or she is in good company! "God [has] chosen the poor of this world to be rich in faith" (James 2:5).

4. The caller should be objective in evaluating wealthy people. Why do they have so much? Do they have a better education or special skills he or she doesn't have? Have they taken better advantage of their opportunities than he or she has? Did they inherit their wealth? Be sure he or she does not accuse all wealthy people of "getting all the good breaks" in life, or of having gotten rich at the expense of others.

5. Recommend renewing his or her own vows of faithfulness to God, determining to love and serve Him whatever the cost. Job said, "Though He slay me, yet will I trust Him" (Job 13:15). We must seek to be rich in faith; it is faith, not riches, that pleases God (Hebrews 11:6).

6. Encourage praying about material needs and learning to trust God to supply them. Paul said, "I know what it is to be in need, and I know what it is to have plenty. I have learned the secret of being content in any and every situation, whether well fed or hungry, whether living in plenty or in want. I can do everything through him who gives me strength" (Philippians 4:12–13, NIV).

7. Encourage the person to continue faithful in the giving of financial resources. This will keep him or her in tune with God's eternal purposes and will bear witness to a committed heart.

Scripture

"Wealth and honor come from you; you are the ruler of all things. In your hands are strength and power to exalt and give strength to all" (1 Chronicles 29:12, NIV).

"For what will it profit a man if he gains the whole world, and loses his own soul?" (Mark 8:36).

"Then he [Jesus] said to them, 'Watch out! Be on your guard against all kinds of greed; a man's life does not consist in the abundance of his possessions'" (Luke 12:15, NIV).

"But God said to him, 'You fool! This very night your life will be demanded from you. Then who will get what you have prepared for yourself?' This is how it will be with anyone who stores up things for himself but is not rich toward God. . . . But seek his kingdom, and these things will be given to you as well. . . . For where your treasure is, there your heart will be also" (Luke 12:20–21, 31, 34, NIV).

Other suggested Scriptures:
Joshua 1:8

REDEDICATION

Background

The Christian helper may have the privilege of praying with another Christian who wishes to rededicate his or her life to Christ. This rededication is usually sought by one who has already received Christ as Savior and Lord, but who seeks a deeper dimension in living for Him.

The desire to rededicate one's life could be based on any of several motivations:

- A lack of fulfillment, perhaps described as a feeling that "there must be more to the Christian life than I have experienced thus far."

- A search for freedom from sin and guilt, because of carelessness in daily repentance and confession.

- A desire to better know the will of God for one's life.

Helping Strategy

1. Permit the inquirer to express fully his or her motive in seeking rededication. The helper who is personally experienced in the will and ways of God will be able to ask relevant questions which will help to focus on the real issue.

2. Commend him or her! Our desire to commit our all to God pleases Him and is rewarded by Him (Hebrews 11:6; James 4:7–8).

3. If indicated, urge the inquirer to confess all known sin and to trust God for cleansing (Hebrews 9:14; 1 John 1:9).

4. Encourage total submission to God in an act of complete obedience, citing Romans 12:1–2 and Ephesians 5:15.

5. Encourage seeking the fullness of the Holy Spirit, citing Ephesians 5:18 and Ephesians 3:16–19.

6. Stress reading the Bible daily, studying and memorizing Scripture passages in a planned and disciplined way (Psalm 119:9, 11, and Colossians 3:16).

7. Focus on making prayer a daily exercise (1 Thessalonians 5:17; Ephesians 6:18–19).

8. Recommend that the inquirer be a witness for Christ on a daily basis:

A. In actions (Ephesians 2:10).

B. In word (Romans 1:16; Philippians 2:16).

9. Ask the inquirer to pray, making a commitment in the light of the above. Then, pray with the inquirer that his or her life may become a daily walk with Christ, resulting in opportunities for service.

Scripture

Joshua 24:15
1 Samuel 15:22
Psalm 43:4
Psalm 107:8–9
Matthew 6:33
Matthew 22:37–38
2 Corinthians 10:5
Philippians 1:6, 9–11
1 Thessalonians 5:23–24
1 Peter 2:11–12

REMARRIAGE

Background

For the Christian, divorce is not an option. The couple promised before God and witnesses that the union of their two lives would be "till death do us part." Paul says: "To the married I give this command (not I, but the Lord): A wife must not separate from her husband. But if she does, she must remain unmarried or else be reconciled to her husband. And a husband must not divorce his wife" (1 Corinthians 7:10, NIV).

There are, however, mitigating circumstances indicated in Scripture: When the Christian's mate is guilty of sexual immorality, such as adultery or homosexual behavior, and refuses to repent and change his or her behavior (Matthew 19:9); when one mate deserts the other (1 Corinthians 7:15).

In both of these exceptional situations, the Bible encourages forgiveness and restoration as the more honorable course. But if no solution can be found on these grounds, then divorce may be an option.

However, the believer who has divorced in these circumstances faces a dilemma when considering remarriage. It would seem that if divorce is permitted in such situations, remarriage would be an option as well. Yet, while many pastors take this position, others do not, all appealing to Scripture.

Helping Strategy

You may face any number of variations of the divorce situations mentioned in the "Background." Try to follow these guidelines:

For the Non-Christian:

1. The first matter of concern to be faced is not remarriage but putting oneself within the circle of the will of God. When a person does this, he or she will have a perspective on himself or herself, and on remarriage, that would never have been there otherwise (Matthew 6:33).

   Ask if he or she has ever received Jesus Christ as Lord and Savior. Explain "Steps to Peace with God," page 11.

2. Encourage the inquirer to begin reading and studying the Bible.

3. Urge him or her to learn to pray and to practice prayer daily, seeking

God's will and guidance. NOTE: The knowledge and maturity acquired through studying the Bible and praying will be indispensable in making a decision about remarriage.

4. Encourage the inquirer to become involved with a Bible-teaching church for worship, fellowship, and Christian service. Urge that he or she seek the counsel of a qualified pastor concerning remarriage.

5. Emphasize, now that the individual is a Christian, that should he or she remarry it only be to another believer (1 Corinthians 7:39) in order to establish a truly Christian home, one that is both Christ-centered and church-centered.

For the Christian:

1. The inquirer should take into account that remarriage is not all that easy! Many questions should be considered:

   - Although I am considered to be the innocent party in my divorce, did I contribute to it in any way?

   - Is there pride and self-centeredness which I haven't dealt with?

   - Is there any resentment and bitterness as a result of the divorce which ought to be dealt with?

   - Do I have the right to think that a new marriage will be a success?

   - Am I now living in the will of God?

   - Am I able to make a truly spiritual contribution to a new marriage?

   - Is God's glory my highest aim in life?

2. If appropriate, present "Restoration," page 17.

3. Urge the inquirer to make sure that he or she is walking in the will of God. This can be determined, in part, by the strength of his or her commitment to read and study the Bible faithfully and to rely on prayer.

4. Encourage the inquirer to get involved in a Bible-teaching church. Urge that he or she seek the counsel of a qualified pastor concerning remarriage.

5. Advise the individual that, if he or she does remarry, Christ must be made the center of the marriage and the home. They should establish a daily family altar where all may read the Bible and pray together.

6. Pray with the inquirer for the realization of God's will and purpose in his or her life.

Scripture

"He has not dealt with us according to our sins, nor punished us according to our iniquities. For as the heavens are high above the earth, so great is His mercy toward those who fear Him; as far as the east is from the west, so far has He removed our transgressions from us" (Psalm 103:10–12).

"Be anxious for nothing, but in everything by prayer and supplication, with thanksgiving, let your requests be made known to God; and the peace of God, which surpasses all understanding, will guard your hearts and minds through Christ Jesus" (Philippians 4:6–7).

"If any of you lacks wisdom, let him ask of God, who gives to all liberally and without reproach, and it will be given to him" (James 1:5).

"Likewise you husbands, dwell with them with understanding, giving honor to the wife, as to the weaker vessel, and as being heirs together of the grace of life, that your prayers may not be hindered" (1 Peter 3:7).

"If we confess our sins, He is faithful and just to forgive us our sins and to cleanse us from all unrighteousness" (1 John 1:9).

SALVATION OF CHILDREN

Background

As children learn about Jesus, His life, His death, and His resurrection, they learn to respond to God's love. Their salvation is desirable, for Jesus said, "Let the little children come to me, and do not hinder them, for the kingdom of God belongs to such as these" (Mark 10:14, NIV). On another occasion He said, "Unless you are converted and become as little children, you will by no means enter the kingdom of heaven" (Matthew 18:3). A child is ready for commitment to Christ as soon as he or she understands the meaning of sin and that Jesus is the Savior from sin.

Helping Strategy

You may explain to the child, as simply as possible, the way of salvation. Use the Bible but make sure the child understands the relevance of each Scripture in the unfolding of God's plan. If you feel that the child understands, lead the child in a prayer to ask Jesus to forgive him or her and to come into his or her heart as Savior. The following outline might be of help as you explain the Gospel:

1. What is God's plan for you? *(Peace and life.)*

   This is God's world. He made it. He made you. He wants you to have peace and happiness. In its very first chapter the Bible says: "God saw everything that He had made, and indeed it was very good" (Genesis 1:31). But when we read about all the trouble in the world—the unhappiness, the badness—we realize that something has gone wrong in God's world.

2. Why can't we live according to His plan? *(Sin.)*

   Instead of living our lives to please God, we have been pleasing ourselves: "All we like sheep have gone astray; we have turned, every one, to his own way" (Isaiah 53:6). This is what the Bible calls sin. Sin is insisting on our own selfish way instead of taking God's way. The Bible says that, "All have sinned and fall short of the glory of God" (Romans 3:23).

3. How does God solve this problem of our sin? *(The cross of Jesus.)*

   When God's Son, Jesus, died on the cross, He took the punishment for sin which we deserved. Through His death we can be forgiven: "For God so loved the world that He gave His only begotten Son, that whoever believes in Him should not perish but have everlasting life" (John 3:16).

4. What must we now do to please God? *(Open our heart and receive Jesus.)*

If you are willing to ask God to forgive your sins, and you receive Jesus as your Savior, you will become a member of God's family: "But as many as received Him, to them He gave the right to become children of God, even to those who believe in His name" (John 1:12).

5. Shall we say a prayer together? If you really want to receive Jesus, I want you to say these words after me:

"Dear God, You have said that I have sinned and need forgiveness. I am sorry for pleasing only myself instead of You. I receive Jesus right now as my Savior and Lord. Amen."

6. Encourage the child to:

A. Read the Bible every day. Tell the child we are sending an interesting book, *Jesus Loves Me,* which will help him or her to understand more of God's Word.

B. Learn to pray to Jesus every day.

C. Try to be loving to his or her parents and other people, as well as being helpful to them.

D. Go to Sunday school and church every Sunday.

Scripture

"For 'whoever calls upon the name of the Lord shall be saved'" (Romans 10:13).

"If we say that we have no sin, we deceive ourselves, and the truth is not in us. If we confess our sins, He is faithful and just to forgive us our sins and to cleanse us from all unrighteousness" (1 John 1:8–9).

"Look! I have been standing at the door and I am constantly knocking. If anyone hears me calling him and opens the door, I will come in and fellowship with him and he with me" (Revelation 3:20, TLB).

SATAN, ORIGIN AND WORK OF

Background

Satan wor̲america in recent years. We need to understand the enemy!
prevale... ...practiced in many countries of the world and has become

...atan?

Wh... allen angel. He was of the highest order of angelic beings,
S... to cover God's throne. God created Satan, but not as an evil being;
...me evil when by his own free will he forfeited his privileged
...n before God (Ezekiel 28:15). Satan tried to make himself equal with
... hoping even to usurp God's position. But instead, because of his pride
... selfish ambition, God cast him out of heaven (Isaiah 14:12–14).

...atan was joined in his rebellion by millions of lesser angels who now serve
as his messengers (see the chapter on "Demons").

Satan is known in Scripture by many names, including: the "tempter"
(Matthew 4:3); the "enemy" (Matthew 13:39); a "murderer" and the "father
of lies" (John 8:44, NIV); the "god of this age" (2 Corinthians 4:4); the
"prince of the power of the air" (Ephesians 2:1–3); the "adversary" and a
"roaring lion" (1 Peter 5:8–10); a "deceiver" (Revelation 12:9, PHILLIPS); and
the "accuser of our brethren" (Revelation 12:10; see Job 1:6–12). These
names reveal something of Satan's nature and mission.

Where Is Satan's Domain?

Satan does not live in hell (nor does he carry a pitchfork!). He is not and
never shall be the master of hell. He will, however, someday be one of its
victims; in fact, hell was made specifically for Satan and the fallen angels
(Matthew 25:41). For the present, Satan goes "to and fro on the earth" (Job 1:7)
and appears in heaven to accuse God's people before Him (Revelation 12:10).

What Is Satan Like?

What do Satan's names reveal about him? Here are three important points
to remember while talking with an inquirer concerning Satan:

- Satan deceives, transforming himself into an "angel of light"
  (2 Corinthians 11:14).

- Satan tempts, as seen in his contest with Jesus (Matthew 4:1–11).

- Satan blinds the minds of unbelievers, hoping to prevent them from
  coming to the light (2 Corinthians 4:4).

The Bible records the ages-long contest between Satan and Christ. Satan controls the world system as god of this world. First John 2:16 describes the spirit of this world: "For all that is in the world—the lust of the flesh, the lust of the eyes, and the pride of life—is not of the Father but of the world."

"Many jokes are made about the devil, but the devil is no joke," says Billy Graham. "Students today want to know about the devil, about witchcraft, about the occult. People do not know they are turning to Satan. They are being deluded because, according to Jesus Christ, Satan is the father of lies and the greatest liar of all times. He is called the deceiver. In order to accomplish his purposes, the devil blinds people to their need of Christ. Two forces are at work in the world, the forces of Christ and the forces of evil. You are asked to choose between them."

Helping Strategy
For the Non-Christian:

It is rare for a nonbeliever to ask questions concerning the devil; however, someone may ask why Christians are so preoccupied, negative, or even angry about the devil. It could be someone seeking justification for a very worldly lifestyle. You may also be approached by someone who will challenge the existence of Satan. In such cases proceed as follows:

1. The Bible teaches that there is a personality behind all the evil in the world: His name is Satan. Share facts about Satan from the "Background."

2. Try to guide the conversation around to Christ's victory over Satan: While Satan is a defeated foe and will someday be cast into the lake of fire, Jesus Christ will reign as King of kings and Lord of lords (Revelation 17:14).

3. Ask the inquirer if he or she has ever received Jesus Christ as Lord and Savior. Share "Steps to Peace with God," page 11. Mention that part of Satan's work is to "[blind] the minds of those who do not believe" (see 2 Corinthians 4:4, PHILLIPS).

4. If a commitment to Christ is made, encourage the new believer to take a positive stand for Christ, start reading and studying God's Word, pray every day, and get involved with a dynamic group of Christians for fellowship, worship, and service.

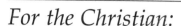

For the Christian:

A Christian may ask questions such as: Just how real is Satan? Can he exercise power over my life? Is he as real as the Holy Spirit?

1. Satan is, indeed, a real person. He is, however, limited in power. The Holy Spirit, on the other hand, is almighty; as a member of the Trinity He is God.

2. The Christian must not take lightly the designs and works of Satan: "For we do not wrestle against flesh and blood, but against principalities, against powers, against the rulers of the darkness of this age, against spiritual hosts of wickedness in the heavenly places" (Ephesians 6:12).

3. The Christian must believe Satan to be a defeated foe: "Greater is he that is in you, than he that is in the world" (1 John 4:4, KJV). Jesus Christ emerged victorious over Satan through His incarnation, death on the cross, and resurrection: "Inasmuch then as the children have partaken of flesh and blood, He Himself likewise shared in the same, that through death He might destroy him who had the power of death, that is, the devil" (Hebrews 2:14).

4. Satan will have no power or influence over the Christian who submits constantly to the dominion of Christ, to the authority and illumination of the Word of God, to the discipline of prayer, and to involvement with a dynamic group of Christian believers. This is what is meant by putting on the "whole armor of God, that you may be able to stand against the wiles of the devil" (Ephesians 6:11).

5. Pray with the inquirer for understanding of Satan and for victory over all concerns and fears about the enemy and his influence and power.

Scripture

Job 1:6–12
Matthew 4:1–11
Ephesians 2:1–3
Hebrews 2:14
1 Peter 5:8–10
Revelation 12:9–10
Revelation 20:1–10

SATAN, RESISTING

Background

Before Jesus began His earthly ministry, He was tempted by Satan in the wilderness (Matthew 4:1–11). Having withstood Satan, Jesus can help us resist him when he tempts us (Hebrews 4:15–16).

Because Christ defeated Satan at the cross, we who acknowledge Him as Savior and Lord have been delivered from Satan's power (Colossians 1:13). Yet our encounter with him is not over; he doesn't give up easily. He is the "accuser of our brethren" (Revelation 12:10); the "enemy" (Matthew 13:39); the "tempter" (Matthew 4:3); and a "deceiver" (Revelation 12:9, PHILLIPS).

In the hymn, "A Mighty Fortress Is Our God," Martin Luther alerts us to be on our guard:

> "For still our ancient foe
> doth seek to work us woe;
> His craft and power are great,
> And armed with cruel hate,
> On earth is not his equal."

We are told to "stand against the wiles of the devil" (Ephesians 6:11), and to resist him (James 4:7). Just how much power does Satan have over believers? What resources must we have in order to withstand his temptations and attacks? The Christian must learn to trust in the finished work of Christ. Satan is a defeated foe: "They overcame him by the blood of the Lamb" (Revelation 12:11). Jesus became a human, "that through death He might destroy him who had the power of death, that is, the devil" (Hebrews 2:14).

The Christian enjoys a privileged position of refuge and security. According to Galatians 2:20, the "old you" is dead and your life is now "hidden with Christ in God" (Colossians 3:1–3). The Christian is in Christ's constant protection and care: "The one who was born of God keeps him safe, and the evil one cannot harm him" (1 John 5:18, NIV).

Helping Strategy

If a Christian feels under attack by Satan or is vulnerable to his wiles or temptations, ask him or her to tell you about it. He or she may be just succumbing to selfish, sinful desires. Satan is blamed for many things for which he is not guilty.

1. Confess all known sin (1 John 1:9) with the understanding that the sin is to be abandoned. "A conscience without offense toward God and men" (Acts 24:16) is the first step in confronting Satan.

2. Be vigilant and "on your guard": "Be sober, be vigilant; because your adversary the devil walks about like a roaring lion, seeking whom he may devour" (1 Peter 5:8). Alertness to Satan's designs and intentions will help avoid encounters with him.

3. Submit to God (James 4:7–8) in two ways:

   A. Resist the devil:

   (1) Have a psychological mind-set against him: "But Daniel purposed in his heart that he would not defile himself" (Daniel 1:8). "Clothe yourselves with the Lord Jesus Christ, and do not think about how to gratify the desires of the sinful nature" (Romans 13:14, NIV).

   (2) Put Satan in his place. When Satan spoke to Jesus through Peter to try to divert Him from His eternal purpose, Jesus rebuked him: "Get behind me, Satan! You are a stumbling block to me; you do not have in mind the things of God, but the things of men" (Matthew 16:23, NIV).

   (3) Use Scripture. When Satan tempted Him (Matthew 4:1–11), Jesus answered devastatingly with three pertinent Scriptures: Deuteronomy 8:3; 6:16; and 6:13. A strong argument for familiarity with Scripture is to be able to resist Satan.

   B. "Draw near to God and He will draw near to you" (James 4:8). Intimate, daily devotional time with the Lord, using His Word and seeking His presence and strength through prayer, will help us resist Satan and result in his fleeing: "Your word I have hidden in my heart, that I might not sin against You" (Psalm 119:11).

4. Overcome Satan by the Holy Spirit: "Walk in the Spirit, and you shall not fulfill the lust of the flesh" (Galatians 5:16).

Scripture

"I have been crucified with Christ; it is no longer I who live, but Christ lives in me; and the life which I now live in the flesh I live by faith in the Son of God, who loved me and gave Himself for me' (Galatians 2:20).

"Put on the whole armor of God, that you may be able to stand against the wiles of the devil" (Ephesians 6:11).

"Since, then, you have been raised with Christ, set your hearts on things above, where Christ is seated at the right hand of God. Set your minds on things above, not on earthly things. For you died, and your life is now hidden with Christ in God" (Colossians 3:1–3, NIV).

"Therefore submit to God. Resist the devil and he will flee from you. Draw near to God and He will draw near to you" (James 4:7–8).

Other suggested Scriptures:

Colossians 1:13

SEXUAL IMMORALITY

Background

We have become overwhelmed by the so-called sexual revolution. It has been romanticized and glorified out of all proportion. That which began in defiance of biblical principles has become the battle cry of the hedonists: "If it feels right, do it—as long as nobody gets hurt."

How ironic this maudlin defense of immorality sounds in the light of its devastating legacy to the nation: millions of illegitimate births, shattered personalities, divorce, abortions, and rampant sexual diseases—some of which are incurable.

God expressly forbids irresponsible sexual behavior, in order to spare us the disastrous consequences: "The body is not meant for sexual immorality, but for the Lord. . . . Flee from sexual immorality. All other sins a man commits are outside his body, but he who sins sexually sins against his own body" (1 Corinthians 6:13, 18, NIV).

Billy Graham says: "Premarital sexual relations are always a mistake. . . . The Bible condemns sex outside the bonds of matrimony. The fact that immorality is rampant throughout the nation doesn't make it right!"

God condemns immorality, but He offers deliverance. In 1 Corinthians 6:9–11, the apostle Paul says that none of the sexually immoral will inherit the kingdom of God. But, he adds, "And that is what some of you were. But you were washed [born again], you were sanctified [cleansed] you were justified in the name of the Lord Jesus Christ and by the Spirit of our God" (1 Corinthians 6:11, NIV).

As with any other sin, God has dealt with immorality through the cross.

Helping Strategy

1. Tell the inquirer you are glad he or she called. Show that you are a caring, concerned person—without being patronizing. Don't be judgmental.

2. Listen with sensitivity and ask questions only for understanding of the problem. Draw no conclusions nor offer any spiritual solutions until you have a complete perspective.

3. Inquire about the person's attitudes toward sex. How he or she feels about it will explain his or her sexual behavior. What were the contributing causes of getting involved? Does he or she feel guilty about this involvement and regard it as sin?

4. Ask if you may read portions of God's Word about premarital or extramarital sex. Emphasize that the Bible is a trustworthy source in regard to moral issues. Read some or all of the following Scriptures: 1 Corinthians 6:13, 15–20; Acts 15:20; Ephesians 5:3; Colossians 3:5; Exodus 20:14.

5. In the light of Scripture, the caller's immoral acts are displeasing to God. To please God, he or she must repent of all immorality and renounce it (read 1 Corinthians 6:9–11). God condemns immoral behavior, but loves us and will forgive us if we confess our sin and, by faith, receive Jesus Christ as Lord and Savior. Share "Steps to Peace with God," page 11.

6. Emphasize the importance of severing any relationships which may have contributed to the immoral behavior: "Do not be misled: 'Bad company corrupts good character'" (1 Corinthians 15:33, NIV). The best place to form new friendships is in a Bible-teaching church. Recommend finding one and becoming involved. Being a committed Christian should be the person's goal. The lack of a vital relationship with Christ is a primary contributing factor to an immoral lifestyle.

7. Suggest seeking a pastor's encouragement and counseling. He or she may need serious counseling for a period of time to experience freedom from temptation and to begin to walk with the Lord.

8. Pray with the inquirer for a complete refocus of mind and life, to the glory of God.

If the inquirer is a Christian, share the section on "Restoration," page 17. Encourage reading and studying God's Word for the purpose of remolding his or her mind and life. As a Christian, he or she should become involved in a Bible-teaching church, where energies can be turned toward serving Christ.

Scripture

"Wash yourselves, make yourselves clean; put away the evil of your doings from before My eyes. Cease to do evil. . . . Come now, and let us reason together," says the Lord, "Though your sins are like scarlet, they shall be as white as snow; though they are red like crimson, they shall be as wool" (Isaiah 1:16, 18).

"Let the wicked forsake his way, and the unrighteous man his thoughts; let him return to the Lord, and He will have mercy on him; and to our God, for He will abundantly pardon" (Isaiah 55:7).

"But sexual sin is never right: our bodies were not made for that, but for the Lord, and the Lord wants to fill our bodies with himself" (1 Corinthians 6:13, TLB).

"If we confess our sins, He is faithful and just to forgive us our sins and to cleanse us from all unrighteousness. . . . And if anyone sins, we have an Advocate with the Father, Jesus Christ the righteous" (1 John 1:9; 2:1).

STEWARDSHIP

(Giving, Tithing)

Background

God's plan is for Christians to support the advancement of the Gospel through tithes and offerings: "On the first day of the week let each one of you lay something aside, storing up as he may prosper" (1 Corinthians 16:2).

The idea of tithing goes back to earliest biblical history. Abraham paid tithes to Melchizedek (Hebrews 7:6). The Law of Moses specified that the Levites should collect tithes from the people (Hebrews 7:5). Though a tenth part of one's income is indicated as the tithe, this should not limit the extent of giving for those who have the means and the will to give more.

The New Testament teaches that Christians should give individually, regularly, methodically, and proportionately to support the local church, the needy, evangelism, and missions (1 Corinthians 16:2).

Giving out of a heart filled with God's love is to be a characteristic of the born-again believer: "But this I say: He who sows sparingly will also reap sparingly, and he who sows bountifully will also reap bountifully. So let each one give as he purposes in his heart, not grudgingly or of necessity; for God loves a cheerful giver. And God is able to make all grace abound toward you, that you, always having all sufficiency in all things, have an abundance for every good work" (2 Corinthians 9:6–8).

As we respond to the needs of God's work, He promises that our own needs will be supplied: "And my God shall supply all your need according to His riches in glory by Christ Jesus" (Philippians 4:19).

Billy Graham comments: "We have found in our home, as have thousands of others, that when we tithe, God's blessing upon the nine-tenths helps it to go further than ten-tenths without His blessing. How you handle your money is an optional matter. God doesn't force you to distribute it one way or another. There are certain biblical principles, however, in a philosophy of Christian stewardship. For one thing, God owns everything. We are custodians, so to speak, of His property. Whatever we give is, by definition, His anyway. Secondly, one's giving ought to be prompted by love—and by a personal commitment to Christ. Thirdly, while Christian stewardship is not based on reward, it certainly recognizes that there's no better investment in terms of return. Jesus talked in Mark 4 about yields which were thirty-, sixty-, and a hundredfold. . . . If tithing was appropriate under law, it is even more so in this age of freedom and grace. . . . Try giving the tithe and more—with joy and even abandon—and you'll see, you'll see!"

Helping Strategy

1. Determine if the inquirer is a Christian. If not, explain that the first gift God expects of us is ourselves. Present "Steps to Peace with God," page 11. Encourage him or her to take a positive stand for Christ, to get into the Word of God, to cultivate habits of prayer, and to become a part of a Bible-teaching church for the purposes of fellowship, Bible study, and opportunities for service.

2. Share the following with anyone asking advice on giving:

   A. Become an active, participating Christian in a local, Bible-teaching church. Being part of a fellowship of believers will provide challenges, along with motivation and perspective, in giving.

   B. Pray for wisdom in your giving, then investigate, so that you know to whom you are giving. Many non-evangelical and even cult-like organizations receive regular gifts from Christians who lack spiritual discernment. Know before you give!

   C. To whom should the Christian give?

      (1) A substantial part of your tithes and offerings should go to your own local church.

      (2) Another portion should be set aside and used for the poor or for those with special needs. This also may be handled through your local church.

      (3) There are many ministries in evangelism, missions, and benevolence which are worthy of the Christian's support. Make provision for some of them.

Scripture

"Honor the Lord with your possessions, and with the firstfruits of all your increase; so your barns will be filled with plenty, and your vats will overflow with new wine" (Proverbs 3:9–10).

"'Bring all the tithes into the storehouse, that there may be food in My house, and prove Me now in this,' says the Lord of hosts, 'If I will not open for you the windows of heaven and pour out for you such blessing that there will not be room enough to receive it'" (Malachi 3:10).

"So when you give to the needy, do not announce it with trumpets, as the hypocrites do in the synagogues and on the streets, to be honored by men. I tell you the truth, they have received their reward in full. But when you give to the needy, do not let your left hand know what your right hand is doing, so that your giving may be in secret. Then your Father, who sees what is done in secret, will reward you" (Matthew 6:2–4, NIV).

"Give, and it will be given to you: good measure, pressed down, shaken together, and running over will be put into your bosom. For with the same measure that you use, it will be measured back to you" (Luke 6:38).

"And my God will meet all your needs according to his glorious riches in Christ Jesus" (Philippians 4:19, NIV).

"Command those who are rich in this present world not to be arrogant nor to put their hope in wealth, which is so uncertain, but to put their hope in God, who richly provides us with everything for our enjoyment. Command them to do good, to be rich in good deeds, and to be generous and willing to share. In this way they will lay up treasure for themselves as a firm foundation for the coming age, so that they may take hold of the life that is truly life" (1 Timothy 6:17–19, NIV).

Other suggested Scriptures:

Romans 12:1

SUFFERING AND ADVERSITY

Background

Why? Why me? Why my family? What is the meaning of this suffering?

These are familiar questions asked by Christians and non-Christians alike. No one is immune to suffering and adversity: "Man is born to trouble, as the sparks fly upward" (Job 5:7). There are the pressures of want, need, sorrow, persecution, unpopularity, and loneliness. Some suffer for what they have done; others suffer because of what people do to them. Many suffer because they are victims of circumstances they cannot control.

Pain is distressing. There can be nights of agony when God seems so unfair and it seems that there is no possible help or answer. Temporary relief may seem adequate, but the real solution to suffering is not to isolate it and try to do away with it, nor even to grit our teeth and endure it. The solution, rather, is to condition our attitudes so that we learn to triumph in and through suffering. When the apostle Paul sought relief from his "thorn in the flesh" (2 Corinthians 12:7), God did not take it away, but reassured him that, "My grace is sufficient for you, for My strength is made perfect in weakness" (verse 9).

Except for physical pain, handling suffering seems to be a question of attitude: "What am I going to do in the face of suffering in order to learn from it and use it for my advantage as far as God's eternal purposes are concerned?"

Billy Graham comments: "Nowhere does the Bible teach that Christians are exempt from the tribulations and natural disasters that come upon the world. Scripture does teach that the Christian can face tribulation, crisis, calamity, and personal suffering with a supernatural power that is not available to the person outside of Christ."

Some of the most pathetic people in the world are those who, amid adversity, indulge themselves by wallowing in self-pity and bitterness, all the while taking a sort of delight in blaming God for their problems.

Job's attitude is an inspiration: "Though He slay me, yet will I trust Him" (Job 13:15).

The sufferer will be blessed if, amid great agony and despair, he or she can look into the face of the Heavenly Father and, because of His eternal love and presence, be grateful. Our response to suffering should be to look beyond it and see God's higher purposes and what He wants to teach us.

Reasons for Human Suffering

- We may bring suffering upon ourselves. Dissipation and lack of discipline bring unhappy consequences. Long-term abuse of our bodies may bring on sickness. Wrong choices come back to haunt us. You may ask the inquirer: "Do you think this is happening to you because of your own bad judgment or excessive actions? What can you do to alleviate your suffering?"

- Sometimes God is taking corrective action because of sin and disobedience. God will correct and discipline His own. Through chastening He proves that He loves us and that we truly belong to Him (Hebrews 12:5–11).

- God may permit suffering so that we learn to respond to problems in a biblical way. Scripture tells us that Jesus "learned obedience by the things which He suffered" (Hebrews 5:8). Our goal should be not merely relief from suffering but rather learning from it (Romans 12:1–2).

- Sometimes God permits us to suffer simply to teach us that pain is a part of life. Nowhere does the Bible say that the Christian will not suffer adversity! Paul points out that it is "granted on behalf of Christ, not only to believe in Him, but also to suffer for His sake" (Philippians 1:29).

  Adversity can be a gift from God. Christ did not try to escape the cross. Hebrews 12:2 says He "endured the cross, despising the shame." Why? "For the joy that was set before Him." Jesus knew that the final word was not crucifixion (suffering) but resurrection (victory). We may suffer briefly, or all our lives. But let us not give up hope or engage in self-pity or bitterness. The end result is what we all look forward to: Being with the Lord in heaven will put everything into perspective!

- God may permit suffering for our well-being: "And we know that in all things God works for the good of those who love him, who have been called according to his purpose" (Romans 8:28, NIV). We must accept this by faith and pray that God's highest good will come as a result of our suffering. Some of the deeper lessons of life are learned only through adversity. We must trust God to work out His own will and purpose in us so that we might be more Christlike (Romans 8:29). There is no redemptive merit in our suffering, as there was in that of Jesus; but if we are faithful under adversity we may be able to share in "the fellowship of His sufferings" (Philippians 3:10).

- Sometimes God permits suffering in order to speak through our life and testimony to comfort others. Jesus said that a particular blind man had been allowed thus to suffer in order that "the work of God might be displayed in his life" (John 9:3, NIV). God might work in your life through suffering to inspire others by your example in handling the adversity. Those who endure adversity can sympathize and identify more effectively with others who suffer. We comfort others in the way we are comforted: "Praise be to the God and Father of our Lord Jesus Christ, the Father of compassion and the God of all comfort, who comforts us in all our troubles, so that we can comfort those in any trouble with the comfort we ourselves have received from God" (2 Corinthians 1:3–4, NIV).

Helping Strategy

For the Non-Christian:

1. Be sympathetic. Listen carefully as the inquirer articulates his or her problems. Guide the conversation so that you can offer spiritual help.

2. Offer encouragement and hope. God loves the inquirer and knows what is happening. He or she is not alone: "When you pass through the waters, I will be with you; and through the rivers, they shall not overflow you. When you walk through the fire, you shall not be burned, nor shall the flame scorch you" (Isaiah 43:2). Tell the person you are glad he or she called, and that, by working together, you should be able to find an answer to the situation.

3. Ask if he or she has ever received Jesus Christ as Savior and Lord. Sometimes God permits affliction in order to get our attention and bring us to salvation. Share "Steps to Peace with God," page 11.

4. Pray with the inquirer for salvation and deliverance.

5. Encourage the inquirer to read and study the Bible. Praying will provide strength and perspective on the problems in life. Offer to send *Living in Christ*, which will provide a good starting place for serious Bible study.

6. Recommend finding a Bible-teaching church. Fellowship with committed Christians will have a maturing influence. The church can also provide opportunities for Bible study and Christian service.

For the Christian:

If the inquirer is distressed because of some tragedy or suffering, discuss possible reasons why God may have allowed it.

1. Sympathize with the caller. Encourage him or her by offering God's comfort. You may share some of the insights from "Reasons for Human Suffering," above. Apply those which seem suitable.

2. If a desire for restoration and rededication seems to be manifest, share page 17.

3. Encourage the person to search God's Word and to pray sincerely that God will reveal His reasons for the suffering:

   A. What is God trying to say to me?

   B. What is He trying to teach me?

   C. What steps ought I to take as a result?

4. If the person is not already involved, encourage getting into a Bible-teaching church. Bible study can lead to deeper understanding of God's will and ways.

5. Encourage him or her to communicate with Christian friends. It always helps to have a listening ear. This will result in comfort, understanding, and strength.

6. Pray with the inquirer personally, asking for deliverance.

Scripture

"Let not your heart be troubled; you believe in God, believe also in Me" (John 14:1).

"And we know that in all things God works for the good of those who love him, who have been called according to his purpose. For those God foreknew he also predestined to be conformed to the likeness of his Son, that he might be the firstborn among many brothers" (Romans 8:28–29, NIV).

"Who shall separate us from the love of Christ? Shall tribulation, or distress, or persecution, or famine, or nakedness, or peril, or sword? . . . Yet in all these things we are more than conquerors through Him who loved us" (Romans 8:35, 37).

"Consider it pure joy, my brothers, whenever you face trials of many kinds, because you know that the testing of your faith develops perseverance. . . . Blessed is the man who perseveres under trial, because when he has stood the test, he will receive the crown of life that God has promised to those who love him" (James 1:2–3, 12, NIV).

"Beloved, do not think it strange concerning the fiery trial which is to try you, as though some strange thing happened to you; but rejoice to the extent that you partake of Christ's sufferings, that when His glory is revealed, you may also be glad with exceeding joy" (1 Peter 4:12–13).

"Yet if anyone suffers as a Christian, let him not be ashamed, but let him glorify God in this matter. . . . Therefore let those who suffer according to the will of God commit their souls to Him in doing good, as to a faithful Creator" (1 Peter 4:16, 19).

SUICIDE

Background

A suicidal person feels he or she has exhausted all possible options. Life has no meaning, no purpose, no future, so why continue to endure its extreme unhappiness, anguish, hopelessness, and despair? The obsessive belief that nothing will ever change for the better leaves him or her feeling helpless, with the conviction that death is the only way out.

Such a person is a victim of depression, tortured with feelings of unworthiness, sin and failure, deep guilt, and the need to be punished. Many things condition this person for the depressed state that can lead to suicide or attempted suicide: anger, envy, jealousy, fear, guilt, self-pity, sexual deviation, drugs, alcohol. It should be obvious to the helper, then, that root causes leading to such a crisis are likely to be deep and possibly of long duration. Many of these do, in fact, reflect back to childhood and therefore point to the need for prolonged professional counseling with a Christian psychologist or psychiatrist.

Although not all the problems of the suicidal person are spiritual, the ultimate problem for any person's life is separation from God, solved only through a personal relationship with Jesus Christ. Without this relationship with Christ, there can be no real solutions or healing. As a person experiences all that is involved in the new life in Christ (2 Corinthians 5:17)—forgiveness, freedom from guilt and fear, a sense of fulfillment and well-being, new motivation to live—forces for radical change are set in motion. This is where the helper can be of real service: guiding the inquirer into a personal relationship with Jesus Christ.

Some people threaten suicide in order to get attention and sympathy. They want someone to listen to their hurt and frustrations. Others are beyond this point and seriously have self-destruction in mind.

It is only natural that you will feel inadequate when confronted with this kind of challenge; however, you should try to help, remembering that our resources come from the Lord. He will be reaching out in love and power through you. Be motivated by the promises of Scripture that "with God all things are possible" (Matthew 19:26), and, "If any of you lacks wisdom, let him ask of God . . . and it will be given to him" (James 1:5).

Helping Strategy

When talking with a suicidal person, two main goals should be kept in mind:

- Share the Gospel as a source of hope. A new relationship with Jesus Christ can bring about change.

- Gather information about the concerned party for possible emergency procedures.

Helping the Suicidal Non-Christian:

1. Unobtrusively, but as early as possible, you should determine if the individual is really suicidal. Has he or she taken pills or poison? Is there a loaded gun which he or she threatens to use? As the conversation develops, try to obtain the person's name, address, and telephone number; the name of a relative living in his or her area; and the name of a pastor and a church. Always solicit information in a casual, friendly way in order to avoid arousing suspicion.

2. Speaking with a suicidal person demands the greatest tact and patience. Be prepared to listen! Let your inquirer do most of the talking until you get the complete picture. Punctuate the conversation with an occasional question to keep it flowing. If he or she makes a statement, seek a further explanation of how he or she feels. Or, ask what has led to that particular conclusion. The phrase, "Tell me about it," is often helpful.

3. As the conversation permits, offer words of encouragement to the suicidal caller. Stress that he or she has called the right place, because we are friends and are willing to listen. Suggest that God can help in revealing solutions and that He really cares and loves.

4. Do not minimize any feeling or conclusion the person may express about his or her problems. He or she should be permitted to vent all the stored-up anger, tension, and sense of desperation. Do not contradict any statement made, except to disagree with the proposed "solution." If he or she says that life is not worth living, believe it! Probably for him or her in this present state, it isn't. Avoid such statements as, "Oh, come now, things can't be all that hopeless," or, "You are not as bad as you would like me to think."

5. Assure the individual that there is a solution for his or her problems and there is hope! If he or she will permit God to intervene, He can forgive all the past, making things right through Jesus Christ. Jesus understands suffering. He was maligned, mistreated, and murdered. He truly cares about what happens to us. He loved us so much that He died for us. Christ will come to us where we are—to our level of need, no matter how sinful and hopeless we consider ourselves to be—in order to lift us up and beyond our despair. Jesus says: "Come to me, all you who are weary and burdened, and I will give you rest" (Matthew 11:28, NIV).

6. Share "Steps to Peace with God," page 11.

7. If the caller receives Christ, offer the assurance that this experience can be the catalyst for real change: "Therefore, if anyone is in Christ, he is a new creation; the old has gone, the new has come!" (2 Corinthians 5:17, NIV).

8. Explain that to help bring about this change, he or she needs to begin to read and study the Bible. Offer to send *Living in Christ* for help in getting started.

9. Encourage prayer, because communicating with God is very important in effecting change. We can turn over to God all our emotions and our problems through prayer: "Cast all your anxiety on him because he cares for you" (1 Peter 5:7, NIV). Also share Philippians 4:6. Suggest writing these references down so he or she can look up the verses easily.

10. Encourage seeking new friendships by identifying with a local Bible-teaching church. This will provide opportunities for worship, fellowship, Bible study, and service, all of which are important in the person's attempt to redirect the focus of his or her life.

11. If you are involved in a telephone ministry center, ask the person if your supervisor might call the following evening. With this offer, he or she will have something to look forward to. Ask what would be a convenient time to call. (PLEASE NOTE: If such a promise is made, be sure to turn over your "Counselor's Report Form" to your supervisor so that it is not forgotten!)

12. Ask if the person would like a visit from a pastor, if such a contact could be arranged. Do not promise that it will happen, but state that we will do what we can. If it seems unlikely that you will be able to set up such a meeting, encourage the caller to personally make such a contact. Whatever the case, suicidal calls should be followed up if at all possible.

13. If the inquirer doesn't make a commitment to Christ, encourage him or her the best you can. Explain that he or she can act on what you have shared at any time. The door of access to God is always open. Recommend making contact with a local pastor for counseling. Immediacy is important.

Helping the Suicidal Christian:

Christians are not immune to suicidal thoughts or attempts. Unresolved or unconfessed sin, or a crisis situation such as a deep disappointment, the death of a loved one, a divorce, loss of employment, loss of health, or a nervous breakdown can precipitate depression severe enough to lead to such an attempt.

1. As with the non-Christian caller, determine as early as possible if the individual is really suicidal. Has he or she taken pills or poison? Is there a loaded gun which he or she threatens to use? As the conversation develops, try to obtain the person's name, address, and telephone number; the name of a relative living in his or her area; and the name of a pastor and a church. Always solicit information in a casual, friendly way in order to avoid arousing suspicion.

2. Remind the Christian that God always loves and cares: "For He Himself has said, 'I will never leave you nor forsake you'" (Hebrews 13:5).

3. Remind him or her also that we are God's children (quote John 1:12).

4. Emphasize the truth that God still forgives. Share "Restoration," page 17, emphasizing Proverbs 28:13 and 1 John 1:9. Confession results in forgiveness and restoration of fellowship.

5. Encourage him or her to look only to the Lord and not at the present problems and circumstances (Matthew 14:27–32; Proverbs 3:5–6).

6. Suggest that it is important to get into God's Word: hear, read, study, meditate, and memorize.

7. Remind him or her that prayer is a valuable resource and an essential part of a Christian's life (1 Thessalonians 5:17; Philippians 4:6–7).

8. Recommend becoming involved in a Bible-teaching church as an important step in recovering emotional stability. Such identity permits fellowship with caring people who worship and work together.

9. The telephone helper could at this point ask if the inquirer would like a call from a supervisor the following evening. This will give him or her something to look forward to. Please give the "Counselor's Report Form" to a supervisor so that the promise is not forgotten.

10. Pray with the inquirer that God will come to him or her with new meaning, with a new measure of hope and trust.

Scripture

Proverbs 3:5–6
Matthew 11:28
Matthew 14:27–32
2 Corinthians 5:17
Philippians 4:6–7
1 Thessalonians 5:17
1 Peter 5:7

TEMPTATION

Background

As the compass needle is affected by magnetic attraction, so the Christian feels the attraction of sin. This is illustrated by Israel's desire to return to the "leeks and garlics" of Egypt (Numbers 11:5); and by Demas, the young man the apostle Paul mentions as having left the ministry because he "loved this present world" (2 Timothy 4:10). Paul describes the Christian as having two natures, the old and the new, which constantly compete for supremacy. The Christian must understand this, and learn to confront this "magnetic pull" of his or her own sinful nature and Satan's wiles.

A paragraph by Billy Graham helps put this into perspective: "God never promises to remove temptation from us, for even Christ was subject to it. . . . There is a sense of achievement and assurance that results from victory over temptation that cannot come to us otherwise. Temptation shows what people really are. It does not make us Christian or un-Christian. Overcoming the temptation does, however, make the Christian stronger and cause him or her to discover resources of power. . . . In times of temptation Christ can become more real to you than ever."

Some Things to Remember About Temptation

- Temptation is common to all Christians: "But remember this—the wrong desires that come into your life aren't anything new and different. Many others have faced exactly the same problems before you" (1 Corinthians 10:13, TLB).

- Temptation is of the devil (Matthew 4:1–11).

- Temptation itself is not sin, but succumbing to it is.

Billy Graham says, "The sin is when we use the temptation for giving in. None of us should deliberately place ourselves in a position to be tempted. Satan will always attack where we are the most vulnerable. 'But each one is tempted when, by his own evil desire, he is dragged away and enticed. Then, after desire has conceived, it gives birth to sin; and sin, when it is full-grown, gives birth to death' (James 1:14–15, NIV). A thought enters; we pamper it; it germinates and grows into an evil act."

- God does not personally lead us into temptation: "Let no one say when he is tempted, 'I am tempted by God'; for God cannot be tempted by evil, nor does He Himself tempt anyone" (James 1:13). But God does *permit* us to be tempted (Job 1:6–12) so that we can face temptation, overcome it, and become stronger: "I have written to you, young men, because you are strong, and the word of God abides in you, and you have overcome the wicked one" (1 John 2:14; see James 1:12).

- No temptation is irresistible: "You can trust God to keep the temptation from becoming so strong that you can't stand up against it, for he has promised this and will do what he says. He will show you how to escape temptation's power so that you can bear up patiently against it" (1 Corinthians 10:13, TLB).

- Whatever we experience, Jesus has been there before us. He "was in all points tempted as we are, yet without sin" (Hebrews 4:15).

Helping Strategy

1. Ask if the inquirer is a Christian, one who has received Jesus Christ as Savior and Lord. If he or she is not, explain "Steps to Peace with God," page 11. No one is strong enough to overcome temptation without God's help, regardless of how high his or her ideals or motives

2. Share ways to confront and overcome temptation:

   A. We must resist the tempter: "Resist the devil and he will flee from you" (James 4:7).

   B. We must submit to God (James 4:7). This we do by:

   (1) Committing ourselves daily to God (Romans 12:1), and daily confessing all known sins, so that there is no unnecessary "buildup" of temptations (Psalm 51:10).

   (2) Subjecting our minds to His control:

   - "Be transformed by the renewing of your mind" (Romans 12:2).

   - "Set your mind on things above, not on things on the earth" (Colossians 3:2).

   (3) The discipline of prayer:

   - "Let us therefore come boldly to the throne of grace, that we may obtain mercy and find grace to help in time of need" (Hebrews 4:16).

- "Pray all the time. Ask God for anything in line with the Holy Spirit's wishes" (Ephesians 6:18, TLB).

(4) Reading, studying, and memorizing the Bible. Dwight L. Moody used to say, "Sin will keep you from this book, or this book will keep you from sin":

- "The word of God is living and active. . . . It judges the thoughts and attitudes of the heart" (Hebrews 4:12, NIV).

(5) Associating with the right kinds of friends—God's people:

- "Do not be misled: 'Bad company corrupts good character'" (1 Corinthians 15:33, NIV).

- "And let us consider how we may spur one another on toward love and good deeds. Let us not give up meeting together, as some are in the habit of doing, but let us encourage one another—and all the more as you see the Day approaching" (Hebrews 10:24–25, NIV).

(6) Putting on the whole armor of God (Ephesians 6:13–18).

(7) Dependence on the Holy Spirit:

- "How much more will your heavenly Father give the Holy Spirit to those who ask Him!" (Luke 11:13).

- "And I will pray the Father, and He will give you another Helper, that He may abide with you forever" (John 14:16).

- "When He, the Spirit of truth, has come, He will guide you into all truth" (John 16:13).

Scripture

"Blessed is the man who perseveres under trial, because when he has stood the test, he will receive the crown of life that God has promised to those who love him. When tempted, no one should say, 'God is tempting me.' For God cannot be tempted by evil, nor does he tempt anyone; but each one is tempted when, by his own evil desire, he is dragged away and enticed. Then, after desire has conceived, it gives birth to sin; and sin, when it is full-grown, gives birth to death" (James 1:12–15, NIV).

"Now have come the salvation and the power and the kingdom of our God, and the authority of his Christ. For the accuser of our brothers, who accuses them before our God day and night, has been hurled down. They overcame him by the blood of the Lamb and by the word of their testimony; they did not

love their lives so much as to shrink from death" (Revelation 12:10–11, NIV).

Other suggested Scriptures:

Matthew 4:1–11
Romans 8:26
Galatians 5:16

TERMINAL ILLNESS

Background

> O Joy that seekest me through pain,
> I cannot close my heart to thee;
> I trace the rainbow through the rain,
> And feel the promise is not vain
> That morn shall tearless be.
> —*George Matheson*

Your inquirer is a very ill person. His or her life is threatened; in fact, he or she may not have long to live. Cancer, high blood pressure, heart disease, kidney failure, or some other critical illness is destroying his or her body. He or she feels alone. Who else has known pain like this?

Successively, though not necessarily chronologically, he or she feels:

- Denial ("This can't be happening to me.")

- Anger ("Why me, Lord?")

- Depression ("There's no hope.")

- Bargaining ("Lord, get me out of this and I'll do whatever You say.")

- Acceptance ("May God's will be done.")

These feelings are not experienced once and then forgotten, but return again and again. They are not abnormal feelings, but are generally characteristic of those facing the "valley of the shadow."

What do you say to such a person? How do you respond? How can you really identify with and help someone who is experiencing a level of suffering and a sense of finality that is probably beyond what you have personally experienced?

Helping Strategy

1. The first thing to do is simply to listen! Listen with empathy to the feelings that are shared. Encourage the person to talk. You may want to probe gently for feelings, some of which lie close to the surface while others may be more deeply submerged.

2. Pass no judgment on the feelings that are shared, even though they may be expressed in anger, self-pity, or bitterness. Just let the inquirer know

that you are hearing what he or she says. Don't appear to be arrogant by saying that you understand the depth of his or her feelings. You can't possibly understand! But you may tell the person that you care. This can be put into words and also conveyed by the tone of your voice, your gentleness, and your capacity for feeling and identifying: "Think too of all who suffer" (Hebrews 13:3, PHILLIPS) as if you shared their pain. This is no time for you to introduce your own experience of pain and suffering; keep the focus on the inquirer.

3. Do not try to be a "spiritual Pollyanna." Avoid cliches and platitudes. Don't tell the person to "keep a stiff upper lip," or to be an example in suffering.

   Do not offer false hopes about healing, or tell the individual that all illness is of the devil and with sufficient faith he or she could be healed. God may or may not heal. These are matters for the Sovereign will. What we can be sure of is that God will *spiritually* heal those who put their faith in Jesus Christ.

4. Don't discourage any reference he or she may make about death. This may be a healthy conditioning of the mind for that which is inevitable. References to death can prepare the way for you, as a helper, to ask if there might be any unfinished business to attend to. This is why we witness: to help prepare people for eternity.

   In a spirit of kindness and concern, you may ask the inquirer, "If you were to find yourself at the gates of heaven confronted with the question, 'On what grounds do you seek admission to God's heaven?' what would you say?"

   If indicated, explain "Steps to Peace with God," page 11. If the inquirer responds affirmatively, share "Assurance," page 15. You might also read other portions of Scripture, such as Psalm 23, John 14:1–6, or 1 Thessalonians 4:13–18.

5. The commitment to Christ should prepare the way to ask whether the person has any other unfinished business, such as relationships (family, friends), financial matters (a will, perhaps), handling of details in regard to the process of dying, death itself, funeral arrangements, and disposal of the body. Encourage the inquirer to take care of all these matters, seeking either pastoral or professional advice in the process.

6. Suggest that the inquirer find out if his or her community has a hospice agency. These agencies specialize in providing reinforcement to patients whose diseases are considered terminal, and to their families.

7. Pray for the inquirer that he or she might have courage and strength to be victorious in pain, committing himself or herself to Him who bore our griefs and our sorrows.

Scripture

Psalm 23
John 14:1–6
Philippians 1:21
1 Thessalonians 4:13–18

THOUGHTS, CONTROLLING

Background

The history of mankind has largely centered around a battle for the mind. What a person *thinks* is of utmost importance: "He who rules his spirit [is better] than he who takes a city" (Proverbs 16:32). "As he thinks in his heart, so is he" (Proverbs 23:7).

Words or phrases relating to the mind, such as *mind, thoughts, the understanding,* or the *heart* occur frequently in Scripture. God wants to control our minds; so does Satan.

Billy Graham says: "*What you believe is important, the development of your mind is important. We are to grow intellectually in Christ. . . . Jeremiah says, 'I will put my law in their minds' (Jeremiah 31:33, NIV). God said to Joshua, 'You shall meditate in it day and night, that you may observe to do according to all that is written in it' (Joshua 1:8). Isaiah said, 'You will keep him in perfect peace, whose mind is stayed on You, because he trusts in You' (Isaiah 26:3). Will you surrender your mind to Christ, to the lordship of Christ? Will you devote your mind to Him?*"

The Bible describes the unbelieving mind as "hostile to God" (Romans 8:7, NIV), blinded because of sin (2 Corinthians 4:4), and morally defiled (Mark 7:20–22). Even Christians should guard against developing "an evil heart of unbelief" (Hebrews 3:12).

The Bible also mentions the "carnal" or worldly mind (Romans 8:6), which can characterize even Christians.

Helping Strategy
For the Non-Christian:

1. Explain "Steps to Peace with God," page 11.

2. Encourage the inquirer to begin to read God's Word. In this way he or she begins to bring his or her mind into subjection to God. Offer *Living in Christ* for help in getting started.

3. Encourage daily prayer. The book of Psalms is filled with the language of prayer. Ask the caller to note Matthew 6:9–13 and Luke 11:2–13, where the Lord's Prayer is recorded. These are good examples of prayers.

4. Recommend seeking a Bible-teaching church for worship, fellowship, Bible study, and opportunities for service.

5. Pray with the inquirer for a renewed mind.

For the Worldly Christian:

1. Share "Restoration," page 17.

2. Emphasize the need for controlling the mind, using these examples:

   A. The Lord Jesus Christ: "Let this mind be in you which was also in Christ Jesus" (Philippians 2:5).

   B. The prophet Isaiah: "You will keep him in perfect peace, whose mind is stayed on You, because he trusts in You" (Isaiah 26:3).

   C. The apostle Paul: "And do not be conformed to this world, but be transformed by the renewing of your mind, that you may prove what is that good and acceptable and perfect will of God" (Romans 12:2).

   ". . . casting down arguments and every high thing that exalts itself against the knowledge of God, bringing every thought into captivity to the obedience of Christ" (2 Corinthians 10:5).

Scripture

"Blessed is the man who walks not in the counsel of the ungodly, nor stands in the path of sinners, nor sits in the seat of the scornful; but his delight is in the law of the Lord, and in His law he meditates day and night" (Psalm 1:1–2).

"Commit your works to the Lord, and your thoughts will be established" (Proverbs 16:3).

"'For My thoughts are not your thoughts, nor are your ways My ways,' says the Lord. 'For as the heavens are higher than the earth, so are My ways higher than your ways, and My thoughts than your thoughts'" (Isaiah 55:8–9).

"Finally, brothers, whatever is true, whatever is noble, whatever is right, whatever is pure, whatever is lovely, whatever is admirable—if anything is excellent or praiseworthy—think about such things" (Philippians 4:8, NIV).

"The word of God is living and active. Sharper than any double-edged sword, it penetrates even to dividing soul and spirit, joints and marrow; it judges the thoughts and attitudes of the heart" (Hebrews 4:12, NIV).

THE TRINITY

Background

The Christian believes in the Trinity: that God is one, yet is three distinct persons—Father, Son, and Holy Spirit. Each person of the Trinity is independent, but never acts independently. Each is a distinct person, but those three persons are one in purpose, in essence, and in nature. The finite mind finds it difficult to comprehend this mystery; it must be accepted by faith: "And without faith it is impossible to please God, because anyone who comes to him must believe that he exists and that he rewards those who earnestly seek him" (Hebrews 11:6, NIV).

The *Apostles' Creed*, a statement of faith accepted by the church down through the ages, begins by mentioning all three persons of the Trinity: "I believe in God the Father Almighty, maker of heaven and earth; and in Jesus Christ His only Son our Lord; who was conceived by the Holy Ghost."

The *Westminster Confession* carries an eloquent defense of the Trinity: "There are three persons in the Godhead, the Father, the Son and the Holy Ghost; and these three are one God, the same in substance, equal in power and glory." (NOTE: The *Confession* has been reworded in modern language.)

The understanding that God is a Trinity is unique to Christianity. Most non-Christian religions are either animistic or polytheistic; the few that believe in one God have no understanding of His being three persons in one. All major pseudo-Christian cults emphatically reject the belief as well.

Helping Strategy

1. Commend the inquirer for wanting to discover the truth about this important issue. Explain that God's Word, the Bible, speaks eloquently of the reality of the Trinity.

2. Challenge him or her to receive Jesus Christ as Lord and Savior. The best way to understand the Trinity is to receive eternal life through Jesus Christ. Explain "Steps to Peace with God," page 11. Some additional Scriptures you may find helpful are: "For there is one God and one mediator between God and men, the man Christ Jesus, who gave himself as a ransom for all" (1 Timothy 2:5–6, NIV). See also Titus 3:5, John 1:12, John 3:36, and passages listed on the following pages in "Scripture."

3. If the inquirer invites Christ into his or her life, share verses from

"Assurance," page 15, and the chapter on "Assurance of Salvation." Suggest the following:

A. Determine to take a strong stand for Christ.

B. Begin to read and study the Bible. Offer to send *Living in Christ* for help in getting started.

C. Seek a Bible-teaching church where he or she can fellowship with other Christians, worship, pray, witness, and learn about "rightly dividing the word of truth" (2 Timothy 2:15).

4. Pray with the inquirer for a faithful walk with Christ and for a full understanding of the Bible.

Scripture

The Bible makes a convincing defense of the diversity and unity of the Trinity. The following is a sampling of the more obvious texts.

The Father:

There is one God and Father (1 Corinthians 8:6).
He is the author of our redemption (Galatians 1:3–4).
He is all-powerful (Ephesians 4:6).
He is unchanging (James 1:17).
He is the Father of our Lord Jesus Christ (Ephesians 1:3).
He is the Father of believers (2 Corinthians 6:17–18).

Jesus Christ, The Son:

He is eternal, from the beginning (John 1:1).
He became incarnate (John 1:14).
He is the author of grace and truth (John 1:17).
He is God's Son, our Savior (John 3:16).
The Father loves the Son (John 3:35).
The Son loves the Father (John 14:31).
The Son and the Father are One (John 10:30).

The Holy Spirit:

God is a Spirit (John 4:24).
The Holy Spirit authored the Bible (2 Peter 1:21).
He guides into all truth (John 16:13).
He is sent by the Father to the world (John 14:26).
He dwells within believers (John 14:17).

He confirms that we are God's children (Romans 8:16).
Believers can be filled with Him (Acts 4:31).

The Trinity Presented Together:

When Jesus was baptized, the Holy Spirit descended and the Father
spoke (Matthew 3:16–17).
Believers are to be baptized and discipled in the name of the Father,
Son, and Holy Spirit (Matthew 28:18–19).

The Unique Ministries of the Trinity in Redemption:

The part of the Father (Ephesians 1:3–6).
The part of the Son (Ephesians 1:6–12).
The part of the Holy Spirit (Ephesians 1:13–14).

THE UNPARDONABLE SIN

Background

Occasionally someone will express concern that he or she may have committed the "unpardonable sin." This person may, in fact, be guilty of a truly grievous sin, such as murder, adultery, incest, abortion, or even something not quite so serious. Over a period of time, the person then develops an obsessive guilt, perhaps not unlike David's when he cried out, "My sin is ever before me" (Psalm 51:3). Some people then associate this guilt with the idea that God cannot possibly forgive them for what they have done.

The inquirer's admission that sin is present, and that it is serious, is to the advantage of the helper. With such a humble admission, the battle for the person's soul is nearly won! There are, however, some misconceptions to be cleared up.

Helping Strategy

1. Immediately encourage the inquirer by stating that you want to help in any way you can. Point out that, in spite of what he or she may think, the Bible maintains that God, in His grace, can forgive any sin if we ask Him to.

2. Define the unpardonable sin in the light of Scripture:

   When Jesus cast a demon out of a blind and mute man, the people were amazed (Matthew 12:22–23). The Pharisees, however, spoke against Jesus, saying that He had cast out the demon by the power of Beelzebub, the prince of demons (verse 24). Jesus answered them as follows: "Every sin and blasphemy will be forgiven men, but the blasphemy against the Spirit will not be forgiven men . . . either in this age or in the age to come" (verses 31–32).

   Ask the caller if he or she is guilty of this sin. If not, offer the assurance that no "unpardonable sin" has been committed.

3. In emphasizing this, however, take care not to minimize the seriousness of any sin which he or she may confess (Galatians 5:19–21). If such an admission of sin is made, emphasize that "the blood of Jesus Christ His Son cleanses us from all sin" (1 John 1:7). To experience God's grace in salvation—which includes forgiveness from sin—a person must admit that he or she is a sinner. See step 2 of "Steps to Peace with God," page 11.

The next step is to confess sin as the publican did: "God be merciful to me a sinner!" (Luke 18:13). Recognizing and confessing sin is a prerequisite to all else that follows. God is in the business of forgiving sin. He sent His Son to the cross that "we might become the righteousness of God in Him" (2 Corinthians 5:21).

Point out that the only sin that is truly "unpardonable" is to reject Christ as Savior.

Billy Graham discusses the "unpardonable sin" as follows: "Perhaps I can venture a definition of what I understand the unpardonable sin to be. It seems to me, negatively, that no one has committed this sin who continues to be under the disturbing, convicting, and drawing power of the Holy Spirit. So long as the Spirit strives with a person, he or she has not committed the unpardonable sin. But when a person has so resisted the Holy Spirit that He strives with him or her no more, then there is eternal danger. In other words, the unpardonable sin involves the total and irrevocable rejection of Jesus Christ. Resisting the Spirit is a sin committed by unbelievers. But it is a sin that, when carried on long enough, leads to eternal doom. Only certain judgment remains for those who resist the Spirit."

---

4. Present "Steps to Peace with God," page 11, and urge the person to trust in Christ without delay, emphasizing that although his or her sin is serious, it is forgivable: "[He] forgives all your iniquities" (Psalm 103:3).

5. If he or she is a Christian, emphasize that a child of God is not capable of committing the "unpardonable sin." Only unbelievers reject the Holy Spirit. Follow the procedure outlined above:

   A. Define the unpardonable sin (Matthew 12:22–31).

   B. Ask if he or she is guilty of the sin described by Jesus, that of blasphemy against the Holy Spirit.

   C. In dispelling the person's doubts, remember not to treat lightly the sin which the inquirer thinks might be unpardonable

   D. Offer the assurance that any sin, no matter how terrible, can be forgiven on the basis of repentance and confession (see page 17 on "Restoration"). Emphasize especially 1 John 1:9. It may not be easy to convince a spiritually insecure inquirer that his or her sins are all pardonable. Be persistent in reiterating God's love, shown in the price He paid on the cross so that sin might be forgiven. If we confess, all sin will be forgiven.

6. Pray with the person that he or she might be able to see sin from God's perspective. God hates sin but loves the sinner; He will forgive any and all sin through the person and work of our Lord Jesus Christ.

Scripture

The Unpardonable Sin:

"He who is not with me is against me, and he who does not gather with me scatters. And so I tell you, every sin and blasphemy will be forgiven men, but the blasphemy against the [Holy] Spirit will not be forgiven" (Matthew 12:30–31, NIV).

The Seriousness of Sin:

"The acts of the sinful nature are obvious: sexual immorality, impurity and debauchery; idolatry and witchcraft; hatred, discord, jealousy, fits of rage, selfish ambition, dissensions, factions and envy; drunkenness, orgies, and the like. I warn you, as I did before, that those who live like this will not inherit the kingdom of God" (Galatians 5:19–21, NIV).

God's Willingness to Forgive Any and All Sin:

"I waited patiently for the Lord; and He inclined to me, and heard my cry. He also brought me up out of a horrible pit, out of the miry clay, and set my feet upon a rock, and established my steps. He has put a new song in my mouth—praise to our God; many will see it and fear, and will trust in the Lord. Blessed is that man who makes the Lord his trust, and does not respect the proud, nor such as turn aside to lies. Many, O Lord my God, are Your wonderful works which You have done; and Your thoughts which are toward us cannot be recounted to You in order; if I would declare and speak of them, they are more than can be numbered" (Psalm 40:1–5).

"Who forgives all your iniquities, who heals all your diseases. . . . As far as the east is from the west, so far has He removed our transgressions from us" (Psalm 103:3, 12).

"He who covers his sins will not prosper, but whoever confesses and forsakes them will have mercy" (Proverbs 28:13).

"If we confess our sins, He is faithful and just to forgive us our sins and to cleanse us from all unrighteousness" (1 John 1:9).

WAR, CHRISTIAN INVOLVEMENT IN

Background

Conscientious Christians have always struggled with the problem of war and its moral implications. Some view war as incompatible with Christianity and therefore unacceptable under any circumstances. People holding this view may point to Scriptures such as Matthew 5:43–44: "You have heard that it was said, 'You shall love your neighbor and hate your enemy.' But I say to you, love your enemies, bless those who curse you, do good to those who hate you, and pray for those who spitefully use you and persecute you."

Other Christians feel that armed preparedness is necessary, and that Christian citizenship obligates us to obey those in authority, serving in the military should a war develop (Romans 13:1; Titus 3:1; Hebrews 13:7).

Philosophically, war is an extension of man's struggle with sin and evil in the world. The apostle James wrote: "What causes fights and quarrels among you? Don't they come from your desires that battle within you? You want something but don't get it. You kill and covet, but you cannot have what you want. You quarrel and fight. You do not have, because you do not ask God. When you ask, you do not receive, because you ask with wrong motives, that you may spend what you get on your pleasures" (James 4:1–3, NIV).

What Should Be the Attitude of a Christian Toward War?

When faced with the possibility of involvement in war, a Christian should:

- Seek to be an instrument of God's peace, praying for it and working for it:

  "Blessed are the peacemakers, for they shall be called sons of God" (Matthew 5:9).

  "I urge, then, first of all, that requests, prayers, intercession and thanksgiving be made for everyone—for kings and all those in authority, that we may live peaceful and quiet lives in all godliness and holiness" (1 Timothy 2:1–2, NIV).

- Seek to please God by presenting your life to Him (Romans 12:1–2) and living in obedience to His Word. As a person finds God's will for his or her life, matters of conscience can be handled with perception from the Holy Spirit.

- Seek to win others to Jesus Christ. Peace begins on the personal level and comes as one permits Him who "is our peace" to control his or her life (Ephesians 2:14). There will be no peace on earth until the Prince of Peace, Jesus Christ, returns to establish it. We should spread the Gospel to all nations in anticipation of His return (Acts 1:8).

- If a person must bear arms, he or she should commit himself or herself to Christ and trust Him for safekeeping from harm, and from the temptations and sins that confront the soldier. Seek to honor Christ in all ways.

Helping Strategy

1. Assure the person that he or she is not alone in being concerned about war; any conscientious Christian is concerned. Say that you are happy to talk with him or her and share as you are able. Sometimes it is much better to confess at the outset that you are not equipped to discuss war philosophically. You are convinced, however, that God is just and does not willingly permit hurt and suffering. God is love. His greatest demonstration of this love is that He sent His Son to die for our sins. He has a plan for everyone's life, including the inquirer's. He wants to share His life, His love, His peace with each of us. Has the inquirer opened his or her life to Jesus Christ, receiving Him as Lord and Savior? If appropriate, present "Steps to Peace with God," page 11.

   Point out that if the person will commit his or her life to Christ, he or she will gain insights and perspective in regard to participation in war. The human conscience is reliable only when it is guided by the Holy Spirit, who indwells the person who has received Christ (1 Corinthians 6:19–20).

2. Reassure the person that you understand his or her apprehensions and are glad to talk and share with him or her in thinking through the issues.

   You would like for the moment, however, to lay aside the concerns about war and return to them a little later. You want to ask life's most important question: Has he or she ever received Jesus Christ as Savior? If appropriate, present "Steps to Peace with God," page 11.

3. Another inquirer may raise the question: How can you believe in a God who permits war when it causes so much human suffering, destruction, and premature death? In addressing such a question, ask the person to consider:

A. War is only one facet of the larger problem of evil which has been with the human race since the beginning. Evil is just as much present in a case of murder. This same evil tried to destroy the greatest human being who ever lived, nailing Him to a cross.

B. The problem boils down to one of moral choices. God wanted a world based on moral values, thus He created mankind with the ability to respond to moral choices. Faced with the moral option of living selfishly or unselfishly, people can and do make wrong decisions. We are free to choose, but we reap the consequences of bad moral decisions. War is one of those wrong decisions.

C. War is the fruit of sin. Sin is the breaking of God's Law. We have not obeyed and do not obey this Law, thus we must face the consequences of our disobedience. We can choose to obey Him by trusting Him not only as our Savior but also as our Lord. "For God so loved the world that He gave His only begotten Son, that whoever believes in Him should not perish but have everlasting life" (John 3:16).

4. Another inquirer may raise the question: Why can't we just refuse to arm ourselves or participate in wars?

Let us reduce the problem to a very practical level in the neighborhood where we live: Would the inquirer be willing to stop locking the doors of his or her house or apartment or automobile? Even in our own country we must safeguard ourselves, our family, and our goods. How much more true this is for nations with conflicting philosophies and cultures! We don't live in an ideal world, but in a world dominated by sinful, selfish desires. Jesus said, "You shall love your neighbor as yourself" (Matthew 19:19). Applied on an international level, this would mean protecting the life, family, home, and property of others just as we protect our own.

Scripture

Prophecy Concerning War:

"He shall judge between the nations, and shall rebuke many people; they shall beat their swords into plowshares, and their spears into pruning hooks; nation shall not lift up sword against nation, neither shall they learn war anymore" (Isaiah 2:4).

"You will hear of wars and rumors of wars, but see to it that you are not alarmed. Such things must happen, but the end is still to come" (Matthew 24:6, NIV).

"And God will wipe away every tear from their eyes; there shall be no more death, nor sorrow, nor crying; and there shall be no more pain, for the former things have passed away" (Revelation 21:4).

Submission to Authority:

"Everyone must submit himself to the governing authorities, for there is no authority except that which God has established. The authorities that exist have been established by God. Consequently, he who rebels against the authority is rebelling against what God has instituted, and those who do so will bring judgment on themselves" (Romans 13:1–2, NIV).

"Therefore submit yourselves to every ordinance of man for the Lord's sake, whether to the king as supreme, or to governors, as to those who are sent by him for the punishment of evildoers and for the praise of those who do good" (1 Peter 2:13–14).

The Reason for War:

James 4:1–3 (see "Background")

THE WILL OF GOD, KNOWING

Background

God has a specific will for the life of each Christian. It should be our highest purpose to determine just what His will is for us and then to do it, whatever the cost.

In order to know the will of God for our lives, we must first know God Himself. We can never know who we are without first knowing *whose* we are. We learn to know God as we submit more and more to His lordship, are obedient to His Word, and are led by the Holy Spirit. In direct proportion to our knowledge of God and our submission to Him, we experience the joy of walking in His will: "Trust in the Lord with all your heart, and lean not on your own understanding; in all your ways acknowledge Him, and He shall direct your paths" (Proverbs 3:5–6).

Billy Graham writes: "To know the will of God is the highest of all wisdom. Living in the center of God's will puts the stamp of true sincerity upon our service to God. You can be miserable with much if you are out of His will, but you can have peace in your heart with little if you are in the will of God. You can be happy in the midst of suffering if you are in God's will. You can be calm and at peace in the midst of persecution as long as you are in the will of God. The Bible reveals that God has a plan for every life and that if we live in constant fellowship with Him, He will lead us in the fulfillment of this plan."

Helping Strategy

Commend the inquirer for desiring to seek God's highest and best for his or her life. Mention, however, that only the child of God can know His direct or specific will for life. Sometimes the non-Christian will express a desire to know the will of God about an important decision or step in life. Point out that the first step in knowing the will of God is to receive Jesus Christ as Lord and Savior. Explain "Steps to Peace with God," page 11.

For the Christian seeking to know the will of God, suggest some principles for knowing His will:

1. Advise him or her to make right any conduct or relationships that may

constitute a barrier against knowing God's will. Sometimes a romantic or business relationship will have to end, or a specific sin will have to be confessed. Share the section on "Restoration," page 17.

Emphasize that the way to God can be cleared through confession (1 John 1:9), while the way to others can be cleared, if necessary, through apologies and restitution.

"Always . . . have a conscience without offense toward God and men" (Acts 24:16).

2. Encourage a willingness to do God's will, whatever it may be or whatever it may cost: "Then He said to them all, 'If anyone desires to come after Me, let him deny himself, and take up his cross daily, and follow Me'" (Luke 9:23).

3. Suggest assembling all the available facts and then filtering all facets and circumstances related to knowing God's will. Tools for doing this would include the person's own intellect and common sense, previous experience, and the counsel of godly friends. He or she needs to consider also his or her own gifts and talents.

4. Suggest that the inquirer seek God's will in the light of revealed Scripture. What principles, commands, or prohibitions apply? Has the Holy Spirit given any motivating verses or promises? "Your word is a lamp to my feet and a light to my path" (Psalm 119:105).

5. Urge praying for God's will to be revealed, and also praying for the spiritual perception to discern it. Isaac's servant said, "As for me, being on the way, the Lord led me" (Genesis 24:27). "Don't worry about anything; instead, pray about everything; tell God your needs and don't forget to thank him for his answers" (Philippians 4:6, TLB).

6. He or she must be very sensitive to the Holy Spirit's leading, asking, is He moving me toward, or away from, a particular course of action?

"But when he, the Spirit of truth, comes, he will guide you into all truth. He will not speak on his own; he will speak only what he hears, and he will tell you what is yet to come" (John 16:13, NIV).

7. Suggest that he or she ask, Am I at peace as I consider the factors involved? Or am I restless and impatient because of uncertainty or inner conflict? "The work of righteousness will be peace, and the effect of righteousness, quietness and assurance forever" (Isaiah 32:17).

8. Recommend allowing room for faith. According to faith, is this the time to proceed, or stop, or wait? What principles in the Scriptures considered apply to his or her situation? (Recommend that the person record the verse references for further study.)

"Commit your way to the Lord, trust also in Him, and He shall bring it to pass" (Psalm 37:5).

9. As an exercise in practical monitoring of progress, suggest preparing a list under the headings of "pros," "cons," and "alternatives." As the Lord, through His Word and through prayer, gives insight, record those insights under one of those three headings.

Scripture

"Has the Lord as great delight in burnt offerings and sacrifices, as in obeying the voice of the Lord? Behold, to obey is better than sacrifice, and to heed than the fat of rams" (1 Samuel 15:22).

"Trust in the Lord, and do good; dwell in the land, and feed on His faithfulness. . . . Commit your way to the Lord, trust also in Him, and He shall bring it to pass" (Psalm 37:3, 5).

"I delight to do Your will, O my God, and Your law is within my heart" (Psalm 40:8).

"For the Lord God is a sun and shield; the Lord will give grace and glory; no good thing will He withhold from those who walk uprightly" (Psalm 84:11).

"If you love Me, keep My commandments. . . . If anyone loves Me, he will keep My word; and My Father will love him, and We will come to him and make Our home with him" (John 14:15, 23).

"Be doers of the word, and not hearers only, deceiving yourselves" (James 1:22).

WITNESSING

Background

The term *witnessing* is commonly used to describe the process of proclaiming the Christian faith to nonbelievers. The term is very appropriate, as Christians tell others of what they have "witnessed" or seen of God's grace and goodness. The apostle John saw himself as a witness of the Gospel precisely for this reason:

"That which was from the beginning, which we have heard, which we have seen with our eyes, which we have looked at and our hands have touched—this we proclaim concerning the Word of life" (1 John 1:1, NIV).

The Christians of the first century "turned the world upside down" (Acts 17:6) because they had a sense of urgency about the message of Christ. Paul said, "Woe is me if I do not preach the gospel!" (1 Corinthians 9:16).

All Christians are witnesses; they are either sharing Christ by life and word, or they are not. Some are negative witnesses; others keep silent about their faith. Each of us needs to seek a more vibrant relationship with Christ so that people will realize that we have been with Jesus (Acts 4:13).

In witnessing, example is essential; our lives must reflect our profession. By our example we establish credibility and build confidence and trust, which prepare the way for presenting Christ. However, we need more than just example. There is no substitute for the witness who verbalizes the facts of the Gospel:

- "God was in Christ reconciling the world to Himself" (2 Corinthians 5:19).

- "I declare to you the gospel which I preached to you, . . . that Christ died for our sins according to the Scriptures, and that He was buried, and that He rose again the third day according to the Scriptures" (1 Corinthians 15:1, 3–4).

- "Salvation is found in no one else, for there is no other name under heaven given to men by which we must be saved" (Acts 4:12, NIV).

A Christian witnesses objectively by sharing the facts of the Gospel, and subjectively by sharing his or her own experiences in Christ. We should not overlook the value and potential effectiveness of our own testimony. The first real impression some people will get concerning Christ's power to transform a life (2 Corinthians 5:17) will be through hearing about what Jesus has done for us. Paul shared again and again his Damascus road experience.

These are ingredients of an effective personal testimony:

- What my life was like before I received Christ.

- How I met Him and received Him (through what instrument and circumstances).

- What life has been like since I received Him.

Billy Graham writes on witnessing: "We are stewards of the Gospel. The power to proclaim the greatest news in heaven and earth was not given to the angels; it was given to redeemed men. Every Christian is to be a witness; every follower of Christ is to preach the Gospel. We can preach by sharing our experiences with others. We can preach by exalting Christ in our daily lives. Sermons which are seen are often more effective than those which are heard. The truth is, the best sermons are both heard and seen."

Helping Strategy

1. In order to witness effectively, an individual must know Christ personally. Ask the inquirer if he or she has received Jesus Christ as Lord and Savior. If appropriate, present "Steps to Peace with God," page 11.

2. Jesus must be real to the Christian! There will be very little to share with someone else if the witness doesn't seek and maintain a close walk with Christ through reading and obeying the Bible and praying. We do not have to be super-Christians to witness, but we must be genuine Christians. Urge the inquirer to be sure he or she is a genuine and growing Christian.

3. Witnessing begins in prayer. Concerned prayer for those who need Christ will spiritually condition the Christian for witness. A prayer list of "prospects," the people you want to reach, is a good way to start. This list may include family, neighbors, an old friend, a new friend.

4. Advise the inquirer to gather all possible data about each person considered a likely candidate for Gospel witness. The more carefully he or she plans the approach, the more effective the witness will be. (The approach could be thought of in terms of rowing around an island, looking for the best place to land.)

5. Suggest beginning with one person. Be natural, caring, and friendly, without being patronizing. Don't overwhelm the prospect by trying to go too far too fast. Be a good listener; most people really want to talk about themselves, their problems, their hurts, and their desires.

6. At this point, the witness may share his or her own experiences with Christ—how Christ came into his or her life and what His presence means.

7. This sharing should lead into the precise moment for the witness to explain God's plan of salvation (see "Steps to Peace with God," page 11). The facts of the Gospel must be applied in such a way that they converge at the point of the individual's need. Sin will have to be squarely faced, Christ's atoning death for sin accepted as the only way to God, and repentance and faith expressed for a person to be born again.

8. Advise the inquirer always to be aiming for a decision—one that is comprehensive, intelligent, and definite. The witness should invite the person, lovingly but firmly, to make a decision based on the presented facts. The greatest service a Christian may render to another human being is to help the person understand the all-important step of surrendering his or her life to Christ.

9. Encourage the inquirer to seal the decision with prayer. If the prospect is sufficiently knowledgeable, suggest offering his or her own prayer of commitment. If not, the witness could guide him or her in a prayer.

10. Following this, the witness should review with the prospect what has actually transpired in order to confirm the decision (see page 13).

11. The ultimate goal in witnessing and winning people to faith in Christ is that they, themselves, may also become effective, reproducing witnesses. In order for this to develop, it will be necessary to continue to dedicate time to the new believer, instructing on the importance of Bible reading and study, explaining the value and practice of prayer, and introducing him or her to committed Christians for fellowship, challenge, and encouragement.

Additional Suggestions for Those Desiring to Witness for Christ

1. Identify with a church where the Bible is preached and taught and where emphasis is placed on personal witness and soul winning.

2. Try to cultivate friendships with other witnessing Christians in order to learn from them: Observe, then do. Evangelism Explosion teaches in its seminars that evangelism is better caught than taught.

3. Enroll in any courses on personal evangelism that are available through your own or another church.

4. Read and study books on Scripture memory, personal evangelism, and witnessing. A few that are available are:

How to Give Away Your Faith by Paul Little (InterVarsity Press)

The Art of Personal Witnessing by Lorne Sanny (The Navigators)

"My Commitment" and *"Steps to Peace with God"* (Billy Graham Evangelistic Association)

Topical Memory System (The Navigators)

"Victory Scripture Memory" (Word Publications)

Personal Prayer Notebook (Tyndale House)

Know What You Believe and *Know Why You Believe* by Paul Little (Scripture Press)

Becoming a Christian by John Stott (InterVarsity Press)

(These books are available at your local Christian bookstore or you may write to Grason, P.O. Box 669007, Charlotte, NC 28266-9007.)

Scripture

"But you shall receive power when the Holy Spirit has come upon you; and you shall be witnesses to Me in Jerusalem, and in all Judea and Samaria, and to the end of the earth" (Acts 1:8).

"Now when they saw the boldness of Peter and John, and perceived that they were uneducated and untrained men, they marveled. And they realized that they had been with Jesus" (Acts 4:13).

"God was in Christ reconciling the world to Himself . . . and has committed to us the word of reconciliation" (2 Corinthians 5:19).

"Always be ready to give a defense to everyone who asks you a reason for the hope that is in you" (1 Peter 3:15).

WORLDLINESS

Background

The Christian who is "worldly" is the one who is devoted to or engrossed in worldly interests rather than in things relating to Christ and His kingdom. The King James Version of the Bible refers to the worldly person as being "carnal," a word which literally means "fleshly." More recent translations use terms such as "unspiritual," "sinful," or "of the world."

The worldly Christian is not concerned about those things "that pertain to life and godliness" (2 Peter 1:3). Rather, he or she is characterized by spiritual indifference, instability, and lack of discipline. He or she is contaminated (James 1:26) and rebellious against God (James 4:4). He or she is a "friend of the world" (James 4:4) and a lover of pleasure rather than a lover of God (2 Timothy 3:4).

The worldly Christian takes a halfhearted stand for that which pertains to the kingdom of God; therefore, he or she easily falls victim to almost any temptation or false teaching that comes along. He or she gives "lip service" to a form of doctrine, but ignores any real substance: "From such people turn away!" advises Paul (2 Timothy 3:5).

The spiritually minded Christian, on the other hand, is one who:

- "Will seek first the kingdom of God and His righteousness" (Matthew 6:33)

- Takes a stand against the "spirit of this age" in order to establish an identity with the family of God

- Enjoys a certain perception and spiritual discernment which comes from prayer and from walking in the Spirit (Philippians 1:9–11)

- Seeks and experiences constant renewal at the foot of the cross (1 John 1:9; 2:1)

- Desires to be "filled with the fruits of righteousness which are by Jesus Christ, to the glory and praise of God" (Philippians 1:11)

- Knows that "to be spiritually minded is life and peace" (Romans 8:6)

Billy Graham comments: "The Bible teaches that we are to live in this world, but we are not to partake of the evils of the world. We are to be separated from the world of evil. When I face something in the world, I ask: 'Does it violate any principle of Scripture?

Does it take the keen edge off my Christian life? Can I ask God's blessing on it? Will it be a stumbling block to others? Would I like to be there, or reading that, or be watching that, if Christ should return at that time?' Worldliness doesn't fall like an avalanche upon a person and sweep him or her away. It is the steady drip, drip, drip of the water that wears away the stone. The world is exerting a steady pressure on us every day. Most of us would go down under it, if it weren't for the Holy Spirit who lives inside us, and holds us up, and keeps us."

Helping Strategy

1. If a Christian inquires about how to be victorious over the world and how to become a spiritually minded person, commend his or her interest in spiritual growth.

2. In order to set the stage for new attitudes and goals, encourage the person to consciously renounce all sinful, selfish desires; to ask forgiveness for them; and to ask God for spiritual renewal: "Choose for yourselves this day whom you will serve. . . . But as for me and my house, we will serve the Lord" (Joshua 24:15).

   Share "Restoration," page 17, emphasizing 1 John 1:9 and 2:1. Also share Romans 12:1, asking the person to make a conscious presentation of his or her life to God.

3. Advise being prepared for adversities, temptations, and failures which come to us all when we determine to keep ourselves "unspotted from the world" (James 1:27). God will not permit temptations to overwhelm us (1 Corinthians 10:13), and He will never leave us nor forsake us (Hebrews 13:5; John 14:16).

4. Recommend faithfully reading and studying the Bible and practicing daily prayer. There is no substitute for these if a person desires to grow in the grace and knowledge of our Lord Jesus Christ. As we practice these disciplines, a hunger and thirst for righteousness begins to develop which will send us back, again and again, to His presence for confession, renewal, growth, and knowledge: "If anyone thirsts, let him come to Me and drink. He who believes in Me, as the Scripture has said, out of his heart will flow rivers of living water" (John 7:37–38). This habitual cycle of thirsting and coming to drink will become an indispensable part of one's life.

5. It is often necessary to change one's lifestyle and circle of friends in order to pursue life in the Spirit without encumbrances. Recommend seeking out dedicated Christian people for fellowship, and building new interests

and outlets through service in a Bible-oriented church: "And let us consider how we may spur one another on toward love and good deeds. Let us not give up meeting together, as some are in the habit of doing, but let us encourage one another—and all the more as you see the Day approaching" (Hebrews 10:24–25, NIV).

6. Pray with the inquirer for genuine commitment. Pray for immediate spiritual victories to confirm that commitment.

7. Finally, challenge the person to set some immediate spiritual goals and to work on them, monitoring his or her progress from victory to victory.

Scripture

"Base your happiness on your hope in Christ. . . . Live in harmony with one another. . . . See that your public behavior is above criticism. As far as your responsibility goes, live at peace with everyone. . . . Don't allow yourself to be overpowered by evil. Take the offensive—overpower evil with good!" (Romans 12:12–21, PHILLIPS; selected phrases).

"Therefore let us pursue the things which make for peace and the things by which one may edify another. . . . It is good neither to eat meat nor drink wine nor do anything by which your brother stumbles or is offended or is made weak" (Romans 14:19, 21).

"Do the good things that result from being saved, obeying God with deep reverence, shrinking back from all that might displease him. For God is at work within you, helping you want to obey him, and then helping you do what he wants. In everything you do, stay away from complaining and arguing, so that no one can speak a word of blame against you. You are to live clean, innocent lives as children of God in a dark world full of people who are crooked and stubborn. Shine out among them like beacon lights, holding out to them the Word of Life" (Philippians 2:12–16, TLB).

"Yet every advantage that I had gained I considered lost for Christ's sake. Yes, and I look upon everything as loss compared with the overwhelming gain of knowing Christ Jesus my Lord. For his sake I did in fact suffer the loss of everything, but I considered it mere garbage compared with being able to win Christ. For now my place is in him, and I am not dependent upon any of the self-achieved righteousness of the Law; God has given me that genuine righteousness which comes from faith in Christ. Now I long to know Christ and the power shown by his resurrection; now I long to share his sufferings, even to die as he died, so that I may somehow attain the resurrection from the dead" (Philippians 3:7–11, PHILLIPS).

"If then you were raised with Christ, seek those things which are above, where Christ is, sitting at the right hand of God. Set your mind on things above, not on things on the earth. . . . And whatever you do in word or deed, do all in the name of the Lord Jesus, giving thanks to God the Father through Him" (Colossians 3:1–2, 17).

"Do not love the world or anything in the world. If anyone loves the world, the love of the Father is not in him. For everything in the world—the cravings of sinful man, the lust of his eyes and the boasting of what he has and does—comes not from the Father but from the world. The world and its desires pass away, but the man who does the will of God lives forever" (1 John 2:15–17, NIV).

SEVEN COMMON QUESTIONS

by Paul E. Little

1. What About the Heathen?

"What about the person who has never heard of Jesus Christ? Will he or she be condemned to hell?" Certain things are known to God alone (Deuteronomy 29:29). On some things God has not fully revealed His plan. This is one instance. The Scripture does offer some very clear points for us to keep in mind.

- God is just. Whatever He does with those who have never heard of Jesus Christ will be fair.

- No person will be condemned for rejecting Jesus Christ of whom he or she has never heard; instead such a person will be condemned for violating his or her own moral standard, however high or low it has been. The whole world—every person, whether having heard of the Ten Commandments or not—is in sin. Romans 2 clearly tells us that every person has a standard of some kind, and that in every culture, people knowingly violate the standard they have (Romans 2:12–16).

- Scripture indicates that every person has enough information from creation to know that God exists (Romans 1:20, ". . . so that they are without excuse"). Psalm 19 confirms this fact. Matthew 7:7–11 and Jeremiah 29:13 relate that if anyone responds to the light he or she has and seeks God, God will give him or her a chance to hear the truth about Jesus Christ.

- There is no indication in the Bible that a person can be saved apart from Jesus Christ (John 14:6). Only He atoned for our sins. He is the only bridge across the chasm that separates the highest possible human achievement from the infinitely holy standard of God (Acts 4:12). We, who call ourselves Christians, must see to it that those who have not heard, hear the Gospel.

- The Bible is perfectly clear concerning the judgment which awaits the individual who *has* heard the Gospel. When that person faces God, the issue will not be the heathen. That one person will have to account for what he or she, personally, has done with Jesus Christ. Usually someone will raise the question of the heathen as a smoke screen in an effort to evade personal responsibility. We need to answer the question. But then, as we terminate the discussion, we should focus on the person and on his or her responsibility. What is he or she going to do with Jesus Christ? For a fuller discussion of the moral law inherent in the universe, see *Mere Christianity* by C. S. Lewis.

2. Is Christ the Only Way to God?

Neither sincerity nor intensity of faith can create truth. Faith is no more valid than the object in which it is placed. The real issue is the question of truth. For example, Islam and Christianity are very similar in the moral and ethical realms, but the two faiths are diametrically opposed on the crucial question: "Who is Jesus Christ?" Islam denies that Jesus Christ is the Son of God. Both faiths cannot simultaneously be true at this point. One is correct; one is incorrect. If the crux of Christianity is false, our faith is worthless.

This question has some emotional aspects. Christians are not being bigoted, prejudiced, or presumptuous when they say that Christ is the only way to God. Christians have no other option because Jesus Christ Himself has said this. We are dealing with truth that has come to us by revelation, through the invasion into human history of God Himself in Jesus Christ.

Some laws and their penalties are socially determined. For instance, being picked up for speeding means paying a fine. But in some other aspects of life, such as in the physical realms, we find laws that are not socially determined. The law of gravity is one such law. In the moral realm, as in the physical, there are laws that are not socially determined. We discern these laws from what God has revealed about the inherent law of the universe. One such law is that Jesus Christ is the only way to God. Dorothy L. Sayers offers some further helpful thoughts on this subject in *The Mind of the Maker*.

3. Why Do the Innocent Suffer?

"If God is all-good and all-powerful, why do the innocent suffer?" Here we have to admit our partial ignorance. We do not have the full explanation of the origin and problem of evil because God has chosen to reveal only a part to us. God created the universe perfect; mankind, through free will, chose to disobey. Evil came into the universe through man's disobedience. Because mankind disobeyed and broke God's law, evil pervades the universe.

We must not overlook the presence of evil in every one of us. If God executed judgment uniformly, not one of us would survive. Suppose God were to decree, "At midnight tonight all the evil will be stamped out of the universe." Which of us would be here at 1:00 a.m.?

After pointing out man's personal problem with evil, we need to know that God has done everything necessary to meet this problem. He came into human history in the Lord Jesus Christ, and He died to solve this problem. Every individual who willingly responds receives His gift of love, grace, and forgiveness in Jesus Christ. C. S. Lewis has observed that it is idle for us to speculate about the problem of evil. The problem we all face is the *fact* of evil. The only solution to this fact is God's Son, Jesus Christ.

4. How Can Miracles Be Possible?

"How can miracles be possible? In this scientific age, how can any intelligent person who considers the orderliness of the universe believe in them?" The real issue here is whether or not God exists. If God exists, then miracles are logical and pose no intellectual contradictions. By definition, God is all-powerful. He can and does intervene in the universe that He has created.

Ultimately, we are being asked, "How do I know God exists?" History records many arguments for the existence of God. However, these have counterarguments, and some evidence seems to negate them. So they are regarded as hints rather than as conclusive proof that God exists.

The greatest indication of the existence of God is His coming into human history. I know God exists, not because of all the philosophical arguments, but because He came into human history in Jesus Christ and I have met Him personally. Our answer begins with Him. His credentials substantiate His claim. The supreme credential, of course, is the fact that He rose from the dead. In helping a non-Christian think through the intellectual basis of Christianity, our best defense is a good offense. One way to stimulate the person's thinking is to ask, "Which of the other three possibilities about Jesus Christ do you believe, since you do not believe that He was the truth?" There are only four possible conclusions about Jesus Christ and His claims. He was either a liar, a lunatic, a legend, or the Truth.

A. *Liar.* Most people believe that Jesus was a great moral philosopher and teacher. To call Him a liar would be a contradiction of terms.

B. *Lunatic.* He thought He was doing right, but He suffered from delusions of grandeur. The hitch in this conclusion is that the clinical symptoms of paranoia do not fit with the personality characteristics of Jesus Christ. The poise and composure which He demonstrated are not characteristic of those who suffer from paranoid disturbances.

C. *Legend.* He never made the statements attributed to Him. They were put in His mouth by overenthusiastic followers in the third and fourth century. Modern archaeology, however, makes it difficult to maintain this theory. Recent findings confirm that the New Testament documents were written during the lifetime of the contemporaries of Jesus Christ. Development of an elaborate legend would have required a more significant time lag.

We also need to consider with the person what it means to prove or not prove God. We can never prove God by the scientific method. But that does not mean that our case is lost. The scientific method as a means of verification is limited to measurable aspects of reality. No one can measure love, hatred, or justice. However, there is a science of history. As we examine the data for Christianity and particularly the evidence for the Resurrection, we find a solid case on which to base our conviction.

These are the ideas we need to suggest to a person who takes the essentially materialistic position, based on rationalistic presuppositions, and claims that because there is no supernatural, miracles are impossible. When someone begins with this presupposition, no amount of evidence will convince him or her of the truth. If you started out by denying that miracles are possible, what evidence would convince you that a miracle had taken place? None. Christ dealt with this problem in Luke 16:27–31. The principle still holds today. The data we have concerning God's visitation to this planet are sufficient grounds for us to believe. When someone refuses to accept this evidence, no additional evidence will convince that person.

5. Isn't the Bible Full of Errors?

"How do you reconcile your faith with the fact that the Bible is so full of errors?" First, ask what particular errors the person has in mind. Ninety-nine percent of the time people cannot think of any. If the person has a specific problem and you do not have the answer, do not panic. Instead smile casually and say, "I don't have the answer to that one, but I will be glad to dig it up for you." If the person has not read the Bible, that is a fair indication of his or her insincerity in questioning it. But do not press this point, and never make fun of anyone or try to argue by ridicule. This only brings the Gospel into disrepute.

The Bible does contain some apparent contradictions. But, time and time again, an apparent contradiction has been vindicated by the discoveries of modern archaeology. Dr. Nelson Glueck, an outstanding Jewish archaeologist, makes the remarkable statement, "No archaeological discovery has ever controverted a biblical reference."

Evolution may be a problem if it leads to an atheistic conclusion for someone. The real issue though is not evolution, but coming to grips with Christ Himself. Ask:

"What conclusion are you drawing from your evolutionary position—that the universe happened by chance? Or are you saying that God created the universe and did so by using certain evolutionary processes? I am not convinced about that particular position, but let us assume for the moment that it is correct. What conclusion are you drawing?"

From there, direct attention to what Jesus Christ has said and done. *How* God brought the universe into being is not so important as *that* He did it. One's presupposition, and not the actual evidence, often determines his or her conclusion. An apparently strong case for a naturalistic position can be made by ignoring the evidence for Jesus Christ. But if a person is going to be intellectually honest, he or she must come to grips with Him. An amazing number of thinking non-Christians have never really thought about the evidence for Jesus Christ.

6. Isn't Christian Experience Only Psychological?

Some suggest that we have faith only because we have been conditioned since early childhood. We have been raised like Pavlov's dogs. But this is an oversimplification; Christians have been converted from every imaginable background. Thousands have had no childhood contact with Christianity. Yet each will testify to a personal encounter with Christ that transformed his or her life. The Lord, Himself, is the only constant factor.

Others assert that spiritual ideals are essentially wish fulfillments. They can be traced to a person's feeling a need for God, creating an image in his or her mind, and then worshiping the mental projection. Objective reality is totally lacking. Religion is called a crutch for people who cannot get along in life. Religious people are self-hypnotized.

What is our objective evidence for our subjective experiences? Christianity differs from autohypnosis, wish fulfillments, and all the other psychological phenomena in that the Christian's subjective experience is securely bound to an objective, historical fact, namely the resurrection from the dead of Jesus Christ.

If the Resurrection is true, it makes all the difference in the world. It is confirmation of God's revelation in Christ, an absolute truth, a historical fact outside of ourselves, an objective fact to which our subjective experience is tied. We need to hold the objective and the subjective in proper perspective. I need to recognize that my experience is based on the solid foundation of an objective fact in history.

Evidence for the Resurrection, by J. N. D. Anderson, is a brief and helpful summary. He discusses the evidence and the various alternatives that have been advanced to explain away the Resurrection, showing why, in the light of the data, each explanation is inadequate.

7. Won't a Good Moral Life Get Me to Heaven?

A student at Duke University said, "If God grades on the curve, I'll make it." Most people will accept the philosophy that all we need to do is our best, and then everything will be all right, or at least we will be able to just get by. This attitude shows an incredible optimism about man's righteousness and an appalling ignorance of God's infinite holiness. God does not grade on the curve. He has an absolute standard, Jesus Christ. Light destroys darkness. The character of God so blazes in its purity that it consumes all evil. In God's presence, we would be consumed because of the corruption in our lives. The perfect righteousness of Jesus Christ is the only basis on which we can come into fellowship with the living God.

Morality is not the answer. From the bum on skid row, to the Joe College type, to the tremendously moral person, all human effort is futile. No one could swim the entire distance to Hawaii. All would drown. No swimming instructions would help. We need someone to take us to Hawaii. This is where Christ comes in.

If you can live a life that is absolutely perfect, you can make it to heaven on your own steam. But no one has ever succeeded at that, nor will anyone ever succeed. All the other religions of the world are essentially sets of swimming instructions, suggested codes of ethics for a wonderful pattern of life. But man's basic problem is not failing to know *how* to live; it is lacking the *power* to live as one ought. The good news is that Jesus Christ, who invaded human history, does for us what we could not possibly do for ourselves. Through Him we may be reconciled to God, we are given His righteousness, and we are enabled to have fellowship with Him in His very presence.

Reprinted from *How to Give Away Your Faith* by Paul Little. Revised edition ©1988 by Marie Little. Used by permission of InterVarsity Press, P. O. Box 1400, Downers Grove, Illinois 60515.

A COMPARISON OF CHRISTIANITY WITH MAJOR RELIGIONS AND CULTS

CHRISTIANS	BUDDHISTS

God

God is omniscient and omnipotent (Job 42:2; Ps. 115:3; Matt. 19:26).	Deny existence of a personal God.

Jesus Christ

He is the unique Son of God who died for mankind's sin (Matt. 14:33; 16:16; John 1:34; 9:35–37; Rom. 5:6–8; 1 Cor. 15:3).	He was a great teacher, less important than Buddha.

Sin

Sin is any thought or deed contrary to the will of God. Mankind is spiritually dead in sin (Rom. 3:10, 23; 5:12; Eph. 2:1).	Sin is anything which hinders mankind's progress. Each person is responsible for his or her own sin.

Salvation

Salvation is through Christ's efforts only (Acts 4:12; Eph. 2:8–10; Titus 3:5).	Salvation is by self-effort only.

CHRISTIANS	CHRISTIAN SCIENTISTS

God

God is a person. He created the universe, and created man in His own image (Gen. 1:1, 26). God, as a person, sees, hears, speaks, remembers, knows (Gen. 6:5; Ex. 2:24; Num. 11:1; Ps. 79:8; 2 Tim. 2:19).	God is an impersonal Principle, not a person. Mary Baker Eddy (founder of the movement) writes: "God is all . . . that soul, or mind, of the spiritual man is God, the Divine Principle of all being."

Jesus Christ

Christ is one with God. Jesus said, "I and My Father are one" (John 10:30). Christians find much evidence of Christ's deity in the Bible (John 1:1; Phil. 2:5–8; 1 John 2:22–23).	Jesus was not God. *Science and Health* states: "Jesus Christ is not God" (p. 361). Christian Scientists consider Christ an outstanding man, a great teacher, but deny His deity.

Matter

What man sees, touches, feels, smells, and hears is real. Jesus demonstrated the reality of matter. He became flesh (John 1:14). He was hungry (Matt. 4:2). He gave others food to eat (Matt. 14:16).

Only Principle (God) exists and every thing else is an "illusion." There is no matter; material things (a person's body, etc.) are not real.

Sin

Sin is real. It originates in the heart and mind of man, and separates man from God. The ultimate result of sin is death (Isa. 59:2; Mark 7:21–23; Rom. 5:12; 6:23).

Sin, evil, and death do not exist. *Science and Health* states: "Since God is All, there is no room for the opposite . . . therefore evil, being the opposite of goodness, is unreal" (p. 234).

The Atonement and Resurrection

Christ's shed blood atoned for mankind's sins (1 Pet. 2:24), and Christ died and rose from the dead in bodily form (John 20:16–17, 20, 27).

Christ's shed blood on the cross did not cleanse man from sin, and His disciples were fooled into thinking Him dead when He was really alive in the tomb (*Science and Health*, pp. 330, 349).

CHRISTIANS

HINDUS

God

God is an external, personal, spiritual Being in three persons: Father, Son, and Holy Spirit (Matt. 3:13–17; 28:19; 2 Cor. 13:14).

"Brahman," the Hindu concept of God, is a formless, abstract, eternal being without attributes. Brahman can be manifest as a trinity and as millions of lesser gods.

Jesus Christ

Christ is the only begotten Son of God the Father. He is God as well as man; He is sinless; and He died for our redemption (Mark 10:45; John 1:13–14; 8:46; 10:30; Heb. 4:15; 1 Pet. 2:24).

Christ is just one of many incarnations, or sons of God. He is no more divine than any other man, and He did not die for mankind's sins.

Sin

Sin is proud, independent rebellion that separates man from God. It is falling short of the standards God has established in His Word. Sin must be punished, and its consequence is death and eternal separation from God (Rom. 3:23; 6:23).

Good and evil are relative terms. Whatever helps is good; whatever hinders is vice. People cannot help "stumbling" over these obstacles as they strive for self-knowledge. If they cannot succeed in this life, they may try again in reincarnated form.

Salvation

People may be justified only through the sacrificial death and resurrection of Jesus Christ (Rom. 3:24; 1 Cor. 15:3).

People are justified through devotion, meditation, good works, and self-control.

| CHRISTIANS | JEHOVAH'S WITNESSES |

God

God is an eternal, personal, spiritual Being in three persons—the Trinity: Father, Son, and Holy Spirit (Matt. 3:13–17; 28:19; 2 Cor. 13:14).

God is one solitary being, Jehovah God. There is no Trinity.

Immortality

People have an eternal, immortal soul (Gen. 1:26; 5:1; Job 32:8; Acts 7:59; 1 Cor. 11:7).

People do not have an immortal soul. The soul is not separate from the body.

Jesus Christ

Christ is divine, a part of the Trinity, God Himself (John 1:1; Col. 1:15–19; 2:9; 1 John 5:7–8).

Christ was not God; He was God's first created creature.

Atonement

Christ's death was the complete payment for mankind's sins (Rom. 3:24–25; 2 Cor. 5:20; Col. 1:20; 1 Pet. 2:24).

Christ's death provides the opportunity for man to work for his or her salvation, which will consist of perfect human life for eternity on an Eden-like earth.

Christ's Resurrection

Christ was physically resurrected from the grave (Luke 24:36–43; John 2:21; 20:24–29).

Christ was raised, not in bodily form, but as a "divine spirit."

Christ's Return

Christ will return to earth physically (Zech. 12:10; Matt. 24:30; 1 Thess. 4:16–17; Rev. 1:7).

Christ returned to earth— invisibly—in 1914 and now rules earth from heaven.

Hell

Hell is the place of eternal punishment for sin (Matt. 5:22; 8:11–12; 13:42, 50; 22:13; Luke 13:24–28; 2 Pet. 2:17; Jude 13; Rev. 14:9–11).

There is no hell or eternal punishment. Those who do not measure up to Jehovah's standards will be annihilated—they will cease to exist.

CHRISTIANS

ORTHODOX JEWS

God

There is one God, existing as Father, Son, and Holy Spirit—the Trinity. Within the one "essence" of the Godhead there are three persons who are coequally and coeternally God (Matt. 3:13–17; 28:19; 2 Cor. 13:14).

The Godhead consists of only one person. "Hear, O Israel: the Lord our God, the Lord is one!" (Deut. 6:4).

Sin

Through the sin of Adam, all humans are born as sinners (original sin) (Ps. 51:5; Rom. 5:12). All people are condemned before God for their sin: proud, independent rebellion against God in active or passive form (Rom. 1:18–23; 3:10, 23).

People are not born in original sin nor are they born good. They are born free, with the capacity to choose between good and evil. Each person is accountable for himself or herself.

Salvation

Mankind is justified before God and obtains salvation through the atoning death of Christ on the cross. Salvation is a gift of God through faith (Rom. 3:24; 1 Cor. 15:3; Eph. 2:8–9).

Anyone, Jew or not, may gain salvation through commitment to God and moral living. Judaism looks forward to an afterlife; however, it does not stress preparing man for the next world as much as guiding ethical and moral behavior in this present life.

Jesus Christ

Christ is the only begotten Son of God, the Messiah predicted in Isaiah 53. Though part of the Godhead, He became a man, lived a sinless life and died to redeem all mankind from sin (Mark 10:45; John 1:13–14; 8:46; 10:30; Heb. 4:15; 1 Pet. 2:24).

While some Jews may accept Jesus as a good teacher of ethics, they do not accept Him as Messiah because: (1) He did not bring lasting peace; (2) He claimed to be God. Jews believe the Messiah will be a human sent from God to deliver Israel from oppression, not a divine being sent to save individuals from personal sin.

CHRISTIANS   MORMONS

God

God is uniquely eternal and all-powerful, the only such being in existence (Ps. 145:13; John 4:24; 1 Tim. 1:17).

God is a material creature who was once human. We who are now human can also, someday, become gods.

The Bible

The Bible, given by God's Spirit, is complete in itself and needs no additions. In fact, additions to the Bible are forbidden (Deut. 4:2; 12:32; Prov. 30:5–6; Gal. 1:8; Heb. 1:1–2; Rev. 22:18–19).

The writings of Joseph Smith are divinely inspired additions to the Bible.

Sin

People are not godlike, but are sinful and separated from God. They can have a relationship with God only through faith in Christ. Apart from Christ, they are lost (John 1:29; Rom. 5:12–19; 6:23; Gal. 3:13; Eph. 2:1–2).

Humans are progressively becoming gods. Adam's sin in Eden was necessary in order to provide parentage for the spirit children of God who were ready and waiting for the experience of earth life.

Salvation

Salvation is a free gift provided by the grace (unmerited love) of God for all who believe and accept His plan (John 12:26; 14:1–3, 6; Eph. 2:8–9; 1 John 3:1–2).

Salvation comes by works; all people will spend eternity on some level of a multistoried heaven, the level being determined by the scope of each person's good works.

| CHRISTIANS | MUSLIMS |

God

There is one God, revealed in Scripture as Father, Son, and Holy Spirit. Within the one "essence" of the Godhead there are three persons who are coequally and coeternally God (Matt. 3:13–17; 28:19; 2 Cor. 13:14).

There is only one person in the Godhead (Allah means "the God").

Jesus Christ

Jesus Christ is the Son of God; He is one with the Father; He is the sinless redeemer of sinful man, through His death on the cross and resurrection from the dead (John 1:13–14; 1 Cor. 15:3; Heb. 4:15; 1 Pet. 3:18).

Jesus Christ was only a man, a prophet equal to Adam, Noah, Abraham, and Moses, all of whom are below Mohammed in importance. Christ did not die for mankind's sins; in fact Judas, not Jesus, died on the cross.

Sin

Sin is proud, independent rebellion against God in active or passive form (Rom. 1:18–23; 3:10, 23).

Sin is failure to do Allah's will, failure to do one's religious duties as outlined in the "Five Pillars of the Faith."

Salvation

Christ died for our sins (1 Cor. 15:3–4).

People earn their own salvation and pay for their own sins.

CHRISTIANS	UNITARIANS

God

God is revealed in the Bible as Father, Son, and Holy Spirit—the Trinity (Matt. 3:13–17; 28:19; 2 Cor. 13:14).

There is only one person in the Godhead. God is not a personal deity and the term *God* refers to the living processes of nature and conscience at work in mankind.

The Bible

The Bible is divinely inspired and is the sole guide and authority for faith (1 Thess. 2:13; 2 Tim. 3:15–17; 2 Pet. 1:19–21).

The Bible is a collection of myths, legends, and philosophical writings.

Jesus Christ

Christ is divine, a part of the Trinity—God Himself. Christ frequently referred to Himself as God (John 8:12–30, 58).

Jesus was no more or less divine than any man.

Sin

People are inherently sinful and there is only one way they can rid themselves of their sinful nature—through faith by the grace (unmerited love) of God (Eph. 2:8–9; 4:20–24).

People are essentially good and can save themselves.

Adapted by permission from Fritz Ridenour, *So What's the Difference?* (Ventura, Calif.: Gospel Light, 1979). See this valuable source for further reading.

SUBJECT INDEX